Pagan in the City

PAGAN IN THE CITY

CASSANDRA EASON

quantum
LONDON • NEW YORK • TORONTO • SYDNEY

quantum
foulsham

quantum
An imprint of W. Foulsham & Co. Ltd

The Oriel, Thames Valley Court, 183–187 Bath Road, Slough, Berkshire, SL1 4AA, England

Foulsham books can be found in all good bookshops and direct from www.foulsham.com

ISBN 978-0-572-03418-4

Copyright © 2008 Cassandra Eason

Cover photograph © Superstock

A CIP record for this book is available from the British Library

The moral right of the author has been asserted

All rights reserved

The Copyright Act prohibits (subject to certain very limited exceptions) the making of copies of any copyright work or of a substantial part of such a work, including the making of copies by photocopying or similar process. Written permission to make a copy or copies must therefore normally be obtained from the publisher in advance. It is advisable also to consult the publisher if in any doubt as to the legality of any copying which is to be undertaken.

Neither the editors of W. Foulsham & Co. Ltd nor the author nor the publisher take responsibility for any possible consequences from any treatment, procedure, test, exercise, action or application of medication or preparation by any person reading or following the information in this book. The publication of this book does not constitute the practice of medicine, and this book does not attempt to replace any diet or instructions from your doctor. The author and publisher advise the reader to check with a doctor before administering any medication or undertaking any course of treatment or exercise.

Printed in Great Britain by Thomson Litho Ltd, East Kilbride

Contents

	Paganism and the Everyday World	7
Chapter 1	Are You a Natural Pagan?	19
Chapter 2	Making the Home a Place of Happiness	37
Chapter 3	Working With the Energies in Your Home	61
Chapter 4	Rediscovering Your Natural Rhythms	85
Chapter 5	The Moon and Your Inner Rhythms	105
Chapter 6	Rites of Passage	133
Chapter 7	The Wheel of the Year – Old Festivals in a Modern World	159
Chapter 8	The Wheel of the Year – from Darkness Back to Light	179
Chapter 9	The Pagan Workplace	199
Chapter 10	A Pagan Treasury of Wisdom and Healing	219
	The Pagan Path	239
	Useful Contacts	241
	Further Reading	245
	Index	253

Paganism and the Everyday World

Have you ever come back from holiday and wished that you could have stayed there forever – even if it rained every day? I moved my family to the rural Isle of Wight from a very comfortable semi-detached house on a new housing estate in urban Reading in Berkshire, not far from London. The move was the result of pure impulse. Driving along a road on the island, through banks of daffodils and primroses one windy, rainy March holiday, the family decided – unusually unanimously for my lively brood of five – that we were going to live in that road. Then it would not matter if it rained, they said, as the sea would always be there and we would not need holidays.

After two years of false starts and setbacks, a house purchase in that road went through. Though the decision was a financial disaster, the daffodils and primroses still bloom every spring and the children experienced a wonderfully safe childhood, with almost every free moment spent on the beach or on the downs. When they grew up, they adopted distinctly non-otherworldly careers in banking and hospitality, but they all still love the countryside and the sea. And I can hear the sea from my garden on a windy day and see it if I stand on a chair in my top back bedroom ('sea glimpses' in estate-agent speak).

Many people make the decision to downsize as I did, to move abroad or live a simpler life, but for others the return to daily routine after a holiday rapidly wipes out the temporary sense of freedom and harmony. This need not happen, however, as in town or country there are basic small lifestyle adjustments that can ensure continuing tranquillity and positive connection with a more pleasurable, less stressful way of life.

Becoming a 21st-century pagan

Pagan comes from the Latin *paganus*, which means country dweller, and has come in the modern world to refer to anyone – city or countryside dweller – who follows the cycles of the seasons, the moon and the sun, rather than becoming a slave to measured clock time and the 24/7 frantic activity cycle.

Even if you live in a high-rise tower block in the city centre, you can be a pagan if you love nature, have a window box of herbs and take regular trips to the nearest green space. You can be a Christian, a Jew, a Muslim, a Buddhist or practise no formal religion and still live the pagan way while holding down a demanding job and juggling home and personal commitments.

I was pagan before I knew the word, even as a child living in the centre of industrialised Birmingham. I still remember our backyard where there was a rose bush and a walnut tree that every year produced a single nut.

Though I am now trained in two neopagan forms of spirituality – as a solitary witch (Wiccan) and druidess (Celtic nature priestess) with the Order of Bards, Ovates and Druids – these are part of my everyday world and are essentially a private way of improving the spiritual and actual quality of my life.

Just as holidays by the sea or in the countryside energise and harmonise stressed bodies and minds, so paganism brings with it a lifestyle and spirituality base that makes it possible to become more in tune with your own innate rhythms, ebbs and flows.

With the decline in influence of conventional formal religions, people are increasingly looking for a spiritual path that has personal meaning and in which they can directly and privately participate at the times when they have the time and inclination.

This book is a practical hands-on guide to bringing the best of the old ways into modern urban as well as rural life. These more natural and established ways of living enable us to prioritise and restructure personal and family life so that we feel more in control of our destiny and better able to live in a way that brings us closer to the reasons we, perhaps many years ago, embarked on our current life path and relationships.

Making personal time and space

Whether you live alone, as I do for most of the time now my children are grown up, are juggling home and work with perhaps the care of older relations or are trying to make your mark on the world and get on the housing ladder, a pagan path can make your leisure time, however limited, more meaningful and restorative.

It can also improve communication with loved ones by creating an oasis of calm and acceptance, which can be hard to find in the activity and technological bias of modern life. Take the ever-present mobile phone that I have occasionally even seen tucked into priest and priestess robes at festivals! Have you seen the television advertisement in which the insistent ringtone interrupts a woman about to reach the peak on a lonely mountain, and another one in which the phone shatters the peace as a solitary man fishes from his rowing boat in the centre of a lake? You are never more than a ringtone away from your work is the gist of the message.

The range of modern telecommunications means that even on holiday in the most remote parts of the globe, some people are still plugged into work and home (I have witnessed computers and games consoles being used on stunningly beautiful beaches). Once the seaside postcard to the folks in the office was the norm and the only communication with home, except in emergencies.

Neo- or new, modern paganism has, of necessity, adapted to the realities of modern living. The original pagans in the pre-Christian societies before the fifth and sixth centuries CE lived in a very different world to neopagans who wear city suits, work on oil rigs or in computer software design companies and dash into a wine bar for a swift drink after work before the long commute home. The weekend family barbecue has become the modern version of the ancient *Blot* or magical feast of heathen tradition, sharing food and laughter (and the odd benign spiritual essence) with family and neighbours.

In any organised group, religious or secular, ancient or 21st century, including paganism, there may be politics, factions, backbiting and 'I have a smaller carbon footprint than you' competitiveness. But, on the whole, nature-based spirituality is caring, people-centred, environmentally aware and gentle, and counteracts the modern 24/7 frantic dash that even our children can get caught up in. It is all about doing one's best, sometimes in difficult circumstances, and 'Thou shalt not' is far outweighed by 'Why not try …' and 'Can I help?'.

The history of paganism

Paganism is probably the oldest kind of religion and was practised perhaps as far back as 30,000 BCE in hunter-gatherer societies. In these times, Mother Earth was seen as the source of all life. She may have been the earliest focus of reverence as the giver and taker of life and the bringer of rebirth, as new plants were seen growing in the earth where human and animal bones were buried and the herds returned annually to graze on the same ground.

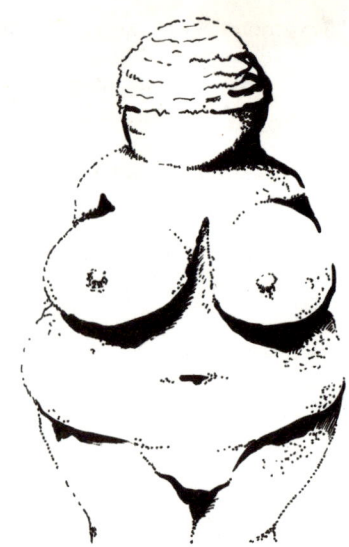

The earliest known Earth Mother figurine, found in Willendorf in Austria, dates from 24,000 to around 22,000 BCE or perhaps even earlier. She is made of limestone tinted with red ochre. The figure is just less than 11 cm/4.5 in high and is, not surprisingly, in the form of a very pregnant woman. Mother Earth may have been given different local names, but the figurines, wherever they are found, have a remarkably similar appearance. Because they have a pointed end, it has been speculated that these figurines may have served as a focus for fertility rites for the herds as well as for humans, placed in Mother Earth herself by the pointed end and carried from place to place when the tribes followed the herds.

Neopaganism

Neopaganism – or new 20th- and 21st-century paganism – is the name for a group of modern polytheistic nature-based religions that encourage people to live in harmony with the earth and one another.

Polytheistic describes a religion that believes in or worships more than one god. While the majority of modern pagans subscribe to the central focus of Mother Earth, there are also a number of different spiritual qualities regarded as divine, which are expressed as a variety of god and goddess forms. In this way, modern paganism is similar to pre-Christian paganism. For example, Airmid, the Celtic Irish healing goddess of medicinal plants and herbs, is a good focus and icon to represent the higher spiritual energies involved in herbal healing or aromatherapy.

Paganism has grown considerably in popularity during the last hundred years and especially since 1951 when the Repeal of the Witchcraft Act in the UK made it easier for people to explore openly other forms of spirituality.

I have sometimes used the words pagan and neopagan interchangeably. Strictly speaking, paganism in modern-world terms refers to an old, unchanged form of nature spirituality like that of Native North America. Neopaganism refers to forms of paganism that have been revived through claiming roots from the past like Scandinavian Astaru or Celtic druidry. Where people in the modern world adopt a lifestyle that takes into account the seasons, moon cycles and so on, even if they live in the centre of a town, I would class them as neopagans. But in practice you will find these terms used interchangeably.

The pagan path to success

Some neopagans draw strength and the energies offered by the seasons into themselves by celebrating the seasonal marker dates throughout the year either alone, with family and friends or as part of a group. However, many pagans who practise as Wiccans, especially those who follow the path of witchcraft, the craft of the wise, and some modern druids and druidesses, additionally absorb into themselves, through ritual, the energies of the earth and the cosmos for personal empowerment. These rituals take place especially but not exclusively at seasonal change points and, in the case of Wiccans, on the full moons that are celebrated through the year. By using these rituals, some pagans attempt to amplify their personal inner potential using the powers within nature (found in herbs, flowers, trees and crystals, the moon, sun and differing weather conditions) as well as the seasonal energies to attain success and fulfilment in their everyday lives and to send healing to others.

Psychologically as well as psychically, by using these underdeveloped but quite natural powers of the human mind, anyone can empower their personal energy field and so make themselves more confident, creative and likely to be noticed in a positive way, and to attract opportunities, love and abundance. The natural world is a treasure store of energies that our ancestors were naturally tuned into as they carried out ceremonies to bring about a successful hunt. Most significantly, it seems from evidence from contemporary hunting societies whose ways have been relatively unchanged for thousands of years, like the Sami reindeer people of Lapland, that nature-based rituals increase their innate telepathic abilities to *know* where the herds will be. Modern life has blunted the ability to tune into these opportunities, whether for love or a new job, and this renewed mind power ability is an optional bonus of practising paganism, even on a personal, informal level.

Creating your own spiritual lifestyle

You may decide to explore or may already be following a more organised pagan path, for example membership of a Wiccan coven that follows the teachings of the Gardnerian or Alexandrian system or a goddess-based structure such as the Fellowship of Isis. The majority of pagans, however, pursue their own private path and perhaps occasionally go along to a special celebration at a sacred site for a collective seasonal festival.

Some forms of neopaganism, like Wicca, can be either very informal, private and nature based or follow more structured, ritual coven practices. The majority of witches are solitary, as I am, and work alone, celebrating the full moon and the seasonal changes with family or friends and possibly going along to festivals or joining in online forums.

Because neo- or modern paganism is so diverse, you can take from any tradition what feels right and good for you and your lifestyle or anticipated lifestyle, to create your own unique path.

Bringing the old ways into the new world

Some neopagan forms of spirituality, unlike Wicca or druidry that have restored ancient practices in a comparatively new way, are derived from traditions that have survived relatively unchanged by the modern world, such as Native North American wisdom and forms of shamanism, an indigenous, often trance-based religion found from Siberia to sub-Saharan Africa. These forms of indigenous spirituality are still practised by the descendants of their original creators in many diverse forms.

It can be more difficult for non-indigenous practitioners to absorb wholeheartedly existing and evolving indigenous cultures' spiritual practices as a faith. The Native North Americans, like other indigenous people such as the Australian Aboriginals, suffered greatly from colonisation, land appropriation and often vicious attempts to overwrite or destroy their culture. A number of contemporary Native North Americans understandably resent people from other lands 'plundering' their beliefs and running what are said to be authentic, often expensive workshops that are a mixture of very different practices of specific Native North American nations with other neopagan beliefs. There are, however, positive and genuine Native North American teachings in books, on the websites of various Native North American nations and provided more directly by indigenous or indigenously trained individuals. Do not be deterred, therefore, if you do feel attracted to Native North American spirituality as your life path.

There is, in the UK, for example, a fabulous stone Native-North-American-inspired medicine or power wheel in Willens Park in Milton Keynes, a town better known for its shopping centre. This is open to anyone for ritual, meditation or just to walk round. In the same park are a Buddhist peace pagoda (like Hinduism and Japanese Shinto, Buddhism could be described as a Far Eastern pagan religion) and a huge turf labyrinth. A labyrinth is an ancient sacred coiled spiral shape found throughout the world that is increasingly being revived as a form of sacred art and focus for personal and collective ritual.

It is a blessing of modern communications systems that, unlike our ancestors, we can access accurate online information about many other cultures and forms of spirituality and visit ancient sites both in our own country and abroad because of the relative cheapness and speed of modern travel.

Using this book

As you work through this book, I would suggest you keep an ongoing notebook or online folder in order to record suggestions and activities that appeal to you. You could also keep a diary with photographs of pagan-based family activities you enjoy and impromptu private rituals or meditations you carry out, perhaps on a beautiful moonlit night or during a day at the sea.

If you already practise a specific form of neopaganism you may adapt some of the practices that you read about here to enrich your current rituals or celebrations.

See Useful Contacts (page 241) for details of various pagan religions and Further Reading (page 245) for books on the subjects that are covered in this book.

Pagan deities

Paganism is, as I suggested earlier, essentially an earth-based form of spirituality, revering the earth as a mother and the origin and source of fertility for land, animals and people, with the father as the necessary generative principle. These male and female principles are expressed in different mythological forms that are remarkably similar in focus in a number of different cultures from Ancient Egypt to Central and Southern America, Eastern and Western Europe, Africa, India, China and the Far East and Scandinavia.

The purpose of different pagan deity characters can be understood as a kind of divine soap opera in terms of the life cycle of humans. It is a matter for personal choice whether you consider all the pagan deities as different aspects of a single all-encompassing deity or of a supreme god and goddess or as distinct deities or higher spiritual forms. This cannot be agreed upon even by eminent theologians and anthropologists.

The pagan deities are believed to reflect the highest values of their culture. Take, for example, Jupiter the supreme Roman sky god, or his Greek counterpart, Zeus, ruler of the universe. Jupiter offered a role model for the ideal emperor who was general, statesman, protector and spiritual leader responsible for the well-being of all his people. He was also the ideal for the ordinary middle-aged man who was soldier, farmer and father of his family. Of course, the myths about Jupiter speak about his shortcomings in terms of fidelity to his consort Juno and his misuse of power for personal gain or vengeance. This is where the pagan deities, female and male, are so fascinating and very human, dealing with real-life issues and feelings, and sometimes getting it wrong. In the modern world, this god-king icon would relate to a middle-aged man struggling with a mortgage, fighting off potential competition from younger people on the career ladder, maybe having a mid-life crisis as he tries to regain his youth and retain his erection and his hairline, and trying to make sense of equality (in a way his grandfather never needed to) and the role of men in society today.

Male and female spirituality

In paganism, male and female deities or evolved spirit forms are both valued. In Wicca and the goddess religions, the emphasis is on the female power bringing forth the new life of the universe, fertilised by the male who thereafter ideally protects the mother and the child (and as god king protects the land, animals and people). Therefore it encourages respect, not war, between the sexes and equality based on responsibility and relative strengths (both emotional and physical) and needs that are not necessarily gender defined. But in re-examining the old roles and continuing to work for female equality, especially in cultures where there is none, real-life dilemmas are raised, such as whether female service personnel who are mothers of young children should be allowed on the front line of fighting or whether it should be left to the individual woman to decide.

Paganism does not teach entrenched attitudes or prejudice but encourages a way of looking at real people and real needs to reach consensus. This respect for equality between men and women may be one of its most socially healing factors.

The pagan deities are very much immanent, part of the world and not above it or separate as with the Christian or Hebrew supreme god. The pagan goddess in whatever form – as the universal mother or a named creatrix goddess – made the world and humans, assisted implicitly or sometimes not at all by the male who was usually her first creation. Therefore all humans, and indeed everything that is created, contain a divine spark. This would imply that we are all potential gods and goddesses or, in less elevated terms, spiritual beings or spirits in a physical body.

Paganism and perfection

In modern life, footballers, film and music icons, members of the royal family like the late Princess Diana, and even reality television stars have taken the place of deities, especially for the younger generation. These superstars, however nice they personally may be, can only offer very shallow definitions of perfection. The emphasis is inevitably on physical prowess, the possession of wealth and media definitions of beauty, and this superstar trend has been linked in both sexes with desires among even pre-adolescents for the body beautiful and a great increase in eating disorders. With older teenagers, the dream of fame and fortune can lead to an obsession for material goods that can spiral rapidly into debt problems, with the ease of obtaining instant credit at age 18.

As we get older we have less-defined worldly icons and may take our images of what is ideal from people we work with or for, beloved family members and spiritual figures, great world leaders or those who have reached the peak of our particular dream. On the other hand, we may stop striving for perfection and understandably focus on surviving; we may even forget our earlier motivating dreams in which we get to star in our very own life movie and ride off into the sunset of happiness.

While the Ancient Egyptians hardly ever portrayed sickness or age in tomb or temple wall paintings or statues and the Greeks and Roman sculpted beautiful marble images of their most beloved deities, more nature-based religions like the Celts did not, until influenced by the Romans, portray their deities in statues at all. They *saw* them in their minds as present in a beautiful landscape, in trees and flowers and as beings able to take the form of birds, deer or horses at will. Early Japanese and Indian nature religions saw their deities as present in sacred rocks and trees.

Working with a neopagan spiritual focus

As part of your travels along a neopagan path, you may start to consider what you are striving for in this life and as your legacy for future generations. You may then think about how you could represent this in image form. Decide what is an ideal male and female higher spiritual or deity focus that for you signifies beauty in the spiritual as well as, or rather than, the physical sense. You can have separate male and female foci or combine them.

This symbol could be a much-loved painting or a photograph of a fabulous sunset, seascape, snow-capped mountains or forest. It could be an image of the place you dream of living one day or your own back garden with a snapshot of the family on the day everyone smiled and the sun shone for more than five minutes, a picture of your wedding day or your first grandchild. It could be a lovely piece of furniture you saved hard to buy or restored from junk, a wooden carving of an animal or bird or a crystal or a ceramic pot. You may find a statue or sculpture of a representative male and female deity, saints, fairies or angels.

Sometimes male divinity is represented in paganism as a horn and the female as a shell or as jet and amber crystals. I use jet for the male but other practitioners prefer amber for the male and jet for the female. You could, Wiccan style, have an ornamental knife and a silver or bronze chalice for the male and female respectively. You could use matching tall white candles in a gold-coloured candlestick for the male and silver for the female or wooden holders for both.

Once you have chosen your focus, or foci, you can start to work with them to enrich your life.

* Find a special place in your home to keep your dream or ideal focus, maybe with fresh flowers and a floral oil or incense and candles that you can light in the evening to create an atmosphere for quiet meditation or reflection.

* Take time to write in your journal a description of your ideal god and goddess with all the qualities you most admire and at the life stage most relevant to you now, whether this is as a wise grandmother or a young maiden huntress or god king.

* If you wish, set them in a culture you feel drawn to and give them names that feel right to you. Over time you can add to the pantheon (deity family) to represent other aspects of your life that you are hoping to concentrate on.

* Choose one god- or goddess-like quality to work on or try out in your daily life and think of a foe, whether binge eating, smoking or a bully who intimidates you at work and how your chosen deity, using mental rather than actual thunderbolts, could begin to make inroads on the problem.

* If this seems hard, light your candle or candles and focus on your symbol of these powers. In time, the icon will absorb the powers you have inside yourself. When you feel a lack of confidence you can look at or touch your icon or icons and draw on the stored strength, amplified by the candles and incense and your own quiet times. It can be good for a woman to work with a male as well as female focus and vice versa for a man.

* Find also an outdoor place that seems to represent the same qualities and draw strength from the earth beneath your feet, the trees or stones you touch and the wind, sunshine, moonlight or rain that transmit the cosmic powers into your own energy field and just for a minute or two borrow a bit of that divinity. Maybe carry a small jet and amber crystal with you as a reminder.

1 Are You a Natural Pagan?

This chapter asks you to consider your own principles by first contemplating your reaction to 14 moral dilemmas. The most common general principles of paganism are then listed and explained. You may find that these offer an alternative perspective or confirm what you already believe. Pagan principles are not in any way weird and reflect what many people instinctively feel and spontaneously follow in their daily lives. Many of us live by pagan principles without realising it and are by nature pagans and love the earth and all her creatures, even if the name pagan is not one that feels right to adopt.

Pagan living is about balance and doing one's best given the circumstances of your life. It should not involve making life more stressful, but is about thoughtful and realistic reactions to threats of global warming, climate change and other social and conservation issues while taking account of the needs and realities of daily living and working. The chapter concludes therefore with a list of ways of introducing pagan principles into your existing life without causing major disruption.

Moral dilemmas

Read through the following list of real-life dilemmas and decide how you would react. Record your initial feelings. There are, of course, no right answers or quick fixes.

You may want to go online to check the latest research on topics such as carbon emissions, endangered species conservation and vegetarianism.

1. What would you do about someone you knew was defrauding the benefits system if you also knew they had been unfairly deprived of what they were morally entitled to by a technicality and were struggling to bring up a sick relative or child with little help.

2. A lazy and manipulative senior colleague is milking the work system for all it is worth, causing major problems that you have to rectify and constantly taking time off for social events while you have to cover for her absence. You have a chance to expose her inefficiency anonymously and would almost certainly get her job,

which you desperately need because you are a single parent trying to bring up a child alone and struggling with money.

3. You find £75 at an airport in an unmarked plastic envelope obviously from a money exchange bureau of which there are a number on the concourse, but with no identifying marks. Three months ago you were robbed of £100 at the same airport.

4. You are asked by a friend to go abroad with her at reduced cost as another friend has dropped out of the trip. You are worried about the carbon emissions of plane journeys and were planning to holiday in your own country. But your friend says the seat will be filled by someone else if you don't take it as it is peak season and the plane would use virtually the same fuel whether you took the seat or not.

5. You are asked to give a donation to a Third World famine area but you have heard from a reliable source that the aid is not getting through and the corrupt local government is pocketing the money.

6. You are campaigning to save elephants in Indonesia. However, locals who were shooting them are complaining that the animals are trampling the food crops and attacking their families and that preventative measures to save the humans' livelihood by conservationists are not working.

7. You are a white couple and are desperate to adopt a baby. There are many children in care waiting for a home, but you are refused because the children available are from mixed races or different ethnic and cultural backgrounds. You argue that it is better to grow up in a loving home than in a care home, but no one will listen. Suddenly you get a chance to adopt a baby from a Third World orphanage through a non-government-approved agency.

8. Your kitchen is overrun by ants from the garden. You have tried to get rid of them without killing them by trying to block accesses but this has proved unsuccessful. Since they are a health hazard, are you justified in killing living creatures if they invade your home?

9. Your daughter who is 17 has a new boyfriend, whom you like, but whose mother regularly uses drugs and has other drug users regularly staying in her home. Your daughter says you are prejudiced against the family because they live off benefits and in social housing and have not had your educational or social advantages. She is threatening to leave home unless you let her stay with her boyfriend at weekends. She says she can influence him away from drugs and help the family.

10 You drive your eight-year-old child to school every day because she is too young to walk along the narrow dangerous country roads alone. If you walked with her you would be late for work and may lose your job. There have been unresolved bullying problems on the school bus by older children and there is no one with whom you can lift share. But what about the environmental issues?

11 Your ten-year-old son has stopped eating meat, cheese and eggs and drinking milk because a friend whose parents are vegans showed him pictures of animals in a slaughterhouse and of chicken embryos. Vegans will not eat or wear any animal-based products including honey, eggs, dairy products, wool or silk. You worry about your son eating a balanced diet at this crucial age as he is anaemic. He refuses to eat pulses and does not like vegetables apart from potatoes. Can you convince him it is not cruel to eat meat or anything to do with animals, as he says? Or does he have a point given the conditions in some battery farms?

12 A woman who has been made infertile by necessary medical treatment has been told by her now ex-husband and the court that she must destroy the fertilised embryos that she had frozen before the treatment since he does not wish to father her children. She argues he is still fertile and can have other children if he chooses, but this is her only chance of motherhood.

13 A woman wants to serve on the front line of action in battle, but she has a small child. Should she go and should she be allowed to go?

14 You live on a fast main road where restrictions stop you parking except at certain times. Should you follow your neighbours' example and concrete your front garden even though this is bad for local wildlife in an area where there is rapidly decreasing green space?

General principles of paganism

Now read through the following most common general principles of paganism. Note that paganism even more than other forms of spirituality involves deciding what is right in response to an actual situation and the people involved rather than relying on set responses.

Which of the principles seem fundamental to you and which do you already follow or could you easily adapt to your lifestyle? Consider the adaptations you would need to make to fit these principles in with the unavoidable demands of your life and the problems you may have in applying them.

Principle 1 All life is connected and operates in a continuing cycle.

This is the most important principle of paganism. The Native North Americans speak of life as a continuous hoop or circle. In 1930 Black Elk, the Oglala Sioux Medicine Man who had been a child at the Wounded Knee Massacre explained:

> *In the old days ... all our power came from the sacred hoop of the nation and so long as the hoop was unbroken, the people flourished. The flowering tree was the living centre of the hoop and the circle of the four quarters nourished it. The East gave peace and light, the South gave warmth; in the West thunder beings gave rain and the North with its cold and mighty wind gave strength and endurance ... The life of man is a circle from childhood to childhood and so it is in everything where power moves.*

Since we know that the fluttering of a butterfly wing in one part of the world subtly affects the vibrations of the universe, each of us has a place in, a responsibility for and an effect on the world. If we can tune into the cycles of nature and the changing seasons, the cosmic and earth energies, our lives will flow more harmoniously from stage to stage. In this way we will not regret the passing of youth or external beauty, fear change or hold on to people and things we have outgrown. Rather we can welcome each new experience and stage of life as precious and valuable.

Our rural ancestors celebrated the sowing and the reaping times as a way of linking with and so increasing or activating their own fertility and prosperity energies and the fertility of the land and animals that if tended brought abundance to the people. This also reinforces the idea that there is not one single life goal but a series of ongoing stages that evolve as we evolve to prevent stagnation.

Most importantly, we transmit our own wisdom and discoveries through the values and traditions we hand on to future generations just as we can learn from both the achievements and mistakes of the past.

Principle 2 *Everyone is equal and so there should be tolerance of and respect for the different lifestyles of peoples of different cultures, ethnic backgrounds, gender and socio-economic groups, even if we do not necessarily share their viewpoint.*

This leads on from the first principle and embraces huge areas such as world peace, the fair distribution of economic and food resources, religious tolerance, terrorist threats and invasion of other lands. It embraces the peaceful coexistence of different cultures within the same country or even town or district, the welfare of older and disabled people, equality between and respect for both the sexes and the removal of prejudices and misinformation. In spite of the modern westernised competitive world, understanding has become more possible through increased communication through the internet, increasingly multicultural societies and the relative ease of travel.

This diversity also involves valuing and preserving the best of local and national customs while drawing on other cultures and their spirituality and celebrations to enrich our own lifestyle.

On a personal level, we may need to re-examine relationships with members of the opposite sex at work and socially in terms of their personalities and merit rather than being sidelined into issues of gender. Above all, we should be confident enough to ask for the respect we deserve in all relationships, based on the value we place on our own worth. (I struggled with this self-esteem issue for years.)

Principle 3 *All life is sacred.*

Humans are not set above creatures, to use the earth and her creatures as a bottomless larder, rubbish bin and money bank. Rather we are the caretakers of animals, birds, fish and insects. They share the same spark of the creator who made them as humans do, whether that creator or creatrix is viewed as an animate deity force or some process triggered by a big bang; also they preceded us in the creation stakes.

A number of neopagans are vegetarian or the stricter vegans. Paganism, however, is not a vegetarian spirituality, but recognises the natural food chain that extends from plants through animals to humans. This food chain continues in those few indigenous hunter-gatherer societies that are unaffected by modern technology, exploitation by middle men and women and the need to supply the mass market. In these societies, animals and birds that are hunted are still accorded respect. In urban or industrialised societies this respect must be shown by ensuring that animals and birds reared for food are well cared for and slaughtered humanely if we do decide to eat meat and eggs.

Principle 4 We have much to learn from other species.

Animals and birds have traditionally symbolised in pure undiluted and idealised forms, the strengths and qualities that humans desire in their own lives: the courage of the lion, the selfless devotion of the dog to friends and family, the single-minded focus of the hawk and the protective fierceness of the mother wolf towards her young and her clan.

For this reason, from Native North America and other societies such as the Australian Aboriginal people comes the concept of totem or power animals, especially intelligent and spiritually wise members of different animal and bird species, who offer to humans a reminder of the need to trust our own instincts and intuitions. These imagined wise and often larger than life specimens are described in indigenous myth as bringers of gifts to humanity such as fire or even assistance with creation.

The concept of power or totem guardian animals and birds as spiritual guardians and icons for humans has permeated other neopagan forms of spirituality and even appears in some modern business assertiveness training programmes.

Principle 5 Harm none by thought, word and deed.

Though this is part of the Wiccan Rede or basic rules of Wicca, it is a more general moral principle to which non-Wiccans can relate and can be applied to every area of life. This principle is much harder to follow than it sounds. If someone is threatening our family or livelihood or has an unfair advantage and is exploiting it or influencing vulnerable people adversely, how far is intervention against them justifiable? (The continuing problems in Iraq at the time of writing this book are an example of this dilemma.)

In neopaganism, this rule involves personal moral choice and responsibility. Though protecting the vulnerable from harm is justifiable, can and should it be achieved without harming the perpetrator? Once you cross your personal moral line of harming none, the boundaries of necessary protection versus justifiable retaliation can become blurred. Harm can even extend to words spoken in retaliation about the office gossip who is making life miserable for a young colleague.

Principle 6 What you send out good or bad is returned to you three times as powerfully.

This is another Wiccan concept shared by many other neopagans.

This takes us back to the idea of the butterfly wing altering the vibes of the universe – we all know how a word of praise or a compliment has an immediate uplifting effect while criticism or sarcasm can be devastating to someone with little confidence.

Neopaganism is unlike the Judaeo Christian and other traditional religions in that there is no supreme deity to whom we can say sorry when we do something bad and we therefore cannot be granted forgiveness through an appointed representative of the deity. Once negative words have been spoken, deeds done or negative thoughts or ill wishes have been released by us into the cosmos, all we can do is try to put right what we have done. If this is not possible, we cannot offload the blame on others or go into denial, but should accept that we got it wrong, live with the consequences and learn from it.

But this principle means more than that. The more good things we do and say, the more we increase the positive vibes in the world. As individuals we can all make a difference in small ways and as a part of the collective and accumulated good vibes of many people focusing on the same event at the same time. Take the example of the now annual worldwide Earth Day that was first observed on 22 April 1970 when about 20 million people in America celebrated the event; as a result came the impetus for national legislation like the Clean Air and Clean Water Acts. Twenty years later, on 22 April 1990, more than 200 million people in 141 countries observed Earth Day and the numbers continue to grow.

As well as the external awareness generated by such events and pressure placed on governments, there is also a huge build up of positive cosmic energy that may make it easier for people generally to work towards goals such as environmental awareness and world peace. We do not understand the way such cumulative energies work but increasing scientific research suggests that we are, as Principle 1 states, all interconnected energy wise.

Principle 7 We can make, or at least can strongly influence, our own destiny by the choices we make.

From Heathenry, a form of paganism now popular as the revived Astaru, Odinnhism or Forn Sed in North America as well as in the original lands of Scandinavia, Anglo Saxon Britain and Germany, comes the belief in Orlog. Orlog is the universal web of destiny to which individuals' personal fates are linked, and which means that everyone's actions are affected by and affect the fate of others. The Vikings and Anglo Saxons spoke of three sisters who wove the web of the world and of the fates of individual beings, mortal and gods.

This principle puts forward the view that what we are and do is influenced by the past. The past embraces both the genetic and family or social values of our ancestors and our own past deeds and beliefs. These beliefs were shaped not only by immediate family and their values from when we were children but by people we have known during our lives and situations in which we have been involved. These past influences may be unconsciously even more than consciously guiding our present actions and attitudes and the values we transmit to those around us.

Even more importantly, each person is responsible by their thoughts, words and deeds for their own future destiny as well as that of their biological descendants and the people they meet. This is an extension of the Wiccan Rede concepts, and emphasises that we have the power to change and make our own destiny and affect that of others for better or worse – a huge responsibility but also a huge opportunity.

Principle 8 We should celebrate or at least become aware of the changing seasons throughout the year as they reflect and regulate our own fluctuating yearly energy patterns and offer a source of power.

This is a more specific version of the main interconnectedness principle. Neopagans in both town and country, like their rural ancestors, generally celebrate the four main seasonal marker points: spring, summer, autumn and winter, which are linked with the changing seasonal solar patterns of daylight and darkness. These rituals, often conducted outdoors by sun or moonlight, may be entirely private or with friends and family. Public celebrations of, for example, midsummer (the summer solstice or longest day) around 21 June (six months earlier in the southern hemisphere) may be organised by a local group of pagans or environmentalists, usually at an ancient sacred site. Larger events are becoming more common throughout the world, for example, the impromptu gathering of thousands of people at Stonehenge in Wiltshire, as are environmental, earth-based or goddess festivals around one of these times.

The summer solstice represents a time of maximum annual sun and light power and on a personal level gives the energy for an opportunity to be created or seized. Alternatively it can be a time for deciding how dreams and ambitions can be achieved perhaps after months of effort planning a career change, house move or long-awaited trip (see pages 164–197 for more on these festivals and others that are important in neopaganism). Pagan seasonal celebrations also counteract more commercialised festivals such as Christmas and Easter and can offer a focus if you do not live with your children all of the time and so cannot celebrate a major conventional festival with them.

Principle 9 Every day is sacred and tuning into the sun's daily movements prevents time from slipping away or passing unnoticed.

For example, each dawn or when you wake can bring a new beginning or renewed hope and can energise and inspire you for the day ahead even if you can only pause for a minute or two before plunging into the daily routine. Otherwise a week can become a month and before we know it another year has passed.

Principle 10 The moon links directly with the inner monthly ebbs and flows that are experienced by men as well as women and if recognised can help you to harmonise your own energy ebbs, moods and flows with the visible lunar cycles in the sky.

Sometimes, when trying to push ahead with a plan, we come up against obstacle after obstacle; when trying to organise an activity for children, they are quarrelsome or have minor accidents. These problems may be due to the waning of the moon. If this is the case, the best option (if possible) is to opt for quieter activities and for getting rid of the obstacles, ready to push ahead in a week or so when the crescent reappears.

A number of naturally fertile women who are blocked from conceiving by anxiety, especially if they are older and feel time is running out, benefit from getting their natural cycles back in rhythm with the moon (see page 106 for more on this).

Principle 11 The human life cycle is marked by natural change points that we need to acknowledge and work through with rites of passage if we are to be able to move through our lives harmoniously and accept and use creatively both loss and gain.

The modern world is strangely devoid of ceremonies except for highly commercialised ones like weddings. Anyone can create and hold a personal ceremony for a particular rite of passage, be it a birth, marriage or divorce, or to mark leaving home after adolescence, a change of career, house move and blessing of the new home, redundancy or retirement.

Pagan weddings or handfastings that may precede or follow a civil ceremony are becoming increasingly popular among non-neopagans. They can be helpful both for divorcees who may still encounter problems with more conventional religions and for people who wish to commit to each other in front of friends and family members rather than in the eyes of the law or in a church that they rarely if ever visit. Equally, if people are not regular churchgoers, a formal baptism ceremony may seem inappropriate. Because pagan celebrations tend to be simpler, they are a good way of getting over the pressures and expense of an elaborate wedding. In Chapter 6 I have described how you can create and carry out such ceremonies yourself, though some people do ask a druid or druidess or Wiccan priest or priestess to officiate and often such ceremonies can be held at ancient sites, such as the Rollright stone circles in Oxfordshire in Central England.

Principle 12 Death is part of the life cycle and is inevitable and so should be prepared for and revered.

In the modern world death is a taboo subject and those who are bereaved may face embarrassment from others who in the days after the funeral try to avoid them or will not speak of their loss. To pagans and neopagans alike, death is just another stage in the ongoing creation, destruction and renewal cycle seen in nature and almost all believe that we are spiritual beings in a physical body. Rather than terrifying threats of hell and damnation if you subscribe to the wrong religion or the prospect of just ceasing to be, the afterlife to neopagans is a stage of beauty, peace and light and a chance to put right what went wrong. But the main emphasis in this book whatever you believe about an afterlife is of leaving your spiritual footprint on the world and ensuring your life is both memorable and remembered even if you do not have family living (see pages 35–36).

Principle 13 Life and spirituality are based on the principle of mutual exchange and giving what is possible and receiving what is needed.

The Heathen principle of *fridh* is another valuable principle of paganism and neopaganism, which involves peace, friendship and social obligations towards family and community. Modern pagan rituals, whether a barbecue, a picnic or my own favourite a 'bring and share' meal, where everyone contributes something, have similarities to the Viking *Blot* festivals, where feasts were shared with the deities. Food is shared with those present and symbolically with the deity or higher spiritual focus, who is pictured as providing the ongoing bounty and blessings. Promises were made at these feasts to honour the gods or in modern terms to do something for others in return for blessings asked. The cosmic exchange principle is simple. You can ask the earth and the cosmos for what you need and then you need to do some practical act of kindness or a small ecological gesture as your way of paying back what you need to take (a sort of balancing of the cosmic bank account).

Principle 14 It is good to be different.

Every human and creature (leaving aside cloning), except for identical twins, is genetically unique and so trying to fit into ideals (whether of the media or of other individuals) if they go against what we really are or want, is ultimately restrictive and counterproductive. What makes you happy and fulfilled may not be what other people consider important or what your family, teachers or those who influence you say you should be doing or aiming for. We all have talents that are of value and our only duty is, where possible, to use those gifts in the way that feels right and authentic – and does some good in the world.

Principle 15 You can and should create your own form of neopagan spirituality that will evolve as you change, learn more of and from nature and meet new challenges.

Even in neopaganism you get people who tell you what you ought to be doing and that you are not a real neopagan, druidess or witch unless you subscribe to their beliefs. I come across them all the time and have only just learned to ignore this form of moral superiority. You are free to do what you want, to celebrate your spirituality where and how you want, either alone or with a group of like-minded friends. Essentially, you need to sign up to nothing, promise nothing (except to yourself and whatever form of higher spiritual form you recognise or the higher more evolved part within yourself) and revere and respect the natural world in its both creative and destructive aspects.

You can make your spirituality part of your everyday world – and it need take no more than five or ten minutes if that is all you have. Your pagan sacred moments will come as you passively allow yourself to absorb whatever natural energies are around you, whether in a ten-minute lunch break in a city square or walking by the sea while the children are building sandcastles or squabbling over the last sandwich. As you walk through the park, your objective is *being* rather than doing, thinking or planning in your head the next hour, day or year.

You may decide to find out about more organised pagan religions such as Wicca or druidry, which have formal training with grades and teaching and sometimes quite elaborate rituals. The formality and level of organisation varies within different traditions and many people, like me, practise even more structured forms of neopaganism alone and in their own idiosyncratic way. (See the list of pagan organisations in Useful Contacts on page 241.)

Principle 16 You can practise neopaganism anywhere at any time.

Ideally, neopaganism is an open-air form of spirituality but you can work indoors with herbs, flowers and crystals. Its temples are ancient groves of trees, old stone circles, near lakes, on hillsides or close to sacred wells that may be thousands of years old. You can equally encounter nature in your garden, on your balcony or at the local recreation ground, where you can use flowers, trees, grass and soil to tune into the powerful and healing energies of the earth. Neopaganism does not need churches, temples or cathedrals.

Principle 17 There may be essences in the natural world that have an objective existence different from our own.

If you are new to nature spirituality or are naturally very logical and left brained, you may want to leave this principle for a few months. But many ordinary down-to-earth people, adults as well as children, have sent me accounts of what might be called fairy beings. Remarkably consistent accounts of these beings have appeared in many different myths, cultures and ages, from old Japan, Ancient Greece and Rome to 21st century urban backyards in industrialised northern towns of England. It may be that fairies are the way the human mind interprets and expresses more abstract essences or energies emanating from trees, flowers, waterfalls and lakes.

Bringing paganism into your daily life

You may have discovered that pagan principles already underlie much of how you live your life, but what follow are further suggestions for adopting a more natural lifestyle.

Do not immediately dismiss those changes that involve time being set aside in your already packed schedule. Some of the apparently essential demands on our time are unreasonable, but we may go along with them to be kind or to keep the peace. It may also be that the original purpose of or need for an ongoing commitment may no longer exist or there may be time-consuming activities or people we have outgrown that could free up precious time for new pleasures and relaxation.

- Spend time studying local indigenous wildlife either in its natural habitat or in conservation or designated wildlife areas, rather than always going to safari or exotic animal parks. The elusiveness of local creatures especially in their natural habitat necessarily makes us slow down and learn that nature is not there to entertain us but that we can be rewarded with an occasional glimpse into their world, which is almost entirely separate from ours.

- If you have a garden, try to leave a small part of it uncultivated. Allow wildflowers and long grass to grow in order to attract wildlife including birds and butterflies. Put up a bat or bird nesting box and feeders. This is especially vital if you live in an area where green space is at a premium or you have had to concrete over part of your garden in order to park your car (not ideal but sometimes necessary).

- Feed wild birds regularly if you have no garden, especially in winter when some people forget them. Patronise and encourage any urban wildlife parks or city farms and take children on organised bat or woodland walks or bug hunting.

- If you can walk or cycle to work you may see birds that you can identify by their markings. It may be that a particular blackbird hops in front of you on significant days when there are special opportunities or challenges at work and this may act as a warning or spur to action. If you have time, stop – the bird may trigger insights from your own deep unconscious about something you are missing. This process was labelled synchronicity or meaningful coincidence by the 20th century psychologist Carl Gustav Jung.

✣ Buy local produce whenever possible, even if you cannot afford organic. Check that supermarkets selling local fruit and vegetables have not sent it long distances to be packaged. Where possible, buy unpackaged food and put cloth or recyclable shopping bags in the back of the car after unpacking the shopping, ready for next time.

✣ If you are buying eggs, ensure as far as possible that they are free range and, if you are buying meat, that it is humanely slaughtered. Even if it means buying a smaller quantity, it is better to buy local and free range – try the farmers' markets that are sprouting up everywhere, even in city centres.

✣ Make trips to country markets part of your weekend and look out for pick-your-own produce or speciality farm shops while you are travelling (getting off the motorways or main roads often saves getting stuck in traffic jams and is much more scenic). There is an amazing amount of free food to be picked in local woodlands, but do get a good book or go initially on an organised trip to avoid poisoning yourself. Be careful of hedgerows where crops may have been sprayed with pesticides.

✣ Watch and plot the moon for a month or two, starting when you first see the crescent in the sky, and noting each moon rise and set. (This will vary from month to month.) You can also find the moon phases in *Old Moore's Almanac*, in local papers under the weather section and in some diaries. Monitor any feelings you have that are not related to current external events in your life, and record when they occur in relation to the moon phase. You may well see a pattern emerging. Men like women can be subject to mood changes affected by the moon and, once understood, these can be used to your advantage. (See pages 110–120 for more on the phases of the moon.)

✣ With 24/7 supermarket and garage openings, 24-hour television and artificial lighting it is easy to get out of touch with the light patterns of day and night as well as the seasonal differences, and this can contribute to burnout and stress-related conditions. To overcome this, try to mark the important times of each day by standing still for just a second or two while facing the sun or the lightest part of the sky if the sun is not shining. Do this at dawn (or when you wake up in the morning), noon (or when you break for lunch), twilight (or when you go home) and midnight (or when you go to bed). If there is a particularly vivid sunrise or sunset, stop what you are doing if possible and watch its beauty.

✣ If you have a highly pressurised job take regular 'sun time' breaks (see page 101 for the chime hours of the day) and where possible try to go home on time (the equivalent of twilight) at least three times a week. It is too easy to do so much regular overtime that it becomes normal working hours.

✤ When you have a spare weekend at home or on holiday try for a day or two to live by the sun, leaving the curtains open so you are woken by the light and lighting candles after dark or sitting outdoors, if it is warm enough, under the moon and stars. Hide the clocks, eat when you are hungry and sleep when you are ready to go to bed. This is a wonderful antidote to binge eating, hyperactivity and insomnia in adults and children. If you practise this at different times of the year (using candlelight on dark mornings when necessary) you will find it easier to relax when you are not working and focus when you are.

✤ Learn to love the dark months and the darkness as well as the light since this, especially the further north you live in the northern hemisphere, is an ongoing reality. Brighten the darkness where possible with candles rather than artificial lighting and make the most of precious daylight hours.

✤ If you can get a short winter sunshine break, make this a priority and economise on other things.

✤ Make experiences a priority over possessions. Parents are under terrific pressure to provide their children with the latest consumables. As a mother of five I often bought 'can't live without' items that gave only short-lived pleasure until the next craze. It is better to spend money on experiences and memories. I know only too well that consumer happiness at 29.9 per cent APR takes a long time to pay back.

✤ Even if you are self employed or juggling work and family, try to keep some time each day and at least one day each week for yourself – your self time. The chore mountain and the unanswered e-mails will still be there and the world will turn without you for a while. The special moments, however, do not return if they are missed. Even if you planned to shop, clean or redecorate, if the sun shines, take off for the day or even a weekend and remember why and for whom you are doing it all.

✤ Walk in all weathers and temperatures, and allow each outing to fill you with its particular energies. The modern world with its indoor sports facilities, central heating and door-to-door car travel can make us less eager to go out in the rain or the wind. But in avoiding these extremes, we can narrow our sensitivity to internal as well as external stimuli and children may not learn the pleasures of wrapping up warm or in waterproofs and enjoying winter outings and rainy day holidays.

- ✤ Spend time being as well as doing and enjoy doing nothing (the hardest thing of all for stressed, overworked adults). Imitate your teenager or your cat for a while. In the modern world, even quiet reverie may be marred by a feeling that you should be practising the latest meditation or relaxation techniques instead of just enjoying the silence or listening to birdsong. From childhood, organised activities occupy more and more time so that we (with or without the family) may need to relearn the joys of a walk in the woods or a day by the sea or in the park without seeking entertainment or themed stimulation.

- ✤ Have technology-free zones and times at home. Nothing is sadder than a family sitting together but using MSN to talk to various friends, playing on personal games consoles or chatting on mobile phones. The dining table is no place for the mobile (very rarely is anything so urgent it cannot wait). We do not need to listen to a news update every half an hour. People who are present should take priority over your boss who wants to check some figures in the middle of your evening or a friend who wants to complain about her boyfriend.

- ✤ Even if you live alone designate your 'do not disturb' times and mean it. Silence is golden and you do not have to watch TV, listen to the radio or read even if you are eating alone. The hardest thing is to learn to do nothing. On a daily train journey try to avoid always reading or using a computer or MP3 player, rather watch what is outside the window as you pass urban back gardens or industrial sites where there may be a tree in blossom.

- ✤ Visit old places of natural beauty, whether old stone circles, cathedrals, caves, healing wells, ruined abbeys or ancient forests and tune into the energies of all the people who have visited and perhaps worshipped at the place over the centuries. Learn the legends of the place so that you can pass them on.

- ✤ Leave positive spiritual footprints and handprints wherever you go by standing and admiring a beautiful view or touching the walls of a ruined abbey. Focus totally on the place and imagine you are leaving footprints and handprints of light. Just as you pick up the sense of peace or wonder from the past, so some day someone will pick up the essence of this moment and of you.

- ✤ Honour your own tribe. Find out all you can about your family past and its stories. If possible, visit the areas or lands your family came from and go to local history or industrial museums in the vicinity. See if you can discover old recipes or local annual events that may still be held. Look in local book or gift shops for reproductions of old books or collections of local fare and customs (often put together by a local historian or folklore expert).

✤ Keep a journal (with photographs and/or illustrations, if you wish) to pass on to future generations or, if you have no family, to a local school or archive.

✤ Celebrate the seasons in your own way, for example by collecting and decorating evergreen boughs on the shortest day of the year – the midwinter solstice around 21 December (six months earlier in the southern hemisphere). Light candles to welcome the sun back as the days very slowly start to get longer. Cook a special meal and invite friends and family to light candles to add light to the darkest of days, a wonderful antidote and break from pre-Christmas stress.

✤ As you become accustomed to the slower rhythms of the natural world, tune into the sounds of nature by listening to the leaves rustling in the wind or the sea dashing on the rocks on a stormy night. Imagine, as the ancients did, that the trees are transmitting messages from the deities or wise ancestors. You may tune into some valuable unexpected information from your wise, yet often inaccessible, inner self.

✤ Touch plants and trees and you may begin to sense and distinguish between different kinds of plant energies. Use both your sensitive fingertips and the palms of your hands that are believed to contain psychic energy centres or chakras. Eventually you may be able to interpret the powerful sensations experienced by touching the trunk of a broad ancient oak and to perceive a very different nature essence or creature from the delicate, almost ethereal, feeling evoked by the first primrose of spring.

2 Making the Home a Place of Happiness

Whether you live alone or house share, live with a partner or a family, the home offers, as it has always done, a sanctuary from the world and a place where you can be yourself, surrounded by the things that you value and love. In this and the following chapter I will suggest ways in which you can put a heart into your home – be it an impersonal city centre apartment or a house on a new suburban estate – so that it feels welcoming and restorative.

Many domestic folk customs practised by our ancestors right through Christian times have ancient roots. These customs continued during the 1800s even as more and more people moved to the towns into small cramped terraced houses. It was not until the Second World War that the real break came with the old ways and with it the increasing mobility of people that gradually eroded the extended family. For all its faults, grandparents, aunts, uncles and cousins living in the same street or sometimes in the same house, provided a sense of continuity and security and ensured the natural transference of the old folk wisdom from generation to generation.

Of course, our ancestors did not have the benefits of essential oils, easily available different coloured candles and polished crystals. We have the advantage of being able to use these to supplement simpler tools such as stones, garden flowers and herbs.

The hearth

Once the hearth was the centre of the home and even in these days when central heating is common, many houses still have a central fireplace with a real or gas or electric flame-effect fire that forms a focal point (*focus*, the Latin word for hearth means centre). If this is not the case in your home, it is easy to make a small hearth-like feature in the main living area by using a wooden or metal hearth surround bought from a DIY store or by marking the area with stones or slate. Any hearth can be kept alive in summer with yellow, orange and red flowers or flowering plants, red crystals or stones and a red candle that can be lit in the evenings.

The history of the sacred hearth tradition

Hearths can be traced back with certainty 125,000 years but may be even older. From pre-Christian times the family hearth was believed to welcome home living family members, deceased wise ancestors and family guardians alike.

The Ancient Greek goddess Hestia was goddess of the hearth and, even on the hottest days, a small flame was kept burning continuously in homes, lit from a sacred brand taken from one of her temple hearths. In the home, prayers were offered to Hestia before and after the meal and small portions of the food were thrown on to the flames. The hearth fire was seen as a symbol of hospitality and in Greece, as in a number of other cultures, women were the special guardians of the fire. This was regarded as an honour rather than a chore, recognising the importance of women as homemakers and earthly representatives of Hestia.

Other traditions included carrying a newborn child round the fire and asking for the protection of Hestia during the early vulnerable days. A bride would also transfer a burning brand from the family hearth to her new home to carry with her the blessings of home.

Gabija, the Lithuanian goddess of the hearth fire, was honoured in a similar fashion by throwing salt on the fire each evening after the main meal and some older Eastern European people continue this tradition.

The sacred flame was constantly kept alight in every city in Greece at a public hearth sacred to Hestia and each new city would take fire from an existing hearth to establish its own. Travellers would ask for a flame from the central hearth to carry with them and it was feared that if the sacred fire of Athens went out then the civilised world would cease to exist.

In Rome, Vesta, the goddess of fire occupied the same role as Hestia, as deity of the family hearth and of the sacred city fire.

Keeping the fire alight

In Western Europe right up until the mid 1900s there was a ritual for the annual extinguishing and relighting of the family hearth fire with a burning coal or brand from the old fire. This traditionally took place at midnight on New Year's Eve or, in places influenced by the Celtic culture, on Halloween (31 October), that once marked the end of the Celtic year. This hearth fire burned from Halloween until May Eve, the beginning of the Celtic summer, but even after that date a small symbolic brand was kept burning.

Some people still keep a small long-burning candle continually alight in their home (in a suitable safe place) except when they go away. In modern times, however, the eternally burning flame is more usually symbolised by a dark candle lit five minutes before midnight on New Year's Eve. Threads are burned in the candle to represent what needs to be left behind in the old year. Then, on the first stroke of midnight, a white candle is lit from the dark one and the dark candle is extinguished to symbolically transfer what is good to the new year. The white candle is left burning until it goes out. The same custom can be used to mark the beginning of a month, the beginning of a week or even a particularly significant period of crisis or opportunity when ongoing strength will be needed.

The heart of the home today

Modern neighbourhood life can be very lonely. Even in a row of houses or block of apartments, the curtains of each home are drawn as darkness falls and only the flicker of the television set indicates life. Family members may be dashing in and out to various activities; teenagers may be hidden away in their rooms, sending MSNs on computers to their friends.

You can start to draw the family back together by creating a special centre or focus where people can gather for just a few minutes each day or an hour or two a week to exchange news and strengthen family ties. If you live alone you can sit by the fire or candlelight, collect your thoughts and restore harmony before doing chores. Five or ten minutes last thing at night after the television or computers have been switched off can help to bring more peaceful sleep. For children, a bedtime story by candlelight in the special place brings the day to a close. (As a working mother of five, I know that this can be hard to do, but it's worth it as the children may settle so much more easily and wake less in the night.)

You can either create an actual hearth, as described below, or, if you prefer, a special place in an area where you would naturally relax, for example round a coffee table (see page 42). The effect is the same.

Creating a magical hearth

By putting symbols of health and abundance around a hearth or focal point you are aligning your own natural health and abundance, and bringing energies via the external symbols to the natural energies around you. It is a bit like plugging into an online network: the more time you spend in quiet contemplation or quiet warm interaction in the area you have created the more the positive energies spread through your home and your life. On a psychological level, creating a beautiful place and a regular if brief time there makes you and others feel more harmonious, less pressurised and so more able to talk from the heart or to let go of the stresses and disharmony of the day. Even a normally noisy or taciturn teenager may occasionally go and sit there quietly alone and you can take that as a cue that you might be welcomed to share their worries or just sit companionably together.

- ❈ If you do not have a hearth you can buy a grate or small brazier to set against a wall, surrounded by a layer of flat stones or slates on which to place your symbolic offerings.

- ❈ Fill the grate or the hearth with symbols of domestic abundance and health. These could include:

  * seasonal flowers and leaves to symbolise the slow natural increase of energy, health and new life and the equally natural falling away of sickness or sadness;

  * corn or some other ornamental dried ears of cereal tied with scarlet ribbon to indicate enough food and practical resources;

  * nuts and seeds regularly replaced and planted for good ideas, optimism and looking ahead even when things seem bad;

  * a small metal container of coal or wood even if you have an electric or gas fire; alternatively a small dish of polished silver iron pyrites and gold-coloured polished chalcopyrite to ensure warmth both actual and emotional;

  * a skein of sewing silk or ball of cotton to symbolise sufficient clothing, practical resources and household goods (though not necessarily designer trainers or handbags);

  * if you are seeking love, two small matching ceramic statues of people or favourite animals or a statue of two entwined figures;

  * if you want a baby, three figures, one much smaller (even if you are using artificial insemination or intend to bring up the baby on your own).

- Among these symbols, position a money pot to attract money and resources and slow the outflow of money. Choose a small traditional brown pottery jar with a lid (any ceramic sugar bowl with a lid can be substituted). Begin your money collection with a single copper or silver-coloured coin and try to add one every day, copper, silver- or gold-coloured.

- If you are not lighting or switching on the fire, once a week light a large red candle (kept in the hearth), preferably on a Thursday or Friday, the days when all things are said to grow naturally.

- Put a pinch of salt in the candle flame or into the open fire to represent health and growing money and leave the candle to burn behind the money pot while you sit there relaxing. When you are ready, blow out the candle and imagine the coins increasing and money opportunities coming into your life. A money-spinning idea may even come into your mind.

- When the pot is full buy something small for the home or family or give the money to charity but always retain a single copper or silver coin from the full pot to start the new collection. Children can enjoy finding ingenious ways to spend the money hoard, even if it is only a pound or two.

- Try to spend a few minutes sitting quietly in the candle- or firelight with those you love at least once or twice a week and, when possible, at the end of the day. Before you scatter into separate activities, talk about your hopes and dreams, and listen to the thoughts and feelings of other family members or invited friends. This short precious time can restore the heart to a home; whether you sit there dreaming with your cat or dog for company or tell your children stories of when you were young and of the family ancestors, you can draw strength from the hearth, as people have done over the centuries.

- If any family members are absent, send them love and thoughts as you blow out the candle or poke the fire. Say their names aloud and send them love and protection.

- Keep the family hearth well tended and replace any dying flowers or other natural items as they decay and bury them.

Creating a special place

If the idea of the hearth seems old fashioned or does not fit in with your domestic arrangements – maybe because you house share and only have a small room to sleep and live in – this alternative can be set up on a small coffee table. It can be as simple or elaborate as you wish.

- ❋ Place a natural-coloured beeswax or white candle on the table, to be lit when you and your partner or family gather in the evening or on special occasions. You can also use smaller candles on these occasions to create background light so that you do not need artificial light. If there have been family disagreements you can draw notches on the candle and allow each person to speak uninterrupted while their notch burns down. This can be advantageous if one or two family members are dominant. If you are alone, play your favourite music and do not do anything, not even read and certainly not text people on your mobile. Let the worries of the day and the future flow into the flame and make this your time, however short, to dream only beautiful visions and imagine the possibilities that will grow into reality.

- ❋ Place a pot of fragrant flowers, herbs or pot pourri or an oil burner on the table. This can help to create a barrier with the everyday world and slow your senses. Choose flowers or oils according to what you need at this point in your life:

  * Rose or lavender will bring tranquillity and heal quarrels.

  * Lilac restores family good humour and affection.

  * Geranium increases love and loyalty.

  * Jasmine helps dreams come true in small ways.

  * Lily strengthens women especially mothers.

  * Patchouli strengthens men.

  * Lily of the valley attracts happiness.

  * Mimosa increases prosperity energies and self esteem even in the youngest or shyest family members.

  * Violet encourages tact and helps to diminish rivalry between family members.

- Place a glass bowl of different-coloured polished crystals on the table. These will release ongoing balanced energies into the area. The crystals need only be small and should be washed under running water every week, and be left to dry naturally. When you sit relaxing, you can hold any individual crystals that you instinctively feel drawn to as these will invariably have the energies or calming properties you need. If there are a number of you sat round the table, ask one person to close their eyes and pick a crystal from the bowl. Without opening their eyes, the person should talk about what it makes them feel. The crystal can then be passed around the others, who each hold it in turn, close their eyes and add their feelings. This works as a great unifier. Suitable crystals include:
    * a red vibrant crystal such as red tiger's eye, garnet or red jasper for strength and energy;
    * orange carnelian or amber for self esteem and connection with others while maintaining personal identity (good if you are a busy mother or career person and have little time for yourself);
    * sparkling yellow citrine for clear communication, focus and increased optimism;
    * green jade for love and gentleness or green aventurine for attracting good luck;
    * blue lapis lazuli or sodalite for wise and kind words and balanced emotions;
    * purple amethyst for healing and spiritual energies;
    * clear quartz crystal for bringing everything and everyone together in unity and for ensuring the flow of the life force of nature through the home;
    * brown tiger's eye for encouraging abundance, prosperity and a sense of well-being;
    * grey smoky quartz or blue grey laboradite for hope even in difficult times and for protection of your home and family;
    * pink rose quartz for kindness and gentle family love and for personal healing of past sorrows;
    * soft cream, yellow or rainbow moonstone to bring you and your home back in touch with the natural cycles of the season;
    * black jet or tourmaline for acceptance of people as they are and tolerance of faults and failings (good for critical partners or know-it-all teenagers).

Meaningful mealtimes

In the modern world, people are increasingly becoming grazers and so families may not often get the chance to share meals together. There is no point in being unrealistic and expecting to change the routine of daily life overnight, but there is much to be gained by making time for a regular meal even once or twice a week with partner, family or friends. Try to ensure that this takes priority over or is at least regarded as equal to other social commitments. The meal could be a barbecue, Sunday tea or lunch, a Chinese meal ordered from the local restaurant or a 'bring and share' supper. A shared takeaway pizza can be just as special as a home-cooked meal you have slaved over for hours – especially if you have a family of fussy eaters.

The origins of food and mealtime magic

Sharing food has from time immemorial been a way of symbolically absorbing not only physical nutrients but also the good feelings of the occasion and the symbolic properties associated with the different foods. This transference of energies is made when the food is eaten.

Many modern food customs date back over two thousand years. For example, writing 'Happy Birthday' on a cake in edible paste stems from traditions of Ancient Greece and the worship of Artemis, goddess of the moon and the hunt. Her festival was celebrated with moon-shaped honey cakes with the crescent moon etched on top. Eating a message wishing a person a happy birthday or indeed a happy Christmas is a way of psychologically absorbing the good luck and happiness of the occasion expressed in the icing or pastry words.

Hot cross buns are still popular in England, particularly during the Easter period. The buns, marked with the cross symbolising the resurrection of Jesus, actually predate Christianity by many centuries as in earlier times the cross signified the old astrological cross, symbol of the Earth Mother. They or similar special small cakes were eaten at the spring equinox around 21 March (in the northern hemisphere), so offering the protection of the Earth Mother and promising a summer of plentiful resources.

The Ancient Egyptians marked small round cakes with ox or cow horns, sacred to the mother goddesses Isis and Hathor, at their springtime celebrations. The practice of decorating small cakes with crosses at the time of the spring festival may have started in Ancient Rome. Evidence comes in the form of two small loaves marked with crosses that were discovered preserved in lava in the ruins of the Herculaneum, a city in southwestern Italy that was destroyed by a volcano in 79 CE. The custom probably came to England with the Anglo Saxons who made and ate small cakes on the spring equinox in honour of Eostre, the goddess of spring who gave her name to Easter. When the Anglo Saxons were Christianised during the seventh and eighth centuries the custom was easily transferred to the new religion. In Christian tradition, hot cross buns made on Good Friday were hung in sailors' homes and churches near the sea to keep sailors from drowning.

The properties of food

The foods listed on the following pages are believed to have particular protective or luck-bringing properties and the majority are nutritionally sound. You can use them in cooking or in the case of fruit or honey in their natural form. This is only a limited list, however, and every food has spiritual significance. Sit with your hands round a bowl or plate containing a favourite food, relax and the meaning will come into your mind. Note these down and create your own list.

Use my list and your own to add ingredients to special meals, for example rosemary to lamb if your teenager has an important exam the next day and cannot focus.

Herbs and condiments

Adding herbs to any food is the easiest way to add special strengths according to the needs of the person or people eating. For example, tarragon or spicy cinnamon are wonderful for giving courage or confidence but wise sage might be better for a hot-headed partner or mini drama kings or queens. Some herbs, such as garlic, are available in salt or paste forms. These are just as effective as the fresh herb. Those not traditionally used in cooking, such as evening primrose and echinacea, can be absorbed from beauty products or taken as health supplements.

Basil	Love, protection against intruders, accidents and attack; brings courage, wealth, fidelity, fertility; conquers fear of flying; good against road rage
Bay	Protection, healing, strength and endurance, marriage, fidelity, loyalty between friends; brings and keeps prosperity in the home
Celery seeds	Potency, money, protection of property, travel opportunities and safe travel
Cinnamon	Success, money, love and passion, assertiveness
Cloves	Protection, love, money, healing, banishes negativity
Coriander	Love, health, healing, protects property and even luggage while travelling if you put the seeds in a sachet in your cases; encourages creativity and optimism. Traditionally pregnant women ate coriander to ensure their unborn children were quick-witted and creative in life
Echinacea	Strength, healing, enhances personal intuitive powers, resists pressures
Evening primrose	Recovers what is lost or was taken away, encourages self-love and self-esteem in women
Fennel	Travel, courage, house moves, protection, healing; especially protects children and animals
Garlic	Protection against human malice and paranormal energies, good health, passion, security from thieves; attracts money
Ginger	Love, passion, money, success, power, promotion and leadership
Horseradish	Banishes negativity, luck in competitions

Lemon balm (Melissa)	Increases abundance and all good things in life; reverses bad luck and grants wishes; promises long life
Lemongrass	Repels spite; good for moves of all kinds; removes what is redundant in your life
Lemon verbena	Trust, family happiness, happy holidays and fun, gentleness, healing, friendship
Liquorice	Love, passion, fidelity, ambition, success, luck in gambling
Marjoram, sweet	Drives away loneliness, alienation and fears of separation or abandonment; increases family loyalty, commitment in love and money flow; resolves divided loyalties, encourages compromise; good for all joint ventures
Mint	Money, love, increases sexual desire, healing, banishes malevolence, protects (especially while travelling) against road rage and accidents
Mustard	Fertility, protection, increases mental powers and good ideas, courage (particularly for standing up to bullies)
Nettle	Protection of the home and family; healing, passion; banishes negativity
Oats	Money, security, stability, restores balance
Parsley	Love, protection, passion, purification, abundance, takes away bad luck
Pepper	Protection, banishes malevolence, overcomes inertia and gives positive focus for change
Peppermint	Purification, energy, love, healing, increases psychic powers; guards against illness of all minds
Rosemary	Love, passion, improves memory and concentration and so good for tests and examinations, banishes negativity, depression and nightmares; preserves youthfulness
Rye	Love, fidelity, prosperity, property
Saffron	Love, healing, happiness, strength, increases psychic powers, reverses the outflow of money
Sage	Long life, good health, wisdom, protection, grants wishes, improves memory and concentration; brings justice, prosperity, career success, healing; good before interviews
Salt	Health, long life, wealth and protection against human and paranormal influences

Sesame	Money, passion, job opportunities
Tarragon	Associated with dragons; courage, new beginnings, shedding the redundant, career, prosperity; regeneration in any aspect of living; helps the user to focus on new targets instead of the past
Thyme	Health, healing, prophetic dreams, overcomes misfortune and brings luck, career opportunities, increases psychic powers; long-term prosperity; drives away fears and helps overcome phobias or addictions; good before a driving test

Foods for health, luck, love and success

Apple	Health, vitality, long life, fertility (especially to conceive a boy), fertility of ideas
Avocado	Inner radiance and outer charisma; promotes well-being on all levels and attracts money and beautiful things
Banana	Fertility, male potency, prosperity; maturity and the middle years
Bread	Sufficient resources including career and property, loyalty between friends and family, health
Carrot	Alertness, awareness of alternatives and cutting through illusion
Cherry	New or young love, growing trust; increases divinatory abilities, fertility, good long-term results from small beginnings
Coconut	Fertility, motherhood, the flow of new life and energies; protection against all negativity, especially psychic attack
Corn	Provision of what is most needed, abundance, generosity, good luck, fertility, beginning enterprises that will bring success in the future
Eggs	New beginnings, conception, birth (of children and of creative ventures), the need to wait for something to come to fruition, revival of what was lost
Fig	Prosperity, sensuality, wisdom, creativity, fertility, harmony and balance
Grapes	Rebirth and renewal, joy, ecstasy, passion, good luck in games of chance; a better lifestyle

Making the Home a Place of Happiness

Hazel nuts	Fertility, wisdom and knowledge, happy long-term commitment, justice
Honey	Nurturing, hospitality and a welcoming home, abundance, creativity, prosperity, health, fertility, whatever is most desired, maternal power and wisdom
Lemon	Cleansing all negativity, logic, clarity of thought; new beginnings and overcoming obstacles; removing addictions and destructive ties from the past; also for good luck and prosperity; travel and house moves
Lime	Justice, new beginnings, new places and people, fresh investment and original ideas; repels spite, jealousy, nasty neighbours or colleagues who take credit for your ideas
Mango	Health, permanence and stability in career, lasting happiness; reliability (good for home or vehicle purchases)
Maple syrup	Long life, health of children, fertility, riches of all kinds, pleasure
Olives/olive oil	Peace and the mending of quarrels, abundance, healing, affection and fertility
Onion	Luck, money, love choices, health, protection
Peach/apricot	Abundance and fertility, the power to grant wishes; attracts love, increases self esteem and a love of beauty; marriage, pregnancy and birth, long life
Pear	New life, health, girls' and women's needs, fertility, conception (especially of a girl)
Potato	Building up any opportunity or path step by step; perseverance; long-term security; valuing simple pleasures and people with good hearts who may not seem exciting
Sunflower oil/ seed/products, also butter	Confidence, abundance, sensual and physical pleasures, riches, happiness; travel or house moves (especially in the summer months)
Tomatoes	Prosperity (keep one on a shelf near heat or a fireplace), health (keep one on a window ledge); replace when soft
Wheat products	Fulfilment of what was started six months earlier; successful completion of projects; long-term gains; successful property renovation or decoration

A mealtime blessing

The tradition of saying a small prayer of thanks before a meal has ceased in most households, but blessing the table and the meal is a powerful but simple way of drawing positive energies to any table, no matter how many or how few people are present.

A blessing is a wonderful antidote to stress if you have been rushing round and are wondering why you are bothering at all for a bunch of ungrateful relatives or friends. It will settle you as well as the place and almost instantly things will start to go right. You will become more confident and in control, even if you are organising a Golden Wedding celebration for 60 people in the garden and it is raining. A blessing can also be calming if you are catering for a difficult relative or colleagues you do not know very well, if you have new neighbours coming for tea or coffee or even a brand new date coming to dinner.

The blessing that follows is based on an old Celtic house blessing from the oral tradition. Blessings tend to evolve as they are handed on, and sometimes I am surprised to find that a hymn or prayer I learned in the industrial Midlands of my childhood in fact has Celtic roots. You can find other house and table blessings in my *Complete Book of Spells* (see Further Reading, page 245). But most importantly you can easily create your own blessings based on the things that are of value to you about the particular celebration and the people who are coming.

- Before setting the table light a single white candle in a holder in the centre of the table and say,

I light this flame in love and peace that this meal/celebration may be filled with peace, tranquillity and harmony.

- Now pass your hands over the table, and the area where people will be sitting if it is a buffet.

- Move the hand you write with in clockwise circles and the other hand in anticlockwise circles. Practise this for a minute or two beforehand in order to get into the rhythm.

✤ As you move your hands continuously say softly aloud or in your mind if you prefer,

> *May blessings and peace, joy and good companionship, kind words and laughter enter my home and my table. Welcome to all who come in friendship and friendship may they take away.*

✤ Leave the candle to burn.

✤ When you have welcomed your guests and are ready to serve the meal, put the food on the table.

✤ Light a second white candle from the first in the centre of the table to transfer the blessings and move the first candle to another part of the room. Leave both burning.

Making mealtimes special

When a guest broke bread together with his or her host in the Middle Ages as part of a meal, it was considered that a bargain had been made involving mutual respect and protection. If you would like to replicate this sense of something special in eating together but are perhaps not comfortable with the idea of using a spoken blessing, there are other ways of making mealtimes special. You may choose, for example, to light a central candle before beginning a meal in order to set the tone for a tranquil meal. You could also suggest to family members who would be receptive that they might like to give silent thanks before beginning their meal, in view of world hunger and poverty even in affluent lands.

Even when eating alone, marking the meal break can help to make eating a more pleasurable occasion. It can become a habit to watch television, work at the computer or read while eating, which makes us less aware of our food. By making even a simple snack an occasion, we can regain a sense of pleasure in food and in eating.

If food is a power issue for children, it can help to make the mealtime into a mini party, by lighting a candle at the beginning of the meal. You could even give each child a candle that they could then blow out at the end of the meal as they make a wish. In good weather, I sometimes turned the main meal into a picnic, where the children could choose from a selection of different foods: cheeses, fruits and berries, cold meats and small cooked sausages, breads of different kinds, chopped raw carrot sticks, nuts and seeds, yoghurts and so on. I found I was not fretting about wasted food as most could be stored and used again. And, yes, lots of the time I resorted to microwave meals – I have even been credited with the invention of the baked bean pizza!

Encountering the guardians of your household

The tradition of protective guardians of a home, whether in a new apartment or a centuries-old building, is found in the myths of many lands and ages. Some people believe that this guardian is an actual essence while others are convinced it is a protective atmosphere or energy that comes from the feelings and energies of people who live in the house now or have lived there in the past. People may picture and describe these feelings as though they were coming from an actual unseen spiritual being. Such descriptions, like those of other nature spirits, are consistent in different lands and it may be that these guardians do have some material reality that is different from the solid human body. They are rarely seen as a physical being, however, except by children who are naturally psychic and adults with developed clairvoyant abilities.

Your own experience of household guardians may have come when sat late at night after a long day or when everyone has gone home after a celebration and you felt the house almost sigh with relief. Alternatively, you may have felt a reassuring presence at night when you return home late and are looking in your bag for your key.

In the following sections I have described how these guardians were and still are described in different parts of the world. The descriptions are fascinating. Even if you are convinced they could not have an objective existence, think of them and work with them as qualities or strengths and you may begin to understand how the legends arose. I will describe them as if they are actual beings, for that is the way they appear in different traditions.

Guardians in the Far Eastern tradition

In the Far East, house guardians are given places of honour. For example, in China every kitchen has a shrine. A picture of the god of the stove or hearth, Tsao-Wang, is placed in a miniature wooden temple over the hearth, facing south. Pictured next to him, his wife Tsao-Wang Nai-nai carries the sayings of the women of the household to the Jade Emperor in the heavens. Each morning, three incense sticks are burnt before this domestic shrine, and offerings of food, flowers and drink are made. This is believed to keep the kitchen safe and to attract good fortune and prosperity to the family home.

In Japan, in the Shinto religion, the kamidana or god shelf serves a similar function. This is set high on the wall in a business premises or home and daily offerings are made to the kami, the divine spirits within nature. Offerings include evergreen twigs, rice wine, salt and rice. After the offerings are made, prayers and thanks are given for blessings and the participants ring the bell hanging over the shrine, bow twice, clap twice and bow once more.

Some westerners adopt these Far Eastern traditions to attract good fortune to the home.

House wights

In Ancient Rome benign household spirits were called the Lare and were honoured each morning by placing offerings of wine, honey, milk, flowers or grain on miniature shrines on the hearth. There were one or two Lares for each household, and also Lares who watched over the neighbourhood and the state. Also honoured by the Roman family were the spirits called the Penates, who were given offerings so that the store cupboard with which they were associated would always be full. They were also entreated to bring wealth to the family.

In Scandinavian, Germanic and Eastern and Western European myth, house wights or spirits are evolved spiritual beings, described almost like individual guardian angels of each home, large or small. There is often just one house wight who is attached to the house or apartment or associated with a building that was once on the site or with the agricultural land that the house was built on. The history of the area may give you a clue. If, for example, you live on a brand new estate in a road called Abbey Gardens, your protective house spirit may have been a monk or nun who loved the place so much they remained as protector. Cats especially are thought to have an affinity with these benign spirits.

House wights often choose a beautiful statue or an amethyst geode in which to settle. You may feel strong but very good energies coming from a particular statue and may occasionally even see small beams of light. Smudge over these weekly with either a lighted Native North American sagebrush smoke stick or a sage or pine incense stick, working in spirals.

Traditionally, a special stone is set on the hearth to act as a focus and home for the house wight. The following steps will enable you to welcome one of these protective essences into your home, either actually or symbolically:

* Choose a small rounded rock from close to (but not actually within) a sacred place, from the seashore or near an old abbey or monastery. Keep it by your hearth or on the table in the centre of your home for a year and a day.

* Smudge the rock weekly unless you have an open fire in which case smudging is not necessary.

* If you prefer, sprinkle round the rock a circle of water droplets in which you have dissolved a pinch of sea salt. Ask for the blessings and protection of the house wight to remain within your home.

* Then after the year and a day return the rock to the place you found it and select a new guardian rock.

* You could alternatively buy a crystal geode – a hollow rock, the cavity of which is lined with crystals. Choose one with tiny purple amethysts or yellow citrines inside, and set it near the centre of your home or on your hearth or close to the stove.

* Whenever there are any changes in the home, people coming to stay, planned redecoration, family news or you are going away for a few days, light a candle near the hearth or the guardian's special place and tell the guardian about what is going to happen. This may sound strange but you will notice that on the occasions when you do this, everything connected with the change seems to work more smoothly.

Dísir

Other more evolved spirits are considered to be attached to the family rather than the actual premises and may move if the family or individual changes residence. The Dísir are considered the spirit ancestral mothers of a specific family in the Scandinavian and Germanic traditions. They are not ghosts as such but, like the wights, are spirits who choose to become part of the natural world and specifically family household essences in order to protect their family through the generations. In this sense they are close to spirit guides.

Each family, or individual if you live alone, has just one guardian mother or Dís. If your own mother is deceased or far away, these are wonderful guardian spirits to connect with by lighting a white candle once a week on Friday evening, the day of the mothers. Your Dís will be especially powerful on Christmas Eve, the night of the mothers, called Modraniht in Anglo Saxon. If you are the mother of the house try to take five minutes out of the celebrations or on a Friday night when the house is still to sit quietly and draw strength from this wise maternal energy.

The Bean-Tighe and Duendes

Similar to the Dísir are the Bean-Tighe, the fairy housekeepers of Ireland and Scotland, and of Celtic people who have settled elsewhere in the world, such as America and Australia.

Bean-Tighe means woman of the house. She guards children and pets, especially during the night, and also encourages exhausted mothers.

The Bean-Tighe would attach herself to a particular branch of the family for generations and would move home with them. Sometimes removal men would ask where the old lady had gone as they were unloading furniture in a new house, only to be told there was no old lady or at least no human old lady in the house.

In Spain and Central and South America, the fairy housekeepers were called Duendes. These were gossipy middle-aged fairy women dressed in green, who attached themselves to households. Unlike the Beane-Tighe, they were sometimes jealous of the mother or women of the home. The individual household Duende would clean because she hated a messy home, but would sometimes throw crockery, move furniture and hide possessions if annoyed. She would, however, protect the family from external harm (only she was allowed to be bad tempered with them).

Calling on the protection of your household guardians after dark

You do not have to believe in house wights to use the following method to draw on their protection, particularly after dark. Whether you fear vandalism or a break-in, feel threatened by gangs of youths roaming outside your home or are afraid at night if you live alone, try this method weekly on a Sunday evening or whenever you feel extra nervous.

- ♣ As darkness falls light two white candles, one from the other.
- ♣ Name one candle for the house wight and one for the family or your personal guardian mother. Give each a private name only you know and use.

- ❀ Let the candles face an uncurtained window that does not have a streetlight directly outside, so that when you light the candles, you can see the flames reflected in the window. If you have no such window, place the candles so they are reflected in a mirror.
- ❀ Say as you light each candle,

> *I call upon (name the guardian). Protect me through the night and turn back any who would do harm, so all is calm until day returns as light.*

- ❀ Now put a pinch of salt in each flame and say,

> *Blessings be on my home and on me/all who are within or in my heart.*

- ❀ Blow out the first candle before you go to bed and carry the second still burning to your bedroom. Blow this one out just before you go to sleep, saying,

> *May the light surround me safe until morning.*

- ❀ Replace the candles regularly but keep the same names.

House elves

For some people these are the stuff of fairy tales. A number of people in Scandinavia, Germany, the Netherlands, Eastern Europe and Russia, however, still acknowledge the presence of these smaller and more tangible luck-bringing essences in their homes and workplaces. These vetter or 'little folk' are said to take practical care of apartments, business premises, cars, pets, wallets, trailers and boats in cities and countryside alike. Some vetter are described as living under floorboards and doorsteps and can be mistaken for mice or even large insects. A dark smoky quartz crystal buried in a small pot of earth or a plant on the doorstep is believed to ensure the vetter will protect your home against natural disasters like fire, floods or storms – and against subsidence.

A number of people, as well as sensing the presence of their house elves, regularly hear them – sometimes all too clearly. Indeed often when householders complain about ghostly activity, it may be the house elf stumbling and grumbling over drinks cans and food wrappers discarded by a teenager in the house.

The following are commonly described forms of house elves. Whether they are objectively true or another way of describing the energy field accumulated around houses and gardens, by making symbolic offerings it may be possible to activate your own innate luck-bringing energies. Once you are sensitised to the possibility of creatures existing parallel to humanity, you may, against all expectations, see or sense a nature essence in or round your home.

Brownies

In English and Scottish folklore, a brownie is a small, industrious fairy or hobgoblin believed to inhabit houses, barns, outbuildings, garages and sheds. Rarely seen, a brownie is often heard at night, cleaning and doing housework; he also sometimes mischievously disarranges rooms. A brownie brings good fortune if he adopts a home. Sometimes several may make their home in a single human dwelling. Cream or bread and milk may be left for him, but other gifts offend him.

The boggart of Yorkshire and the bogle of Scotland are hostile, mischievous brownies, similar to the larger German kobold. According to the Brothers Grimm, who were great folklorists, a real kobold called Hodeken was witnessed living with the Bishop of Hildesheim in the early 1800s.

Gnomes

Described in the folklore of much of Northern and Western Europe and Scandinavia and taken by settlers to America and Canada, gnomes, like dwarves, were said to live mainly underground or in deep forests. They were famous as metal workers and apparently had wives and families and were all very strong, but they jealousy guarded their treasure.

Gnomes in gardens both private and public are regarded as slightly more sociable, though they are attached to the plants and wildlife and not the owners of the land. Males have usually been described with a peaked rather than a pointed red cap, wearing blue or green with boots made from birch bark. Females may be seen in green and often have headscarves. The gnomes may or may not have white beards. Gnomes are said to care for the earth, the minerals and metals, the roots of plants and for forest or garden wild animals and birds.

A resident garden gnome is believed to attract luck and prosperity to your home and encourage plants to flourish. To attract the favour of gnome energy, buy a gnome figure, if possible a plain brown or grey clay one. The creation of a gnomery should see your garden positively shoot up. Burying a coin in the earth directly beneath a gnome statue is thought to attract a slow inflow of money into your life and prevent too fast an outflow.

Domovoy

In Slavic and Russian mythology, the domovoy household spirit or the grandfather as he is called is described as a very small old man with a long white beard or as resembling the oldest male of the household. He originated as part of an ancestor cult and so has something in common with household guardians. He cares for and brings luck to the home and can, it is said, appear suddenly as a cat or a dog, a snake or a rat. His wife is called Domovikha. A domovoy can live near the oven, in the hearth or under the doorstep and rarely goes outdoors. He is said to bring prosperity to those who work hard and are not extravagant; if angered he can be very noisy at night. If invited he will travel with the family to a new home and transfer good luck.

Living with and attracting house elves

If you buy a house and it seems dark, cold and unfriendly, it may be that the household nature essences have moved out. Your personal family guardians (Dísir) will have come with you, but the household elves are the practical ones who fix the atmosphere of the house by making it feel lived in and alive. Whether you describe this as elven energy or a general sense of well-being, you'll notice if it is missing.

Superstitious unscientific nonsense? Maybe. But if you do attract benign elf energy to your new dwelling, watch your everyday luck increase in small but significant ways and notice how DIY seems to go smoothly. Follow these steps to attract the house elves into your home:

- ✤ House elves of all kinds traditionally love shiny things, so keep a dish of old earrings, crystals, bits of costume jewellery in a dish near the hearth. You will find, maybe coincidentally, that your jewellery, keys and trinkets stop going missing once you do this.

- ✤ Hang shiny crystals or old necklaces from a tree if you have one in the garden to attract garden nature spirits to make your flowers grow and protect your boundaries.

✤ Hang strings of bells or small wind chimes just inside the front door to attract the house elves into the house.

✤ If your family luck hasn't been particularly good recently or there has been a lot of clattering in the night, lost car keys and electrical goods blowing fuses for no apparent reason, don't call for the ghost buster. Instead prepare a tiny bowl of sugared or honeyed white porridge or pudding with cinnamon and a pat of butter on top (any rice pudding or breakfast oat porridge you make for the family is fine). Leave it overnight in an outbuilding like a garden shed or put it by the guardian stone on the hearth. Next morning give it to an animal – it is said the house elves only eat the essence. Scandinavians still do this on Christmas Eve and sometimes on Thursdays – the day of the tomte, their house elf.

3 Working with the Energies in Your Home

The previous chapter looked at the energies of the home in animate form, as guardians. Here we will look at the same principles in terms of more abstract energies that accumulate in the home as people interact there, whether as visitors or residents.

A happy home will reflect those who live there and spread the happiness so that it becomes the natural mode. A very old abbey, for example, where different generations of nuns or monks lived in contentment will create a sense of peace for all who visit.

By contrast, when you walk into a home or an office, it is easy to sense if there has been a quarrel just before you arrived even if everyone is smiling. Such feelings can linger in the energy field of the place and if there is consistently a lot of sadness or anger in a particular location, it can continue to affect people's moods months or even years later.

The energy field of the home

Picture every home and every room within the home having an invisible energy field or aura around it. This energy field is made up of all the events that have happened in the house, the conversations, the quarrels and the words of love as well as the energies released from the furniture and artefacts that have been used over the years and even by different generations if they are inherited. Each room will also possess its own kind of energy, either Earth, Air, Fire or Water or a mixture of these. For example, the kitchen will have lively Fire energy because of the stove and the shiny pots, pans and utensils. However, softer counterbalancing Water and Earth energies from the water in the sink and green plants will help to prevent you getting too hot and bothered while cooking or accidentally cutting or burning yourself.

As you live in a home you absorb the household energies into your own personal energy field and so you want to make sure that they are positive harmonious ones and that each room feels right for its purpose. The same is true of workplaces and in time you will learn to sense if a room is out of balance and requires some form of counterbalance (see Chapter 9 for similar information for the workplace).

If everyone in the family is stressed and irritable, you might need extra Earth to calm them down, for example in the form of a thick green or brown cloth (Earth colours) on the dining table. Crystals of the different elemental kinds, fragrances and colours can be kept ready for when there is a need for some Fire to get a lethargic teenager moving or gentle flowing Water power to soften the critical words of a bitchy neighbour. See pages 74–81 for suitable ways of introducing particular elemental energies into your home.

The four elements

If you already know the Chinese Feng Shui system of energy balancing you will not find huge differences with this method. The main difference is that it is based on the four westernised elements, Earth, Air, Fire and Water, from which it was once believed everything came and was made. Feng Shui works with the five Chinese elements of water, metal, earth, fire and wood.

The westernised elemental system originated in the philosophy of Ancient Greece, for example that of Empedocles who lived in Sicily in the fifth century BCE. Plato, who lived in the first century BCE, tried to explain the four elements mathematically and Hippocrates, the Greek doctor who was writing around 400 BCE, linked them with human health and well-being. But ordinary people through the ages have worked with the real physical elements: salt, flowers and herbs for Earth; fragrant smoke and feathers for Air; candles and fires for Fire and water or fragrances (sometimes homemade) for Water. This everyday application will be the emphasis of this chapter.

Clutter clearing

If your home is very cluttered, the aura or energy field of the home will be dull, blocked and stagnant – as will your personal energy field.

Clearing the clutter means throwing away what is not needed or wanted and finding a place for what is needed. People associate clutter clearing with Feng Shui but, of course, the principle of spring cleaning dates back thousands of years. My mother used to say, 'A place for everything and everything in its place' and certainly we had never heard of Feng Shui in the industrialised Midlands in the 1950s.

A home may look tidy but still be cluttered. Clutter is not just the things left on tables, on shelves or on the floor, but those things that are hidden too. The contents of drawers, cupboards and storage areas also contribute to the energy flow, even though you cannot physically see them.

You have to be realistic when you set out to clear the clutter. If you live in a cramped apartment or a small room in a shared house or have a lot of family members including serious hoarders, then your home will never be minimalist. I have a family of five and though they have officially left home, their junk still reminds me daily of their presence.

Life will become more harmonious as you make progress, and the small improvements will soon accumulate. Imagine not having a forest of coats fall down when you open the front door and not tripping over trailing spaghetti-like wires and a magazine mountain every time you plug in the computer or answer the phone. Imagine knowing precisely where the car tax documents are.

In the process of decluttering, you may unearth family photographs you really love or which reveal your family history. All sorts will emerge from cupboards and drawers: missing paperwork you have been fretting about, children's favourite toys, an old ring you had mislaid, a replacement part you bought for a much used but broken gadget and never got round to fitting or maybe some new curtains you never unwrapped. Your home really is a treasure trove and this emphasis can persuade reluctant children or partners to dig deep to see what they can find.

Where to begin

Clutter takes years to accumulate and may have come from several people and more than one home. It is not therefore going to be cleared in a day or even a week or month. You still have to work, cook, send e-mails, make love and packed lunches, argue, go to the gym and supermarket, take the children to after-school activities and visit relatives and friends. You need a realistic timetable for clutter clearing rather than trying to do everything in one fraught weekend and giving up.

Above all, make clutter clearing fun with good music, nice things to nibble and planned short regular breaks away from the mess. If you live alone, ask a good friend along to help and you can do the same with their place on another occasion.

What to keep

Imagine you were moving in six weeks to a house or apartment half the size of the one you now have. What would you take with you as a priority? Now imagine you had to move everything abroad, again in six weeks' time and had to ship everything as freight. Would you really take all your old dolls, your old faded school photographs and birthday cards from when you were three? If these are important, what could you leave behind instead?

Decision-making is crucial. You either want something or you don't, and so you should either keep it or get rid of it. That may sound obvious but some practitioners advise having a box for items you are uncertain about. I think that if you have a box for 'maybe I'll keep it' or 'I'll decide later', you will only need to sort the same things twice and you are unlikely to be any more decisive next time around.

The following steps will help you to organise and make the most of those possessions that you choose to keep:

- Create a collage made up of your best photographs or make several collages, one for each family member to show their ongoing life. My daughter Miranda made a picture wall for my 50th birthday, with pictures right from when I was a baby looking the image of the English wartime leader Winston Churchill up to the present day.

- File any special photos or mementoes you want to hand on to future generations in albums or as slides as well as on CDs for the computer. Add labels and anecdotes so that the collection comes alive and to help your descendants to share your life experiences. Getting out the old albums is a lovely activity on family get-togethers, especially when older family members can fill in the gaps in family legends.

- Display the best pictures on a family shelf or table near the centre of your home.

- Bind precious love letters, poems or family documentation and file these and diaries in a lidded box with dried lavender or roses to be opened by future generations or you whenever you are feeling sentimental. If you wish, write a letter to your descendants about this day when you started to put your life in order and include any insights you have gained. Keep the letter in the box.

- Look objectively at any paintings, pictures or ornaments you have on display. Do you have atmospheric pictures of abandoned houses, a beggar in a deserted street or empty deserts? If you seek abundance or business success, replace these with prints of flowers, fruits, marketplaces filled with stalls and smiling people.

✤ Don't feel that you need to be minimalist in order to achieve free domestic psychic energy flow. Personal or family treasures, those things that you love and have emotional or spiritual value for you, are one of the best sources of positive energy, and you need to display them to allow the energies to flow round and from them. Rather than hoarding your best china or jewellery, enjoy it. Saving something to hand on after death means the possessor misses out on its positive energies, and it may not be valued by a future generation. I regularly buy my daughters relatively inexpensive small heirlooms for them to wear now – a silver locket, a coral or jade bracelet (the latter for my daughter called Jade) – which gives me and them immense shared pleasure.

Spring cleaning all year round

Once you have cleared your clutter or at least sorted one room, you can begin cleaning. Again be realistic as to what is possible; trying to do too much may leave you stressed out which is totally counterproductive. Doing what is realistic will in itself create more harmonious vibes than trying to attain perfection.

If you have small children, they are likely to be uncleaning as you clean, so put them in old clothes and given them their own scrubbing area out of harm's way.

Cleansing festivals

In almost every culture, physically cleaning the home has long been an important prelude to festivals at transition times of the year.

The spring-cleaning tradition is associated with the spring equinox around 21 March (in the northern hemisphere) that indicates the beginning of lighter days and warmer weather. This is a logical time for physically cleaning the home after the winter. The fortnight-long Persian or Iranian New Year celebration or *Nowruz* that begins on the spring equinox is preceded by cleaning floors, drapery, furniture and ceilings, and is called *khooneh takouni*, which translates as shaking the house. Before the beginning of the annual Jewish Pesach or Passover, which commemorates the freedom of the Israelites from the Egyptians, and is celebrated in March or April each year, the home is cleaned. Even crumbs of leavened bread made with yeast are removed as leavened bread is forbidden during the Feast of Unleavened Bread that occurs on the second day of the festival.

Of the many New Year's Day celebrations held worldwide on 1 January, one of the most traditional is the Celtic-influenced Hogmanay in

Scotland. This is named after the pre-Christian solar hero giant of the north, Hogmagog. On New Year's Eve the thorough cleaning in Scotland is called *redding* and even fireplaces are swept and polished clean, and divination practised with the ashes. Then the house is spiritually cleansed to remove any bad luck from the previous year by burning juniper. This is done with all the doors closed to keep the house sealed; the doors are then opened to bring in fresh air. The house is then considered ready to bring in the luck of the new year.

Like Hogmanay, the Chinese New Year requires that each household should be thoroughly cleaned before New Year's Day to remove any bad luck from the old year. Afterwards, on the eve of the festival, all brooms and cleaning equipment are put away and all dirt is carried out of the back door. It is not swept as this is believed to sweep away a family member's affection, and the back door is used as taking the dirt out of the front door might take away prosperity. The Chinese New Year falls on different dates each year, but always between 21 January and 20 February, generally on the second new moon after the midwinter solstice around 21 December.

Modern and traditional cleaning methods

With increasingly busy lives and modern household appliances, we do not spend the hours our great-grandmothers and even older grandmothers did, working lavender polish into furniture, making soap or scrubbing floors with a herbal infusion. I can remember as a child, pounding the washing and rubbing polish in increasing circles into tables, chairs and dresser, worn smooth with age, until I really could see my face in them.

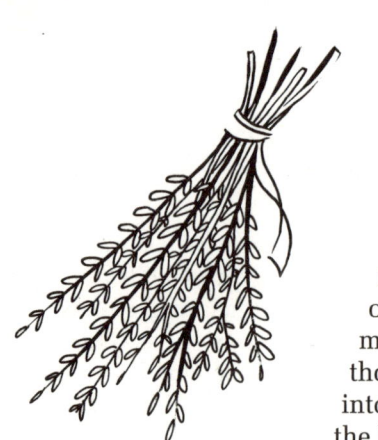

I have no illusions about the hardships of earlier times, but in using the old ways, along with our vacuum cleaners, and where possible buying more natural herbal products rather than those packed with chemicals, we can tune into the physical connection of purifying the home in a deeply instinctive way.

Psychic vacuuming

The modern equivalent of the broom used by our ancestors is the vacuum cleaner.

Before you clean up, sprinkle fine lavender, dried rose petals or a flower-scented talcum powder (even one of the floral floor-freshening powders if you can get one with natural ingredients) on floors. Then vacuum the floor first in anticlockwise and then clockwise circles to remove not only dust and dirt but any lingering unhelpful energies or lethargy. As you vacuum clockwise, picture light flowing into the floor, carpets and furnishings, and filling them with fresh spring-like energies. End if you wish by spraying the room with one of the oil and water mixtures described on page 80.

Magical polishing

When you have time and if possible before your first spiritual cleansing of your home, buy a tin of lavender-, pine- or rosewood-scented beeswax polish. You can pick this up at country fayres, farmers' markets and in the few remaining old-fashioned grocery stores (I have one such store at the end of my road called Orchards that has been in the same family for more than 80 years).

Polish furniture with a soft cloth. As you work, visualise the needs of your family and make wishes for a happy and safe home. You can recite a Celtic blessing (see page 82) aloud or in your mind or repeat these words like a soft mantra,

> *None harm, all calm, make this a home of peace and harmony,*
> *so may it be.*

Children enjoy helping with polishing, and you may even sense a great-great-grandmother working by your side.

Washing away negativity

Amazing promises are made about modern cleaning products, but herbs such as tea tree, eucalyptus, lemon and pine have equally antiseptic and cleansing properties and smell beautiful. You do not need to make herb infusions or mixes to wash your floors unless you wish (see page 80 for how to do so) but can take advantage of the fragrances of essential oils added to hot water or to your favourite natural cleaning products. These are increasingly easy to find as people worry about the environmental effects of the over-use of chemicals.

Follow these steps to wash the negativity out of your home:

❋ Add 10–15 drops of cedar, lemon, pine, rosemary or tea tree oil to a medium-sized bucket of hot water and mix it well.

❋ Wash the front and back door steps with a traditional scrubbing brush dipped in the water, marking in your mind's eye a barrier that will prevent stress or bad feelings from being carried over the threshold. If there is a lot of negativity round you or unpleasant neighbours add a pinch of salt and pepper to the water.

❋ Using the water and oil mix, work next on the bathroom and kitchen or cloakroom, any area where there are water outlets that can drain out luck or happiness.

❋ Then sweep out any yard or patio areas in anticlockwise circles with a broom and wash the area with a bucket of water containing 10–15 drops of eucalyptus or tea tree oil, using your broom in clockwise circles to draw up boundaries of protection.

❋ Finally tip any remaining water down an external drain to allow the negativity to flow away.

❋ According to old European custom, stand your broom, bristles up, outside the door for protection of your home.

Spiritually cleansing your home

After you have cleared and cleaned a room, you are ready to clear its energies. You can repeat the spiritual purification of an area or your whole home whenever there has been a quarrel, minor illness that lingers or misfortune or if you or a family member has a major project or endeavour, whether a job interview or an ongoing aim such as trying to conceive a baby. Spiritual cleansing is also very effective after a house move, at New Year and when the seasons change, around 21 March, 21 June, 21 September and 21 December.

❋ You will need a heatproof tray on which to carry your tools and a small table in each room on which to put the tray while you work.

❋ Cleanse one room a day or each weekend. If you prefer, even if you have not finished cleaning the other rooms, go through the whole house or apartment while you are set up with the equipment. Morning is a good time and Sunday is a good day, but fit in with your timetable and lifestyle.

- ✤ Though some space-clearing experts advise that you open the doors and windows before beginning, if it is cold outside or windy this is not practical and would detract from the harmony of the occasion.

- ✤ Open the main entrance door to the outside of the home briefly before you begin and when you have finished, whether you are cleansing the whole house or just one room. If you are cleansing the entire house you need only open the door once at the beginning and once at the end.

- ✤ Open individual room doors inside the home and, if practical, leave these open during the cleansing and empowerment. But if, for example, you have a dog that would run round and knock things over, open and close the room door briefly before and after the cleansing ritual.

- ✤ If it is a lovely sunny day, open the windows after the ceremony and leave them open for a short while if it is safe to do so in your neighbourhood.

Using the four elements for spiritual cleansing

Each substance is related to one of the elements, but particular types of substance can also convey the powers of another element. For example, all crystals are a natural Earth substance, but by choosing an Air-related crystal, you can bring Air energy to a room to counterbalance another element that is in excess. Equally, fragrances belong to the Air element, but certain flowers or herbs will strengthen particular elemental powers, such as orange for fire power. In this way, all four elements are interconnected. By using various candle colours and fragrance oils you can, with practise, create a perfect elemental balance and, in time, this will become totally instinctive.

The behaviour of people in your home will often indicate the elemental excesses or deficiencies that are present. Alternatively, see pages 210–215 for the symptoms of these excesses or deficiencies relating to the workplace, which can also be applied to the domestic scene.

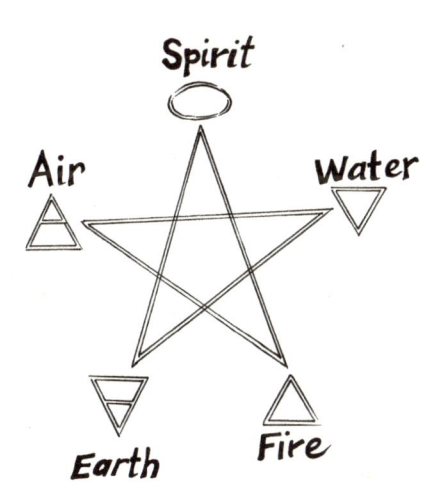

Earth

Areas that will benefit most from Earth input: Dining room, living/sitting room, children's bedrooms, basement, shed, garden and workshop

Substances: Salt, flowers, herbs, leaves, clean rich brown soil, coins, bread, corn and wheat, fabrics, nuts, clay, grass, ceramic statues especially of animals, pot plants, miniature trees, coloured sands and ornamental gravel, fruit, berries, pot pourri, copper jewellery, crystals and gems

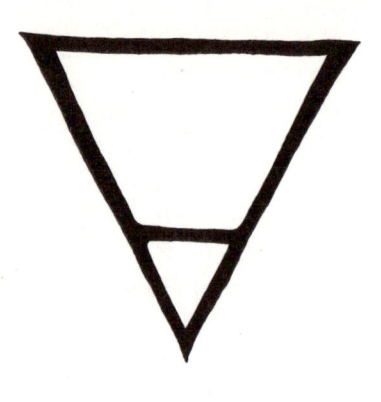

Colours: Green or golden brown

Crystals: Most agates, especially moss and tree agate, amazonite, aventurine, emerald, fossils, jet, malachite, petrified or fossilised wood, rose quartz, rutilated quartz, smoky quartz, red and golden tiger's eye, all stones with holes in the centre

Fragrances: Cypress, fern, geranium, heather, hibiscus, honeysuckle, magnolia, patchouli, sagebrush, sweetgrass, vervain, vetivert

Related sense: Touch

Use Earth to attract: Protection, security and stability, a steady infusion of money and banishing debt, success with official and legal matters, a happy home life, contented family and pets, respect for the family ancestors, family traditions and cultural heritage, successful house renovations, love of traditional work practices and crafts, hospitality, inter-generational harmony and welcoming additional family members whether they enter the family by birth, remarriage or adoption

Counterbalance excess Earth with: Air

Air

Areas that will benefit most from Air input: Study/home office, playroom, teenage and younger male bedrooms, attic, balcony, a hobby or fitness room

Substances: Incense or smudge, fragrant flowers, wind chimes, bells, fragrances and fragrant sprays, feathers, long scarves, wind, bubbles, seeds, feathery grasses, statues of fairies or birds, mobiles of butterflies, dream catchers

Colours: Yellow or grey, also purple

Crystals: Amethyst, angelite, blue lace agate, citrine, danburite, diamond, Herkimer diamond, lapis lazuli, sapphire, sodalite, sugilite, turquoise

Fragrances: Acacia, almond, anise, benzoin, bergamot, fennel, lavender, lemongrass, lemon verbena, lily of the valley, peppermint, sage, sandalwood

Related sense: Smell, hearing

Use Air to attract: Skill in passing tests and examinations, learning, travel, changes and improvements in career, especially self employment, justice, just rewards for efforts made, advantageous house moves, money-spinning ventures, curiosity, health and healing, anything to do with science, technology or the media, new beginnings, following opportunities, meeting new helpful people

Counterbalance excess Air with: Earth

Fire

Areas that will benefit most from Fire input: Kitchen, dining room, hearth, living/sitting room, garage, places where finances are sorted, bedroom of couple seeking passion or to conceive a child

Substances: Candles, beeswax, flames, ash, fibre optic lamps, clear crystal spheres, anything gold, mirrors, oranges, sun catchers, natural sunshine, sunflowers and all golden flowers, dragon statues especially in metal, mobiles and images of dragonflies, gold jewellery

Colours: Red, orange and gold

Crystals: Amber, bloodstone/heliotrope, boji stones, carnelian, clear crystal quartz, garnet, lava, iron pyrites, obsidian, ruby, topaz

Fragrances: Allspice, angelica, basil, bay, carnation, cedarwood, chamomile, cinnamon, cloves, copal, Dragon's Blood, frankincense, juniper, lime, marigold, nutmeg, orange, rosemary, tangerine

Related sense: Vision

Use Fire to attract: The fulfilment of ambitions, dynamic leadership, all creative and artistic ventures, religion and spirituality, success in sports and competitive games, fame, wealth and unexpected good fortune, courage, pleasure, passion and the consummation of love, the removal of what is no longer needed, protection against vicious attack or threats

Counterbalance excess Fire with: Water

Water

Areas that will benefit most from Water input: Bathroom, laundry room, relaxation areas, bedrooms for quiet sleep and for teenage girls and young women, conservatory or garden room, any area with a water feature – from a mini fountain to a swimming pool

Substances: Water, milk, wine, sea shells, crystal spheres, fragrant oils, flower and tree essences, bowls of water, silver jewellery, mermaid, fish and dolphin statues especially in glass, anything made of glass (mirrors are Fire), fish in tanks, silk, transparent drapes, silver bells on cords

Crystals: Aquamarine, aragonite, coral, all fluorites, green jasper, jade, mother of pearl, ocean jasper, opal, pearl, watermelon tourmaline

Colours: Blue or silver

Fragrances: Apple blossom, apricot, coconut, eucalyptus, feverfew, heather, hyacinth, jasmine, lemon, lemon balm, lilac, lily, myrrh, orchid, passionflower, peach, strawberry, sweet pea, thyme, valerian, vanilla, violet

Related sense: Intuition

Use Water to attract: Love, committed relationships, trust, romance, friendship, helpful friends, the mending of quarrels, protection of those far away, quiet sleep, good dreams, adapting to changing circumstances, fun and spontaneity, family celebrations, respecting everyone's opinion and feelings, spiritual values, healing using the powers of nature, long-distance travel especially by water

Counterbalance excess Water with: Fire

Using the four elements to purify your home

Fire/light

Fire/light is the most powerful and effective tool and can be used alone for a quick and effective cleansing or as the first element in a more general psychic cleansing involving all four elements. The main tool of light and Fire is a candle.

- ❈ In the room to be cleansed, light a natural beeswax or white, lilac or soft blue candle in a heatproof holder so you can carry the candle round the room.

- ❈ Alternatively, use a small tea light in a foil container, like those you put under an oil burner. Set it on a small heatproof plate and surround it with fresh flower heads and small clear quartz and amethyst crystals (my favourite). This gives you a good mix of healing and life-giving energies and balances the fierce Fire, especially in a smaller home.

- ❈ Light the candle or tea light in the centre of the room. Raise it upwards slightly and slowly to draw together the room energies and then carry it into the four corners in turn, beginning with the one nearest the door and moving anticlockwise. This is to reach the stale or negative energies that accumulate in corners.

- ❈ You can either work in silence, or if you prefer, in the centre and at each corner, say,

> *May only goodness, light, laughter, loveliness*
> *and peace remain here.*

- ❈ When you have visited all four corners of the room return to the centre of the room, raise the candle or tea light on its plate upwards again and revisit the four corners, this time in a clockwise order. Again, you can either do this in silence or repeat the words above.

- ❈ Carry the candle from room to room if you are cleansing more than one room and when you have finished (one room or the house) say,

> *Blessings be on this house and all who live or enter here.*

- ❈ Leave the candle alight for the next two stages of purification.

At any time after an argument or a difficult visitor you can carry out a simple purification, for example by lighting incense or a candle in the centre of every affected room and using simple words such as,

> *May all be restored as it was before.*

Air/fragrance

Incense or smudge is the purest form of fragrance cleansing and can follow the candle ceremony or be used separately. Traditionally in Europe and Scandinavia, lavender, bay, pine, sage and rosemary herbs would be regularly burned on the main hearth fire to remove negative feelings, repel sickness and attract health and harmony to the home. These are all good fragrances to use in modern spiritual cleansing.

Other protective and cleansing fragrances include sandalwood, probably regarded as the best purifier of all, basil, cedar (as smudge), cinnamon, frankincense, juniper, lemon, lilac, lily of the valley, myrrh, orange, patchouli, rose, sagebrush (as smudge), sweetgrass (as smudge), tarragon, thyme and ylang ylang.

These are all dual function fragrances and will energise any area of the home as well as purifying it.

See page 77 (for incense) and page 78 (for smudge sticks) to choose the most suitable fragrance for your home and situation. See page 76 for information on the different forms of incense available. Then follow these steps, which are the same whether you are using either kind of incense or smudge sticks.

- ❋ Light the incense stick or smudge from the candle flame or add the first granules to the white hot charcoal.

- ❋ Standing inside the room, raise the incense stick, incense dish or smudge upwards as you face the door of the room and say,

    By the powers of the sky/the angels be blessed.

- ❋ Then pass the incense downwards towards the ground and say,

    By Mother Earth be blessed.

- ❋ As before, walk round the four corners anticlockwise. If you have a smudge stick or incense stick, hold it in the hand you write with and make anticlockwise spirals as you walk. With an incense dish, use your hand or a feather to waft the smoke as you walk.

- ❋ In each corner, raise and lower the stick, smudge or dish and repeat the words you used previously.

- ❋ Return to the centre and repeat the raising and lowering actions and words.

- ❋ Now repeat the process in a clockwise direction, visiting all four corners and returning to the centre of the room.

- ✻ Finally face the four corners of the room in turn while still standing in the centre, holding the stick or dish steady at waist height and finally raise it upwards and downwards in silence.
- ✻ Return the stick or dish to the table.

Burning incense

There are two kinds of incense:

- ✻ Combustible incense comes in the form of sticks and cones, which are instantly activated when the end is lit. Sticks are easy to use and the fragrant smoke that is released can be directed where needed by holding the cool end of the stick in the hand you write with as you move round the different areas to be cleared. Cones can be lit and carried around on a heatproof dish.

- ✻ Non-combustible incense is the kind you burn on a lighted circular charcoal disc with an indentation in the centre, in a heatproof ceramic or metal dish. When the charcoal goes white, it is hot enough to burn small quantities of incense at a time (you can top it up as needed).

You can buy ready-made loose granular or powdered incenses and these burn directly on charcoal. However, you can easily make your own by using a mortar and pestle as used for grinding garlic or fresh herbs and pounding dried flowers or herbs. Supermarket herbs in glass jars are excellent in homemade incense as are dried lavender heads and rose petals. (For the qualities associated with particular herbs, see pages 46–48, for flowers see page 42.) You can also used the dried flowers from a bouquet as a way of remembering a special occasion and the good wishes of the sender of the flowers.

So that your incense will burn well, mix the powder with some granular resin (three parts powder to one part resin). Experiment and note your favourite recipes. Creating your own incense mixes is not only fun and easy but means you can use the proportions of each of the flower or herbs to bring the qualities you most need in your home and life. You can also burn granular incenses like frankincense or myrrh on their own on the heated charcoal. You will need to be careful carrying the granular incense.

Choose from the following resins and granular incenses, according to the quality required:

Benzoin	Money, success in career or learning, for all examinations and tests, for speculation and good luck, for new opportunities and for help in times of need
Dragon's Blood	Love, protection and passion, male potency, power, enduring love, material success, for overcoming seemingly impossible odds or opposition; also for reversing bad luck, especially financial
Frankincense	Courage, joy, strength and success, for safe travel, travel and house-move opportunities, prosperity, happiness, self-confidence, creative ventures, good luck, health and leadership qualities
Gum Arabic (acacia)	Secret or new love, optimism, making new friends, family matters, better communication, happiness and well-being, for keeping secrets, for finding what has been lost or taken
Myrrh	Healing, peace, protection, inner harmony, reconciliation, environmental concerns, for mothers and children, for animals, for increased psychic powers
Orange	Love, fidelity, abundance, fertility, marriage, health and happiness
Pine (pinon or collophony)	Healing, fertility, purification, protection, increased inflow of money, for returning hostility to its sender, for new beginnings, for cleansing homes psychically against hostility from troublesome neighbours or external spite or attack
Sandalwood	Healing, spirituality, contact with guardian angels, passion, wealth; also enhances sexual magnetism and commitment in love; enhances self-esteem and a positive body image

See Further Reading (page 245) for books about making and burning your own incenses.

Burning smudge

These fragrances are readily available commercially or you can make your own (see my *Complete Book of Natural Magick* – Further Reading, page 245 for instructions).

Cedar	Cleansing and prosperity; removes negativity from situations, homes and artefacts; good when you move into a new home so you will be happy there; brings abundance and financial good fortune; if burned regularly, cedar is said to keep sickness away from the home and family and to connect with guardian spirits and angels
Juniper	Cleanses negativity after a quarrel or a critical visitor; will bless a new home; protective of you and family members while travelling – against accidents, sickness, road rage, terrorism or violence; an antidote to bullying; for new beginnings and New Year's Eve cleansing
Sagebrush	Health and wealth, empowerment, long life, prosperity, good health, wisdom, protection; speeds justice towards a positive resolution, grants wishes, improves memory; aids success in career, examinations and tests; drives away all negativity from whatever source, human or paranormal; white sagebrush is also good for cleansing and empowering the human aura or energy field
Sweetgrass	Positive energies, gentleness and healing, good for women of any age, living alone or with children or with older parents; also a gentle purifier of grief, sorrow and abuse for men and women; brings reconciliation and hope in difficult times; a giver of abundance of good things not just money; promises better luck; protective (unburned sweetgrass braids or bundles are hung over doorways and entrances)

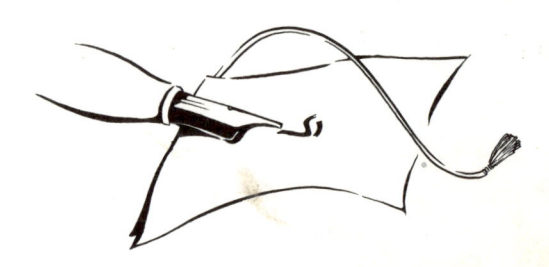

Earth/salt

Salt is found naturally both as rock salt that is mined or extracted from salt marshes and by evaporating seawater. It was one of the earliest items traded and is associated with protection, health and prosperity.

Because salt was historically regarded as the one totally pure substance, it also assumed religious and spiritual significance throughout the ages as a symbol of purity and incorruptibility. Salt was also used in holy water to ward off evil and to increase physical strength and powers of fertility. It is still used in the preparation of holy water.

The most traditional salt purification uses salt that has been mixed with water:

- Mix a few pinches of sea salt with water in a deep bowl about the size of a large cereal bowl or small round serving dish.
- Use either sparkling bottled water or water from a tap that has been left to run so the water is bubbly.
- Stir the salted water three times clockwise with a silver-coloured knife and then make a cross on the surface of the water, asking for blessings from your guardian angels or, if you prefer, the blessings of light and goodness.
- Put a candle in the centre of each room as you work.
- Sprinkle a few drops of salt water in the four corners of the room, moving clockwise in silence.
- Before you leave the room, say,

    Go from this place all that is sad and left from the past that is not joyous, and depart likewise all sickness and misfortune.

- If this is the only room you are working with blow out the candle, otherwise carry it to the next room and blow it out at the end of the whole ritual, sending blessings to whoever needs them.
- If you sense any disturbing paranormal energies, when you have finished blessing the corners with the salt water, carry the still lighted candle into each corner clockwise in turn or where you sense, or a child sees, the ghostly presence. Say in each place,

    Friend, remain in peace or go with blessings.

- After you have cleared the room or the whole house, tip the salt water away under a running tap.

Water

Water is mainly combined with salt (see previous page), but you can use it in the form of a protective and empowering spray. You may choose to buy natural non-aerosol sprays or colognes in lavender, rose, sandalwood, orange or lemon from a pharmacy, a gift store or by mail order. These can be expensive, however, and you can easily make your own spray using a small bottle of essential oil or the relatively new perfume oils that while not cheap are of good quality and can be diluted.

Follow these steps to make an essential oil spray and use it to bring harmony to your home:

- ✤ Add 10–15 drops of essential or perfume oil to 450 ml/¾ pint of water in a pump-action spray bottle.
- ✤ Set the spray in the centre of the room on the table.
- ✤ Raise it and, moving away from the table, turn towards the four directions clockwise, starting facing the door.
- ✤ Spray a fine mist in all four directions (shake the mixture first), then returning to face the door and standing in the centre of the room, spray upwards, but slightly to the side so you do not directly inhale the mix.
- ✤ Finally spray close to the ground.
- ✤ Say afterwards as you put the spray down on the table,

> *May blessings be on all and may order be restored*
> *and harmony, so let it be.*

- ✤ Choose your fragrance according to the results you wish to achieve:
  - * If your home is happy, spray a harmonising fragrance, such as chamomile, jasmine, lavender, melissa (lemon balm), neroli (orange blossom), rose or ylang ylang. You can also use these fragrances if difficult relatives or neighbours are expected and again when they have left.
  - * Other more potent neutralisers of negativity are bergamot, eucalyptus, lemongrass, peppermint, pine and thyme that also encourage optimism and positive communication between family members.
  - * Citronella is excellent not only for keeping away flying insects (also used in scented candles and torches for the garden), but for deterring over-curious neighbours, visitors who outstay their welcome or emotional vampires.

* Rosewood spray is good for easing tense atmospheres and stressed individuals, especially if volatile teenagers or adults with mid-life crises are present in the home. It helps soften potential criticism or sarcasm and counter mood swings, hormonal or otherwise.

* If sadness, resentment or lethargy has penetrated the house, make a stimulating mix of 3 drops of orange essential oil, 2 drops of lemon oil, 3 drops of lemongrass oil and 3 drops of lime or melissa (lemon balm) oil with 450 ml/¾ pint of water. Spray as a fine mist in living areas.

House blessings

The simplest and most effective method for bringing peace and harmony to your home is with a spoken house blessing. A blessing can be used on moving into a new home to clear any sadness lingering from those who lived in the house before you and to welcome the Dísir family ancestors so you can make it quickly feel like your home.

Blessings are also helpful before the temporary or permanent arrival of new or previously absent or estranged family members or friends. Use blessings to change family or personal luck if you have experienced a difficult patch and after a party or gathering, even if it was friendly, to harmonise the free-floating energies and settle the home down again.

House blessings may be as old as the first dwellings and can be spoken and/or involve actions common to many cultures such as candle lighting or sprinkling salt water.

The Celts created very homely spoken blessings, often based around the importance of the love of the family. You will find lots of variations of the same blessings as they belong to an oral tradition. Collect or create your own blessings for different occasions. Note down any that you come across or hear. You can write them in a leather or cloth-bound blank book to pass on to future generations or to give to a child setting up home on their own or with a partner.

A blessing for a visitor

One of my favourite Celtic blessings is one of the old circling blessings and is attributed to St Columba, the Irish saint who lived on Iona in Scotland and died in 597 CE. You can recite this as you walk in circles round different rooms or round a bedroom to be used by the visitor or new arrival.

> *The peace of god/the goddess, the peace of men,*
> *Be on each window and each door,*
> *On the four corners of the house,*
>
> *Upon the four corners of the bed,*
> *On everything the sun shines on,*
>
> *Upon each thing the eye takes in.*
> *And safe in love may you go forth*
>
> *And safe once more return.*

This is also a lovely blessing if someone is going away for a time.

A blessing when lighting a fire

Another favourite adapted Celtic blessing of mine is one you can say when lighting a candle or switching on or lighting the fire at night or after an absence from home.

> *I kindle my fire this evening, without fear or envy of any who walk*
> *beneath the good sun this day.*
> *I kindle this flame in my hearth and my heart for food on my table,*
> *health in my home, and love to my neighbour, my foe and my kindred*
> *and god/the goddess over all protecting.*
> *May you/I be protected.*

A blessing for an unfamiliar place

I sometimes use the following blessing when I stay in a hotel or unfamiliar place to make me feel at home.

> *Circle this place/room, Mother, Father, keep harm without,*
> *keep peace within.*
> *Circle this place/room, Father, Mother, bless this as my home this day.*

A blessing for changes in the house or family

You can also use a more elaborate blessing before any major family change such as remarriage or the birth of a new child as well as when you have had major work or redecorating done in your home.

- ❦ Use water, if possible, from a well or natural source like Malvern or Buxton Spa waters that have a long healing tradition. Put the water in a unglazed ceramic bowl.
- ❦ Stand outside the threshold of your house, facing inwards with the front door open.
- ❦ Sprinkle water all along the doorstep, saying,

    Blessings on all who enter here in peace and friendship, blessings on all who live within these walls. May they never know fear, never know hardship, never know sickness, but always love and security and the ever flowing abundance of the earth.

- ❦ Next sprinkle water on any external downstairs window ledges, saying,

    May the light of the sun shine through this glass and fill the hearts of all within with hope and inspiration.

- ❦ Tip the remaining water on the path or land outside and say,

    And may the gentle rain bring growth and wash away all that is not lovely or of worth.

- ❦ If there is any earth outside your house, bury a large unpolished amethyst as a symbolic house protector from all harm, burglary and natural disasters. If there is no earth there, bury the amethyst below a green growing plant in a plant pot inside the front door.
- ❦ Leave the front door open and then step over the threshold without touching the place you sprinkled the water, refill the bowl and sprinkle water at each inner threshold repeating the blessing or creating one of your own.
- ❦ Finally bless the table, or tables in each room by sprinkling drops of water all around, saying.

    May there be food enough, welcome, warm hearts, cheer and shelter this day that whatever there is may be shared willingly in the knowledge that the earth will provide of her abundance.

- ❦ You can adapt the words if you live alone or share a house.

4 Rediscovering Your Natural Rhythms

Even in the centre of a city, it is possible to connect with the natural changing rhythms of light and darkness through the year and the passage of the moon through the month and to become more aware of their effects upon our moods and energy levels. This chapter looks at how you can return to the natural rhythms of the day.

The physical effects of lack of sunlight in the winter, especially in northern lands can be manifest as an illness called Seasonal Affective Disorder. This was first described by the sixth-century Goth scholar Jordanes who called the condition, common then as now among modern-day Scandinavians, short day sickness.

At the other end of the spectrum with 24/7 lighting, round-the-clock supermarket opening and the potential for 24-hour access to the television and internet, many people are suffering spiritually from the adverse effects of excess artificial light and sound that can cause insomnia and an inability to relax. By surrounding ourselves with noise and stimulation, in the form of television, work or even coffee, on dark winter evenings, we are denying the natural sleepiness, which would make us want to go to bed much earlier. This can make us irritable or depressed as we are going against the prevailing ebbing light energies of the day and our corresponding bodily biorhythms.

Finding your natural rhythms

The Native North Americans, the Australian Aboriginal people and both Celtic and some modern-day druids and druidesses spend regular time alone in the wilderness to reconnect with and get messages from nature. There are numerous retreats and spiritual journeys organised with the same aim, but you can as easily go alone into the countryside or with a friend or the family. Nor do you need deprivation of basic comforts to experience spiritual enlightenment in nature. Real pagan living is about simple pleasures, relaxation and bringing the best of the old ways into your world without feeling you have to endure undue hardships.

During the week or a weekend around the seasonal change points – 21 March, 21 June, 21 September and 21 December – or any time when you feel that work is taking over or you are too stressed to enjoy a day or evening off, literally stop the clock and create some time out of time. Spend a day or two – or longer if you can – close to the natural world (if possible, away from home), following the natural light patterns of your chosen time of year.

You can rent a cottage, chalet or caravan on a quiet site quite cheaply out of peak holiday season. For midsummer and maybe spring and autumn equinox you could go camping in a forestry or nature reserve area. If you have to stay at home, be strict about not answering phones or inviting in neighbours and make sure you spend as much time in the open air as possible. Local botanical gardens, parks, woodlands or country parks can be very magical and spiritual.

Preparing for your time out of time

If you have responsibilities that may distract you while you are away, try to make plans for them to be dealt with so you can forget them. Designate a friend or relative to look after the children – although they make wonderful companions on this experience if you take them with you – or keep an eye on the house. They will sort out any minor crises on your behalf in your absence and will know where you are if they need to reach you in a real emergency. I have found that letting go of life temporarily is harder for me than the people I leave behind – they really do not need me as much as I imagine.

Pack only what you need – don't load yourself down with too many things that aren't important. Don't take any toys, electronic games or gadgets, books or puzzles.

Making the most of your time

Try to arrive at the place you will be staying early enough to settle in and explore. Start as you mean to go on – slow down.

When you go to bed, stop all the clocks, unplug and switch off phones, switch off computers, televisions and radios and keep it that way for 24 hours at least.

Leave any curtains open at night so you will wake with the light. If you wake and it is still dark and you do not want to go back to sleep, light a small lamp or go out in the darkness for a walk if it is safe to do so. You may see nocturnal wildlife still scurrying around.

Books, even sudoku puzzles, can be a distraction from listening to the inner signals from your body, reacting to the outer light patterns and allowing messages from nature to filter gradually into your psyche. If you want to write your great literary work this time out of time may inspire you, but for now open yourself to whatever happens. This is hard in a world where we are used to consulting diaries or personal organisers to structure even our leisure time.

Home or away, do not use the weekend to discuss fraught issues or try to solve money or relationship problems if you are with family or a partner. Your only task is *to be* and not to do, *to listen* rather than talk, and *to be still* and observe rather than take action. You may find a love relationship that has soured or become temporarily cold may revive when there are no external distractions or trouble making by outsiders.

Fully experiencing time out of time

What do you want to do? Do it or do nothing – just sit and watch the world go by. Wasting time is not doing nothing but doing things you do not want to do or spending time fretting about what needs to be done or went wrong in the past. Time out of time is about escaping from the past and the future, just for this short creative withdrawal from the world. It is about enjoying now.

- **Commune with nature:** Focus on being outside and doing things that bring you closer to nature. Do simple things: walk in the woods, crunch through autumn leaves, swim or paddle in a natural water source as opposed to a water park; in winter, collect evergreens to take back home to decorate the house for Christmas. After any initial complaints of boredom because they don't have their electronic games, children will soon be playing with sticks, stones, shells or making tree houses and you can help them create bivouacs out of branches, ford streams or light fires to cook over.

- **Eat simply:** Eat and drink when you are hungry. Eat natural, easily prepared food that even fussy eaters will not argue about or ready-prepared food that does not need cooking. Time out of time is not about one person cooking and clearing and getting stressed while the others commune with nature – get everyone to help.

- **Enjoy the weather:** Do not be deterred by bad weather. As my mother used to say, 'You won't melt in the rain', and if you have spare clothes you can enjoy getting thoroughly soaked.

- **Cherish the silence:** Whether alone or even with others, have periods of silence – again very hard for modern people. Look for cloud pictures in the sky or the patterns made by wind and overhanging trees or clouds reflected in water; listen to the rustle of leaves in the trees or the sound of the sea. Accept whatever you see, hear or feel or just enjoy the experience.

- **Free your imagination:** If you are alone in your daily life, use this time to learn to love silence rather than fear it. I am discovering in my now almost-empty nest that I do not have to turn on the half-hour news update or play music to break the silence, and I am actually less lonely than when I was in an unhappy relationship. In creative silence, imagination grows and nature's sounds, such as birdsong, are sweeter than the finest mobile phone ringtone.

- ✤ **Embrace the dark:** Go to bed when you are tired or when it gets dark, or light a candle or lamp and sit in the darkness watching the light patterns on the walls. If you are with others, tell old stories, legends and myths softly in the darkness. If there is a moon or stars look up at them and you may see a shooting star or make out the constellations. Create other animal and bird forms in the star patterns and choose your special star.

When you go back to the world it will still be turning and will not have noticed your absence. But you will know as you check your messages – most of which will not be as essential as you thought – that there is a world beyond the clock and you can step off the hamster wheel and rediscover it again any time.

Experiment at different times of the year with time out in nature so you get to know from the inside the rhythm of the changing day and night, heat and cold.

The energies and associations of the sun

The sun has long been worshipped, in classical tradition as the magnificent sun gods Helios and Apollo who drove their golden sun chariots across the sky. In the Celtic and Northern traditions and among the Australian Aboriginals, the Sun Mothers emphasise the nurturing power of the sun and often, according to myth, take an active part in the ripening and harvesting of the crops. In the Baltic, the sun goddess Saule would be seen in the summer walking among the growing crops, her golden hair streaming down her back. The Egyptian sun god, Ra, was considered all-powerful.

The sun is vital to humanity. For without the sun there could be no life, no growth or fertility. Yet in excess it can be a destructive force. It affects winds, weather and (like the moon) the tides. The sun can be gentle, empowering and healing or it can beat down over parched deserts, burn skin and wither crops.

Traditionally the sun, the moon and other planets have crystals, herbs and elements that have become associated with them over many centuries. These are believed to reflect the same properties as the heavenly body, for example confidence and energy are considered strengths associated with the sun. Some sun herbs have bright yellow flowers, like St John's Wort and chamomile that in the northern hemisphere bloom around midsummer. The following associations can be used to reflect the properties of the sun.

Element: Fire

Colour: Gold

Day of the week: Sunday

Metal: Gold

Crystals: Amber, carnelian, diamond, clear crystal quartz spheres and rainbow quartz, tiger's eye, golden topaz

Herbs, incenses and oils: Angelica, calendula, celandine, chamomile, cinnamon, cloves, eyebright, frankincense, juniper, mistletoe, olive, rosemary, saffron, St John's Wort

Flowers: Any yellow or golden ones, but especially sunflowers, marigolds and golden carnations

Trees: Ash, bay, birch, laurel, palm, walnut

Archangel: Michael

Use sun energies for: Personal fulfilment and ambition, power and success; to help to increase the flow of the life force, enabling you to assert or strengthen your identity and individuality; for innovation of all kinds and new beginnings; for energy, joy, health, prosperity, spiritual awareness and self-confidence; to bring wealth and prosperity where there is poverty and failure; to help break a run of bad luck; for all matters concerning fathers.

The four daily solar periods

The daily solar change points are dawn, noon, dusk/twilight and midnight (the time of the invisible sun when it is at full height on the other side of the world). Once you are aware of these times, you can draw strength from them, whether you work at or from home, commute or travel longer distances, are part of a big company, are on a regular night shift or have retired.

You do not have to rise with the dawn at four o'clock in summer but can celebrate dawn whenever you wake. Dawn is the time of new beginnings and renewed energy and can be a helpful boost if you have been awake with a teething infant or are going through a bad patch and dread the morning.

Lunchtime, however brief, is your noon, the time of full power or getting back on track mentally if the morning has proved frustrating or for refreshing yourself for the sustained effort of the afternoon.

Going home can be designated your dusk or closing down period and if you often work late or are wrapped up in regular evening children's activities, it acts as a reminder to slow down occasionally and go with what your mind and body are saying rather than being totally at the mercy of your timetable.

Going to bed, the everyday equivalent of midnight, marks the transition between one day and another. It is a crucial but often forgotten period when you need to prepare for sleep by spending time winding down rather than working, sending MSN or text messages or doing chores until you fall into bed exhausted yet restless.

Each of the four daily marker points is the equivalent of a mini season: dawn for spring, noon for summer, twilight or dusk for autumn and midnight for winter.

In winter in the northern hemisphere, dawn is far later than in summer and dusk is far earlier. This also means that except on the equinoxes, 21 March and 21 September, you do not get equal divisions between the four daily solar change points. Depending on where you live you may have almost continuous daylight at the height of summer and a true midnight sun. When I was staying in Sweden around midsummer in 2007, even though I was in the central lake lands rather than the north, the sun only went down for about an hour each night.

Marking the daily solar periods

When you have time, try to mark the four points of the day fully, focusing on what each marker point currently signifies to you and on some of the needs it symbolises that are relevant to you right now. (Your time out period may be the ideal opportunity to do this.)

Try for a few days marking the four transitions of your day even briefly and you will notice that your energy levels avoid the customary sudden energy dips mid afternoon that demanded an instant sugar lift. Gradually too you will feel generally more in control of your life and emotions and find that sleeping and waking become more natural and harmonious. If you carry on for a few weeks or months, you may start to wake just before the alarm and gradually be able to dispense with alarms and wake naturally and harmoniously.

Go out at sunrise, noon and dusk and experience the different energies and emotions that flow through you whether you are on a sunny seashore or city street. We all have our favourite times of day, evening and night, but those we like less may also have their strengths to offer.

Walk out in sunshine, especially as it appears unexpectedly on a winter day, splash in puddles of sunlit water after rain or paddle or swim in the light pools in the sea or a swimming pool. Observe sunlight rippling on water, or sunset colouring the leaves crimson as it catches a tree.

Sit in pure darkness at midnight without switching on the light or even a candle and embrace the velvety darkness. If you are afraid of the dark, as many adults are, do this just for a minute at first with your hand on a light switch and gradually your fear of the blackness will lessen.

Buy four small crystals to represent the four segments of the day: citrine for dawn/when you wake up, carnelian for noon/your lunch break, amethyst or moonstone for dusk/going home and garnet or jet for midnight/going to bed. Keep these in a drawstring bag that you carry with you and take each crystal out at its special time each day. Once a week, when you are at home, wash them first thing in the morning and set them in a circle all day from dawn until dusk to represent the circle of the solar day.

The four solar periods will now be looked at in more detail. Each day, try to choose one of the suggested activities for each marker point (more if you have the time).

Dawn/when you wake

Dawn varies each day. Its precise time can be found in a diary or the weather section of a newspaper. Dawn-tide energies last from when you wake until about half an hour before you break for lunch. The same is true of the other periods in that they decline in strength half an hour before the next period. In this time, you will experience transition energies.

Every dawn is a spring equinox written small, a resurrection, a birth of new hope. Today is the day you anticipated with excitement or feared in many sleepless nights or anxious moments. So walk into the dawn with courage, knowing that this day will be absolutely the best one ever, because you will make it so.

In the winter months the actual rising light energy band from dawn to noon is quite narrow and so should be maximised. Within dawn energies you can initiate projects, spend time forward planning, send e-mails before the system gets clogged up, capitalise on all those brilliant ideas you carried over in your subconscious from sleep, and generally launch yourself on the first tide of the day. People are usually more open, fresh and optimistic during this period.

Of course there will be times when you wake late and in a panic because you were exhausted when you went to bed or you are irritable because an infant or pet has woken you much earlier than you would have wished. But, ideally, how would you like to begin each day and how can you adapt some of those ideals to give a better start to the working day as well as to days off? How too can you refocus a start that was less than ideal?

- ❇ Try waking five or ten minutes earlier and if you do not yet wake naturally and must be up by a certain time most days, try to find a gentle way, perhaps an alarm that plays harmonious music, to ease the transition.

- ❇ The way you begin the day sets the tone, so if it is light and fine weather, try taking your early morning drink outdoors or lighting a candle indoors if it is still dark.

- ❇ Rather than switching on breakfast television or the radio, sit quietly near fragrant plants either outdoors or in, or light floral oils. Allow your dreams to recede gently, taking anything from them that is of use and pushing away any lingering fears from a bad dream. The more you work with your dawn and midnight, waking and going to sleep, the less nightmares you will have and the more gentle the transitions between sleep and waking will become.

* Dawn is a good time for meditation, even if you only have a few minutes. If you don't meditate, try relaxing, breathing softly and regularly and focusing on a lovely flower, a lighted candle or a patch of early light even for five minutes. Allow the mind to clear of racing thoughts and give the new day a chance to unfold in its unique way.

* Afterwards, focus on two or three good things you hope to do or achieve in the day ahead. These need only be small. However many things you are not looking forward to, try to plan something pleasurable.

* Look towards the sunrise or the lightest place in the sky or, if it is dark, promise yourself just a minute or two when the sun finally does rise to tune into the ascending light.

* Identify something special about this moment when you get up. Are the birds singing, is there some new growth in the garden or on an indoor plant? Do the icicles on the window make beautiful patterns? Is the sun breaking through the mist? Is your baby gurgling or your toddler singing? Is the moon still in the sky as it will be during the waning period? Are there any lingering stars visible – perhaps even Venus the morning star, which is considered especially lucky?

* Can you make time for a short walk, cycle ride or swim? These are all so much more refreshing than exercising in a brightly lit gym before work or exercising along with a video.

* Can you get the children ready early so they can enjoy a few quiet minutes of play or reading rather than always watching breakfast cartoons or frantically dashing round trying to find school bags or sports equipment? Modern life discourages forethought and encourages panics and mini crises, most of which can be avoided and with them the stress that is not helpful to begin a new day.

* Finally face the rising light or your candle positioned in the east of the room (the traditional direction of dawn) and say aloud,

> *I am (name yourself to establish your place in the world).*
> *I greet the morning and this morning I go into the world*
> *with the intention of ...*

Name those small pleasures or goals that will make this your day.

✤ If you wish, hold your dawn crystal between your cupped hands as you speak. My favourite is sparkling yellow citrine that is the crystal of the Archangel Raphael, the traveller and supreme healing angel, and a crystal associated with new beginnings and called the merchant's stone because of its traditional link with commerce. Then you can take your dawn crystal with you to work, in the drawstring bag, or keep it at home if you are working there.

✤ Try to sit and eat breakfast either alone or with others. Eat something quick, nutritious and easy rather than snatching toast on the dash or while watching television. Get everything ready the night before, and the calmness in family members will make mornings so much easier.

✤ Before you start work, fill a glass with filtered or bottled spring water and if you have access to natural light, put the water where light will shine on it. If you only have access to artificial light, add two tiny clear quartz crystals or citrines to the water. Cover the glass and leave until noon when you can use this sun water.

✤ Use dawn energies to focus on:

* travel
* initiating a project or new beginnings in any aspect of your life
* optimism
* reversing bad luck
* improving health
* improving career prospects
* house moves
* improving financial matters
* finding new love and trust.

Noon/when you have lunch

Noon-tide energies operate from about 12 noon through to 4 pm, though in wintertime you may start to feel the dusk energies drawing in from early afternoon.

Noon itself is recognised as the most powerful solar marker, though the day may get hotter after noon and the energies will then move into overdrive. Each noon forms a mini midsummer solstice of peak power. Even in midwinter in lands where it barely gets light, you can tap into the maximum power of this period by surrounding yourself with lots of light, sparkling crystals and, if necessary, lamps rather than harsh overhead lights.

You can adapt this marker point to when you take a break from work which you should aim to do whether you are at home, travelling or in an office. This noon or lunch break time should be sacrosanct, except in an emergency, and should be long enough for you to eat your lunch away from your workspace and to get out in the fresh air – unless there is a tornado blowing.

- ✤ If it is a hot day, find a place with greenery and water to eat your lunch and refresh your psychic energy to maximise the opportunities of the afternoon.

- ✤ If possible, after you have eaten, fit in the now popular 20-minute power nap (or sit quietly with your eyes closed for a few minutes visualising the stars going out one by one).

- ✤ After your nap, splash your sun water (see page 94) on the centre of your hairline, the centre of your brow, the centre of your throat and your inner wrist pulse points and drink the rest. As you touch each of these major energy points say in your mind,

    > *I absorb the full power of the sun and I leave for the cosmos to bring to fruition anything that did not go well this morning.*

    If you really cannot stop, at least try to carry out this ritual.

- ✤ Take your carnelian crystal out of its bag and hold it in your hand to call the angelic energies of noon, the Archangel Michael of the sun. Then name two or three small new goals and at least one more small pleasurable moment you seek by the end of the working day. Put the crystal back in the bag.

✤ If you are at home, make a definite break and if with children or caring for relatives either go outdoors or make lunchtime a special occasion. Save children's television for giving yourself an extra 20 minutes peace to rest or meditate but definitely not to clear up – you can do that later. Self time is precious if you care for others. If alone, indulge in that power nap or relax in a fragrant bath.

✤ When you feel refreshed, and before returning to work, assess whether you need to change the tempo or mood of the day or at least to change your own mood and refocus if you can't change the mood of others.

✤ Picture the successful completion of the day before you step back into the fray.

✤ Use noon-time energies to focus on:

   * creating a sudden burst of power or confidence

   * bringing a fast or large infusion of money

   * major promotion or career advancement

   * the consummation of love

   * a permanent commitment in love, a married relationship or fidelity

   * loyalty

   * business partnerships

   * sending absent healing for serious or acute conditions

   * the successful resolution of a court case or official matter

   * sending urgent or major healing

   * joy.

Dusk/when you go home

Dusk also varies each day according to the time of year. 'Never let the sun go down on anger,' my late mother used to say. This is the daily message of twilight, the mini autumn equinox that falls each day. What is gained and what is lost all merge into the darkness and with them we should allow resentment and regrets to drain away and also be pleased with ourselves for what we have achieved during the day, however modest.

The hardest thing in the modern world is to call a halt to the working day, whether you work at home or not. People are working longer hours than ever and productivity actually dips as the hours increase.

After school can also become a frantic dash of going to other children's houses or organised activities and, as in working life, the sheer volume of demands on your time can diminish the quality of what you do. As Bert, a local pagan wise man who helps me with my garden, says,

Think of your life as a torch beam. The more you try to cram in, the wider the circle your personal light must cover; the higher and further away the torch beam must be held to cover the wider area, and so the centre, what really matters, is left without light.

So dusk is about priorities, what is lost and what is gained, what should be abandoned and what is precious and so given priority.

You may go home long after dusk has fallen in winter or before dusk in summer, but the energies represented are the same. Even if you are self-employed or are at home with children, marking this point will help you to relax into any unavoidable unfinished work or chores, and acts as a mini recharging of your batteries.

* Whenever you can see dusk from the window take a minute or two to breathe in the sunset light and exhale (as sighs between your in breaths) any tension, regrets or annoyances from the day so you end on a positive and gently creative note. Do this even if you have to carry on working after dusk.

* Raise the palm of the hand you write with towards the sunset or a lighted candle, saying,

    Flow from my life what is not lovely, peaceful and of worth. Flow from me, go from me, leave only harmony. Blessings be on my home, on my life and (name anyone you wish) this evening.

* Try to take five or ten minutes of quiet contemplation, if necessary after you have given the family some food and settled them down or before leaving work at the end of the working day as you are tidying up, especially if the workplace is quiet.

* Take time to relax with your family. I can now see that some of the things I considered so vital to finish before doing this, took time from appreciating the people and precious moments I was working for.

* Take your amethyst or moonstone crystal from its bag. Hold it in your hand and call on Aftiel the silver angel of twilight or if you prefer Gabriel, Archangel of the moon, who rules over dusk, to help you move into the next part of your day with peace and love in your heart. Return the crystal to the bag.

✤ Either at work before you leave for home or when you get home, put a little rose or lavender essential oil well diluted with almond or olive oil into a small dish (7–10 drops of essential oil to 30 ml/ 1 fl oz of carrier oil). If you are at home, go outdoors and face the direction of the sunset, the waning light, or if it is dark or is getting dark, light a small purple candle. Place the index finger of the hand you do not write with in the oil and name what you wish to leave behind from the day. Anoint the centre of your hairline and the centre of your brow with the oil mix. Dip your finger into the oil again and state what you would like to take with you to tomorrow from the day. If it was a truly awful day, say,

Let all be set to rest.

✤ If you have experienced a really tough day, scatter a few seeds on any nearby earth or grass or tub of soil, saying,

What takes root may grow, for the rest this is neither the time nor place and so I let it go in peace.

✤ Have a dark ceramic pot or jar with a lid near the front door and some pre-cut brown threads. Tie a piece of thread in a knot to represent any annoyance or anxiety that you are finding it hard to leave outside the home and put the knot inside the pot. Continue until you feel free. You can encourage other family members to do this, explaining that they do not have to name the frustrations out loud. When all the knots are in the pot, put a pinch of dried rosemary in too and put on the lid. When the pot is full, bury the knots under a fragrant plant, wash out the pot with hot water and start again.

✤ If you have not done so already, light a candle as it gets dark – one for yourself and one for every other family member. Light each candle from another as people come home. If anyone is absent overnight, light a small white candle for them in the centre of the others and extinguish them all before bedtime with a spoken blessing for each person if the candles are still alight. Children can blow their candles out with a wish when they go to bed.

✤ Use the dusk energies to focus on:
  * letting go of regrets, anger or guilt
  * psychic and physical protection
  * reducing pain and illness
  * reducing debt
  * justice and just rewards
  * love in maturity
  * home and family matters.

Midnight/when you go to bed

Just as sunset began a new day for the Celts and Vikings, so in the modern world midnight is the transition point.

'The darkest hour is before the dawn' is a popular saying that rings true. But in another time zone the sun is shining brightly and we know, unlike our distant forebears, that the sun does not disappear into the sea or back into the womb of the Earth Mother to sleep until morning. Nevertheless, each morning when the sun reappears it is a small miracle and affirmation of hope.

Midnight heralds the new day, 10 pm is the healing hour and can draw on midnight energies, but whenever you go to bed, early or late, try to let the day drift peacefully towards its ending so you may sleep calmly and not lie awake tossing and turning or writing mental lists and worrying how tired you will be in the morning if you cannot go to sleep.

- ✤ Switch off mobile phones, computers, games consoles, televisions and DVD players at least 15 minutes before bed (preferably more).
- ✤ Work indoors unless it is a clear fine night in which case find a safe, sheltered spot in the garden. Light a dark coloured candle and, looking into the flame, say,

    The sun will rise again. But for now I consign all to the flame: worry, fear, pain, loss, joy and achievements of this day and those concerns that rightly belong to tomorrow.

- ✤ Hold your garnet or jet crystal in your cupped hands as you look into the flame. Send love, healing or forgiveness to anyone who needs it and ask for quiet sleep and protection during the night for yourself and for any loved ones. Drop just a few grains of salt into the flame so it sparkles as you speak and then blow out the candle and go to bed. If you wish, set all four crystals in a circle next to your bed.
- ✤ Pass the hand you write with slowly down the centre of your body from the centre of your hairline ending at the base of your body between your legs. Imagine a blue velvet curtain passing in front of you and all round your whole body enclosing your feet and arms, closing down your chakras or inner psychic energy centres. This is like drawing the curtains at your windows and ensures you are not disturbed by free-floating psychic energies or worries while you sleep.
- ✤ Use the energies of midnight to focus on:
    * sending healing (10 pm is the healing hour) especially for chronic conditions and pain (see the Midnight Aett on page 103)

* forgiving yourself and others
* accepting what cannot be changed
* contacting absent family members and friends telepathically
* connecting with wise ancestors, guardian angels and spirit guides
* banishing anything that is harmful in your life or that of loved ones, from bad habits to destructive people. To do this, ask that any who plan or do harm or send bad thoughts to you or loved ones be bound during the night from malice; send them peace and kindness. This binding can be helpful if you live in a dangerous area and fear break-ins.

The Aetts of the day and night

Even more subtle but just as valuable as the major sun points in the day are the ancient Aetts or Anglo Saxon and Scandinavian eight markers within each day. These eight divisions are the same in winter and summer and form the unchanging rhythm behind the changing sun and moon patterns. They bring order, stability and a way of measuring the energy ebbs and flows within each day, in earthly terms as opposed to the more cosmic lunar and solar biorhythms. The eight divisions made the transition from the pre-Christian to Christian world and in rural places survived for hundreds of years until the Industrial Revolution that took place in Europe and especially England in around 1760–1840.

These divisions (or tides) are not something you would mark every day but occasionally when you have a day off, you could work with some of the Aett times that are relevant to your life.

* If you have a particular need or area of concern, each of the three-hour periods is favourable for specific enterprises. Therefore, you could use a certain Aett three-hour period to put a venture into action or to contact someone related to the need.

* Alternatively, light a candle at the beginning of the Aett, saying the need aloud in order to bring it out of your thoughts and into the realms of possibility.

* Right in the middle of the Aett, put a pinch of salt into the flame, while repeating the words you used earlier. Salt is the traditional substance for bringing desires to actuality.

* At the end of the Aett time, blow out the candle, imagining the light strengthening your purpose, repeat the words and end with,

So shall it be.

Chime hours

The chime hours (3 am, 6 am, 9 am, 12 noon, 3 pm, 6 pm, 9 pm and 12 midnight) and the five minutes before and just after them, are said to be the most powerful time of each three-hour period. The energies build up and fall away from the central point, thereafter rising towards the next period of energy. The chime hours are named after the chiming of the church or town clock or the small musical peal that was once a feature of many areas in Europe dating back to Saxon times. Those born on or close to a chime hour (especially midnight) are considered especially psychic and intuitive and able to look backwards and forwards in time.

The power of the Aetts

Each three-hour period has special energies that are good for particular endeavours. Use the lists below and possibly a small chiming clock and you can start to work with the Aetts. Some of the periods coincide with the dawn/dusk, waking/sleeping energies and enable you to fine tune these times. Midnight and noon are the same in both systems, but the Aetts do work on the actual hours rather than regarding midnight and going to bed as synonymous. You can mix and match the two systems according to your focus and what fits best with your free time on a particular day.

4.30 am–7.30 am: Morning-tide is the time of awakening, fertility and new beginnings. The chime hour begins at 6 am. Use its energies for starting something new and all matters concerning infertility, conception, pregnancy and birth of both babies and projects. This Aett can be a good time to make love if you are having conception anxieties or to get up early and put the finishing touches to your novel or some craft work you hope to sell.

7.30 am–10.30 am: Day-tide is the time of work and money-making. The chime hour begins at 9 am. Use its energies for solving money problems, money-spinning ventures and actively seeking alternative approaches and new contacts. If you work flexi time, operate from home or can go into work early, this can be a time of maximum productivity and creative success, when you are less likely to get interruptions. If you are at home with children they may be in daycare or in a relatively good mood and happy to play while you do something creative.
Alternatively, take them outdoors and take a notebook or palmtop along with you. I did some of my best work scribbling down ideas sitting on a bench during this Aett period while the children were happily occupied

in the playground or in the local country park watching the early morning rabbits and taking a picnic breakfast. (My children have always been very early risers.)

10.30 am–1.30 pm: Midday is the time of endurance and perseverance. The chime hour is 12 noon. Use its energies for persisting with matters that are proving wearisome, catching officials between meetings, doing the hard work and assembling necessary information for pushing through ideas, and for research, if doing boring detailed work or checking your facts. It is also a good period for persisting with unhelpful people – take them out to elevenses or lunch to raise their blood sugar and bonhomie.

The middle of this period may alternatively coincide with a break from work when it is important to restore your own blood sugar energies for the rest of the day by actually stopping and moving away from your workstation. The habit I have of working through lunch and eating at the computer is actually counterproductive in terms of stamina and can lead to irritability and reduced productivity.

Use this break to get into the fresh air and to give yourself a brief time out to restore your natural stamina. The inspiration will then follow during the next Aett.

1.30 pm–4.30 pm: Undorne is the time for change, transformation and illumination. The start of the chime hour is 3 pm. Use its energies for exploring new horizons and travel plans. This is the time for booking holidays or planning trips, exploring new markets for your products, selling yourself and communicating persuasively, both personally and electronically.

If you want to move house, change jobs or get promotion, focus at the chime hour by putting a pinch of dried rosemary in the flame of a blue candle and naming any place you want to visit or your desired new job or location. Then blow out the candle and picture yourself in the location or job you desire. Apply immediately afterwards.

4.30 pm–7.30 pm: Eventide is the time of the family, of home and reconciliation. The chime hour begins at 6 pm. Use the energies for questions concerning children of all ages, domestic matters, marriage and partnerships. This is a time for strengthening and resolving existing relationships and, if you have a particular concern, for talking it over, visiting or contacting a person who is being cold or unfriendly or making a family time if you have all been busy and not had time to talk. Send a gesture of reconciliation, whether a small gift, a letter or an e-mail at the chime hour for maximum effect or drop dead leaves or petals off a bridge while saying, 'Water under the bridge' and letting anger or resentment, however justifiable, go.

7.30 pm–10.30 pm: Night-tide is the time for love, passion and learning, which may seem a strange mix, but all involve intensity. The chime hour begins at 9 pm. Ideal for students or anyone who has a test, interview or examination the next day, this is the time most favoured for any learning or research. However, it may also be the time people are on a date, chatting online, looking for love or spending time rekindling a passionate connection with a husband, wife or settled lover if everyday life has got in the way.

Lots of the traditional folk spells were practised at this time or at midnight. So, if you are meeting someone special or hoping to find a partner, use your favourite fragrance or rose or lavender natural cologne after a bath and put a single drop on your heart and one on each breast and on your navel before you dress so your radiance and charisma will shine through. As you do this, say,

Love come to me. Love stay with me, willingly, eternally, devotedly and faithfully. So must it be.

10.30 pm–1.30 am: Midnight-tide is the time for healing and restoration of mind, body and spirit. The chime hour is midnight. This is a natural time for letting go of the day and of worry and this Aett will coincide with the solar midnight/going to bed. The energies, therefore, are the same. However, it is additionally a good time to send healing of the mind, body or a troubled spirit, whether to yourself, a loved one or someone absent. Try this simple ritual:

* Holding a rose quartz crystal, face in the direction of the person's home or room. To heal yourself, close your eyes and picture yourself well and happy. You can also send healing to animals and places by the same method.

* Name the sick person and say softly,

    May you/I be healed and relieved of your/my pain/illness/sorrow.

    (Adapt the words to the need.)

* Breathe in slowly three times and, after each in-breath, breathe softly out on to the crystal.

* Breathe in slowly again three times and after each breath blow three times softly and slowly in the direction of the person or imagine the breaths enclosing you in a pink sphere of light.

✤ While still holding the crystal, repeat the dual cycle three times, ending with,

> *May all be blessed and restored to harmony.*

✤ Wash the crystal under running water and leave it to dry.

1.30 am–4.30 am: Uht is the time of sleep and old age. The chime hour begins at 3 am. Use its energies for concerns about elderly relatives and ageing, and for calm sleep. You will not often be awake at this time, unless on night shift, when it is a good time to take just a few minutes relaxing and letting the restorative energies of this tide wash over you. If you are awake worrying or caring for a sick relative or child, light a small white tea light or candle in a safe place and say,

> *I float my concerns on the tides of the night that (name person you are concerned about) will float gently to morning and awake renewed with the light. So may it be.*

Leave the candle burning for just a minute or two and then blow it out very gently.

5 The Moon and Your Inner Rhythms

In early societies, the moon was regarded as a mother and early people believed that she also brought fertility and growth to the animals, plants and people as she grew each month. Her appearance and changing shape throughout the month, as observed from earth, is still regarded symbolically by pagans as reflecting the birth of the moon child and growth of that child into the moon maiden as the crescent moon waxes or increases. You can even see the moon woman in the sky, bulging pregnant in the week before the full moon.

The full moon then symbolically becomes the mother. As the moon wanes or decreases in size, the moon mother becomes the wise grandmother who dies with the end of the cycle as the moon disappears from the sky. In the dark of the moon or new moon, in the two and a half days when the moon is not visible in the sky, the old moon is reborn in an ever-continuing cycle.

This moon imagery even today symbolises a link with the life cycle of humans as they move from youth to age, with the fertile woman's monthly menstrual cycle and, more generally, with the monthly mental and spiritual emotional ebbs and flows experienced by men and women alike. It is this last aspect I will focus on as the most useful expression of lunar energy in the modern world.

Can the moon affect us?

There is great ongoing controversy over whether the changing monthly moon physically affects the human mind. Some research suggests that the moon – especially the full moon – does have physical effects on human moods and behaviour. Most notable is the work carried out at the University of Miami during the 1970s, in which a psychologist, Dr Arnold Lieber, and his team studied 1,887 cases of murder committed in Dale County in Miami from data that covered 15 years, between 1956 and 1970. They also took into account a similar number of cases from Cuyahoga County in Cleveland, Ohio. In both sets of data the murder rate sharply increased just before the full or the new moon approached and declined just as significantly during the first and the last quarters of the moon.

An earlier report from the American Institute of Medical Climatology on behalf of the Philadelphia Police Department discovered that other crimes such as arson, theft and dangerous driving also sharply increased around the full moon. No one really knows precisely how this might work, but Dr Lieber speculated that because the human body contains a high proportion of water, human emotions, like the earthly tides, may be subject to hormonal moon tides.

Another theory is that there are increased positive ions or atoms in the air at the time of the full moon. Despite their name, positive ions are not good for health and may be linked to hyperactivity, depression, anger and also migraines and some allergies such as asthma.

The moon and fertility

In Native North America, as in other indigenous societies, women traditionally shed the old womb lining during the dark of the moon when it was not visible in the sky. At this time the menstruating women lived apart from the rest of the tribe in a specially constructed moon lodge, resting, dreaming and contemplating, while the older women cared for the family. Menstruating women were considered sacred and to have prophetic powers at this time. The full moon was ideally the time of peak fertility, hence the practical association with the full moon and passion in the superstitions of different lands.

This menstruating with the moon cycle still occurs among women in those few societies where there is no artificial light and where the old traditions remain strong. Of course, withdrawing and resting during menstruation is an impossible ideal for most modern women, but in our anxiety not to treat menstruation as an illness, sometimes women who do suffer pain and bad Premenstrual Syndrome (PMS) can push themselves too hard. Nowadays, women often regard the process as a nuisance rather than a sacred sign of their moon wisdom.

From my own work with women, I have discovered that in some cases women who are anxious to conceive may benefit from getting back into rhythm with the natural lunar cycles. This may even begin to regularise their menstrual cycles, which are positively affected psychologically as a result of a new awareness of the moon phases. It is interesting to note that women living in boarding schools, colleges and convents often find that their menstrual cycles harmonise with each others' naturally. Lunar menstrual harmony may increase naturally over the months if you relax and just focus on the moon in its different phases and spend lots of time watching it, relaxing and breathing in its light. You may discover as you work with moon energies month by month that your menstrual cycle spontaneously comes more into alignment with the moon cycles and as a result PMS becomes less intense if it occurs during the natural waning or letting go period. Moon awareness also helped me psychologically during the menopause.

If you are having problems conceiving, some of the traditional moon spells may relax you and help to bring back joy and spontaneity to lovemaking, even if you are having fertility treatment or intervention. I have suggested some of these in my *Complete Book of Spells* (see Further Reading, page 245).

The moon and plants

Although the effects of the moon on humans may be disputed, strong experimental evidence of connections between plant growth and the moon confirms what farmers have known for many hundreds of years. One example is the work done at Northwestern University by Professor Frank Brown, Professor of Biology. He demonstrated in extensive studies during the late 1950s that seedlings absorb more water at the time of the full moon than at the new moon and, as a result, germinate faster and grow more successfully than those sown at the new moon. This is just one of numerous lunar plant growth effects that have been investigated and proven (see Further Reading on page 249 for books on this fascinating area of study).

The energies and associations of the moon

Throughout pagan spirituality, especially Wicca, there are a number of traditional lunar associations. These are listed below and can be used to help you explore the energies of the main moon phases or to focus on those areas related to the moon that you feel need attention in your life. Use the associations either as background at home or as you focus for five or ten minutes on a particular need.

Make a start by lighting two lunar fragrance incense sticks in a holder that keeps the sticks upright (and the smoke therefore goes straight up). Watch the coiling patterns of smoke as you breathe slowly. This enables you to access the deeper parts of your mind where many of the solutions to dilemmas exist just out of reach of the conscious mind. It should also calm you and thus enable you to flow with aspects of life that cannot be changed at present.

Element: Water

Colour: Silver or white

Day of the week: Monday

Metal: Silver

Crystals: Moonstone, mother of pearl, opal (unpolished green or pink ones are very cheap), pearl, selenite; also white or pearly sea shells, especially double ones

Animals/birds: Bat, heron, moth, owl, snake, wolf

Herbs, incenses and oils: Camphor, coconut, eucalyptus, iris, jasmine, lemon, lemon balm, lemon verbena, lotus, mimosa, myrrh, poppy, white lily, white sandalwood, wintergreen

Flowers: Any with small white flowers or which are especially fragrant at night

Trees: Alder, eucalyptus, mimosa, willow

Archangel: Gabriel

Use moon energies for: Home and family matters, especially those concerning the mother, children and animals; fertility, all the ebbs and flows of the human body, mind and psyche; safe travel and travel opportunities, especially while travelling overseas, by sea or staying away overnight; psychic development, clairvoyance and meaningful dreams, healing, gardening and keeping secrets

Understanding the phases of the moon

The cycle from new moon to new moon lasts 29.5 days but because the moon has an irregular orbit, the rising and setting of the moon will vary each day and the length of the moon month can likewise vary by up to a day. The cycle of the moon can be divided into either three (see pages 110–114) or eight phases (see pages 117–120).

You can follow the different moon phases in the weather section of a newspaper or diary, but what you see in the sky and what you feel are always your best guides to using moon energies. In order to follow the monthly journey of the moon, watch her in the sky, not just for one month but for several. Even in town you can use buildings as markers and will notice slight variations in position as the months pass, because of the moon's irregular path.

Catherine Yronwode has one of the best moon information sections on the internet (www.luckymojo.com/moonphases.html) and describes a simple method of telling the approximate moon phases if you are totally unfamiliar with the concept.

She says if the moon is shining in the sky in the evening when the sun sets, it is waxing (increasing) and each night rises a little later and gets a little fatter. The full moon rises almost at the same time as the sun sets. If the moon is not in the sky when the sun sets, she says, but rises long after sunset or you can see it faintly during the day the following day, rising again a little later and looking thinner each day, you know it is waning (decreasing).

Note that the lunar calendar provided by Catherine Yronwode is for California, so you may need to adjust the times for your local time zone. The moon phases are also available in *Witch's Almanac*, *Old Moore's Almanack* and *Raphael's Ephemeris*.

Working with the phases of the moon

For a few months note down when you feel unduly active or depressed for no apparent reason. Check the moon phase on these occasions and you may find that particular days of the waxing or waning cycle affect you strongly either positively or negatively each month. Other people may be less affected. Each of us, men as well as women, may react in a slightly different way to the fluctuations of the moon according to our unique make-up.

Becoming aware of the moon and structuring personal and family life, where possible, round its phases, does result in smoother flowing days and calmer evenings. Pre-school children and hormonal teenagers seem especially responsive to moon cycles.

Like the moon, you and any children, pets or plants become more dynamic and charged as the moon increases in size. This effect is also noticeable with moonstones and topaz. You will not see a physical change in the crystals but as you hold them will feel the difference in energies with these lunar barometer crystals. Any moon crystals are good for centring your emotions if you feel out of synchronicity with life.

As the moon wanes, you and any children will lose energy and enthusiasm. This is the spirit and body's way of telling you to slow down and regenerate where possible. I am convinced that hyperactivity, PMS and irritability increase if we run counter to waning moon energies.

Of course, you can't ring into work and say that you are not coming in because the moon is waning. However, you can cut down on non-essential tasks, postpone redecorating until the moon waxes again and change exercise regimes to bring in more natural methods such as walking or swimming. As I discovered in my own family life, it was not a good idea to take children to theme parks where they would be whirled upside down on dangerous rides on the waning moon – tears and fights inevitably occurred. Save the more dynamic activities for the waxing period and on the wane enjoy quiet walks and candlelit evenings.

Lunar energies differ from solar energies since they build up gradually and so are good for more sustained efforts or aims that may take several months to fulfil. This is especially true of the full moon where energies are similar to the solar noon tide but last much longer. For extra power, focus on a need or take practical steps towards fulfilling it when the sun and the moon are in the sky at the same time. This occurs regularly, for example, a waning moon and dawn sun appear together, and is particularly effective for bringing balancing energies or different factors in your life.

The three phases of the moon

The following lists indicate the areas of your life that you can effectively focus upon and suggested activities for each of the three phases of the moon. These phases are particularly good to use if you are looking for a broad sweep of energy. If you want more subtle divisions, refer to the eight phases of the moon (see page 117). Choose the method of lunar division that works best for you or, if you prefer, use both methods at different times according to your needs. If there is a difficult or long-standing issue you may need to focus for several moon cycles.

1 The waxing moon

This is usually calculated from the crescent moon to the night before the full moon. Waxing moon energies correspond with solar dawn energies.

Use the energies of the waxing moon for focusing on:

❉ making a new beginning

❉ working towards a longer-term goal

❉ improving health

❉ gradually increasing prosperity

❉ attracting good luck

❉ enhancing fertility

❉ finding friendship, new love and romance

❉ hunting for a job

❉ making plans for the future

❉ increasing psychic awareness.

Waxing moon activities

❉ On the night of the crescent moon, turn over a silver coin three times and then bury it under a plant that symbolises money such as basil (see the list of meanings on pages 42 and 46–48). As the moon waxes, so will money-making opportunities slowly come into your life for you to develop. Like all moon rituals, this seems to work both by sensitising you to opportunities and also making your personal energy field more visible so others offer you chances to develop your talents in this way.

❉ Set gold or silver jewellery and coins in a small dish on the night of the crescent moon and light a silver-coloured candle next to the dish. Leave the candle to burn through and wear the jewellery through the month to draw opportunities to you. For love, use a silver locket or ring.

❉ Put a tiny moonstone in half an eggshell on the windowsill in your bedroom. Leave it there from the new to the full moon to bring fertility and fresh growth of all kinds into the home and your life. If you want to conceive, prick the moonstone with a silver pin on the night of the full moon and make love. In the morning, put the pin with the moonstone inside the eggshell. In either case, put the other half of the shell on top, wrap it in a silk scarf and place it in a drawer to incubate for the rest of the moon cycle. Repeat on the next crescent moon using a fresh eggshell for an ongoing wish or need. Bury the old shell and wash the moonstone under running water.

- ✤ To attract love or increase the commitment of an existing lover, light a silver candle in front of a mirror just before you go to bed on the three nights before the full moon. If possible, catch moonlight in the mirror. Look over the candle into the mirror and call the love who will make you happy (or your lover by name) to you before the next crescent moon. Blow out the candle and as you do so you may see in the mirror, according to old folk custom, a fleeting image of your love.

- ✤ Use the crescent moon energies to start a new venture, whether plunging into writing your novel, taking up painting, joining a gym, mastering your new computer software or buying and listening to language CDs.

- ✤ Book an active fun holiday if possible to be taken or at least started during a future waxing moon period (or go as soon as possible, taking advantage of last-minute prices).

- ✤ Use the waxing moon for outings that involve physical activity, adventure such as camping or trekking or visiting new places.

- ✤ Get up early every morning during the waxing moon period and use the extra time to give your day a flying start and avoid last-minute panics.

- ✤ Begin redecoration and aim to end this phase before the full moon.

- ✤ Apply for new jobs or plan relocation or a career change.

- ✤ If there's someone you really like, ask them out or start to get to know them better on or just after the crescent moon.

- ✤ Try at least one new activity or visit one new place during each waxing moon (see also waning moon activities, page 115) . After a year, your life should be much more how you want it, even if only in small ways.

2 The full moon

Purists calculate the time of the full moon as the very second when the moon is at its fullest but, in practice, its energies are powerful for 24 hours before the full moon time and during the week after the full moon, though these decrease the further from the full moon you are.

The energies of the full moon correspond with noon solar energies.

Use the full moon energies to focus on:

- ✤ fulfilling an immediate need

- boosting power or courage immediately
- actually changing career or location
- protecting yourself psychically or emotionally from malice
- healing acute medical conditions
- raising a large sum of money that is urgently needed
- consummating love or conceiving a child
- making a permanent love commitment
- attracting good luck
- having make-or-break talks in a relationship that is looking shaky (risky but maybe better than uncertainty)
- initiating action for justice, whether through the legal system or by putting right an injustice in your life that bugs you
- taking a major step towards fulfilling an ambition or dream
- asking for promotion or a major job interview.

Full moon activities

- Because the time around the full moon can cause restlessness, it is important to channel your natural desire for change and action to avoid irritability tipping over into bad temper or change for change's sake. If you do discuss relationship issues, set boundaries and avoid recriminations.
- Do something decisive and positive. Send off your novel, propose to the guy or girl of your dreams, audition for a starring part in the local drama production, ask your boss for more money or suggest how your talents might be better used.
- Use the surge of power to carry you to the crest of the wave. If there is something you want to get rid of, use the days after the full moon that are still very potent to carry you on the tide of change.
- Go all out to clear seemingly insurmountable obstacles while the energies are unstable.
- Leave for a major trip or long-distance travel to minimise delays and ease regrets at leaving.
- If you want to move, put your house on the market just before the full moon. The waning moon on the day after will diminish the strong psychological pull that holds the home to you and which can be reflected in unconsciously not inspiring viewers to buy it.

- ❊ If your house is already on the market, use the day before and the day of the full moon for some personal advertising initiative or some personal empowerments such as 'the house is sold and we are on the move' spoken outside your home in the full moonlight.

- ❊ Apply for necessary and realistic financial assistance on the full moon when boundaries are less rigid. You can also use this time to speculate or gamble, but only take chances on the day of the full moon, as good luck energies start to wane immediately afterwards.

- ❊ Apply for a course or job you think is beyond you, while the powerful cosmic tide increases your confidence and charisma.

- ❊ Make healing moon water on the night of the full moon.

  * On the night of the full moon (it rises around sunset) set a silver-coloured or clear crystal bowl outdoors where the moonlight can shine on it.

  * Half fill it with sparkling mineral water or bubbling tap water.

  * Surround the bowl with pure white flowers or blossoms or small moonstones.

  * Stir the water nine times moonwise (anticlockwise) with a silver-coloured paper knife. Ask the moon to bless the water and those who use it.

  * Leave the bowl outdoors overnight, covered with fine mesh.

  * In the morning use a glass jug and filter to pour the water into small blue or frosted glass bottles that you can keep in your fridge or a cool place until the next full moon night.

  * Any water that you have not used during the month, pour into the ground before the moonrise on the full-moon night.

- ❊ Drink a few drops of moon water daily for a month starting on the morning after the full moon. This will help to put men as well as women in touch with their own bodily rhythms and cycle of energy ebbs and flows.

- ❊ Moon water helps a woman who wishes to conceive by helping her to get in tune with her natural cycles. It may help her body to become more receptive in cases where anxiety is blocking or making a physical problem worse (even for IVF or artificial insemination). Anoint your breasts and womb with the water before lovemaking, which should be as spontaneous as possible. Do this for a month or two if you are following an ovulation plan or before any fertility treatment (if this is allowed under the treatment).

- ✽ Add a few drops to a bath to attract love or a particular lover before going out on a date or online to talk to possible partners.
- ✽ Use moon water in a soothing hot drink before going to bed to help relieve insomnia.
- ✽ Sprinkle the water round the bed of a child or adult who suffers bad dreams.
- ✽ Sprinkle a little round plants that are neglected or abused (for example, used for cigarette butts in the reception area of an office).
- ✽ Add to the water of sick or pregnant animals and birds or any you have adopted from a rescue centre.

3 The waning moon

The waning period extends until the waning crescent disappears from the sky.

The energies of the waning moon correspond with dusk or twilight solar energies.

Use the waning moon for:

- ✽ removing pain and sickness
- ✽ removing obstacles to success and happiness
- ✽ lessening negative influences
- ✽ reducing the hold of addictions and compulsions
- ✽ banishing negative thoughts, grief, guilt, anxiety and destructive anger
- ✽ protection against the envy and malice of others
- ✽ ending relationships gently.

Waning moon activities

- ✽ Before the waning moon rises in the evening, bury a dark stone in soil where nothing grows or in a small plant pot filled with soil that you can tip away. The stone symbolises what is best left unsaid and any anger, resentment or bitterness that is holding you back. If you can bear to, send a blessing to the person, organisation or situation that has hurt or wronged you. If you can't bring yourself to do this, keep your silence.

- ✤ Full moon water is especially good during the waning moon period for helping the body to fight chronic conditions and pain. Rub it into painful spots anticlockwise or anoint the centre of the brow.

- ✤ Another healing remedy is to follow the old European folk custom of catching the rays of the waning moon in a silver dish filled with water. The nights following the full moon are ideal as the moon is still bright. If there is no moonlight, work in darkness and light a small silver candle so the light reflects in the bowl of water. Wash your hands in the water and say softly,

    > *I wash my hands in your waning light. Take from me sickness/sorrow/pain this night, kind grandmother.*

    If using a candle, blow it out and tip the water away outdoors. You can repeat this ritual for more than one night if you wish and can name someone else who is sick.

- ✤ Use the waning moon nights towards the end of the first week after the full moon to give up smoking or binge eating or overcome any other fears or phobias as this is a natural time for the pull of an addiction to weaken.

- ✤ If you have debt problems use the waning moon period to get advice so that by the time the waxing moon comes you will have a strategy in place and can slowly begin to resolve the problem.

- ✤ During every waning moon period give up something, however small, that you no longer want in your life or an activity or person's company that no longer gives you pleasure. It might be a fear or an obstacle that holds you back that will take effort and patience to overcome, but this will free up space and time in your life to take up new things as suggested in the waxing moon period. This cycle keeps your life fresh and open.

The dark of the moon

There is a fourth short and very inactive stage that corresponds with the midnight solar phase. The two and a half to three days after the waning moon phase are called the dark of the moon when the moon is so close to the sun that it is invisible. This is a good time for planning, for meditation and for any detoxifying programmes. As this is the time of the rebirth of the moon it is also a very satisfying period for sex.

The eight phases of the moon

The more subtle eight phases of the moon are the cosmic version of the earthly daily Aetts (see page 100) but divided over the moon month of 28 or 29 days. It can be useful to think of these eight phases in four periods:

❧ Period 1: days 1–3

   * new moon

❧ Period 2: days 4–14

From when the crescent first appears in the sky to the day the full moon rises. The light increases from right to left during this period. The closer to the full moon, the more intense the energies and the larger the moon disk. (Gibbous means protuberant.)

   * waxing crescent
   * first quarter
   * waxing gibbous

❧ Period 3: days 15–17

   * full moon

❧ Period 4: days 18–28 or 29

The moon decreases from right to left until, finally, the crescent disappears from the left. About two and a half days later the crescent reappears on the right as a silver sliver again.

   * waning gibbous
   * last quarter
   * waning crescent

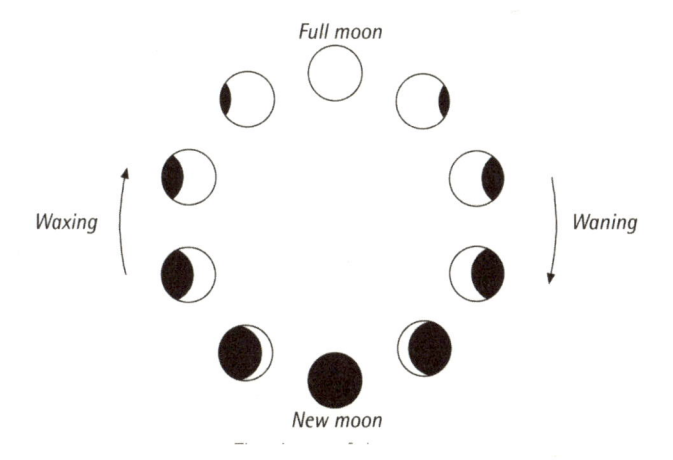

1 The new moon, days 1–3

Equivalent to the midnight tide of the Aetts, the new moon (or dark of the moon) rises at dawn and sets at dusk. Because the sun and moon are in the same part of the sky, the sunlight obscures the moon in the day. At night the moon is on the other side of the earth with the sun and you will see nothing.

This corresponds with the dark of the moon (see page 116) that follows the three phases of the moon, and this is the point at which the two systems are identical.

Day 1 is especially good for meditation or for spending some quiet time walking in the countryside or sitting quietly by water.

Some months you may glimpse the crescent moon on day 3 in which case you can merge the two energies of the new and crescent moon.

2 The waxing crescent, days 4–7

The first quarter or crescent is very slender at this time and is most easily seen at sunset close to the place where the sun sets.

The crescent moon rises mid morning and sets some time after sunset. During this period, the moon can be seen on a clear day from moonrise to moonset.

Use its energies to set plans in motion, for matters concerning animals and small children and for optimism, new love, family joy, making wishes and the gradual growth of money.

3 The first quarter, days 8–11

The moon rises about noon and sets about midnight. The moon can be seen from rise to set.

Use its energies for improved health, good luck and courage, attracting or increasing love, employment issues, house moves and to increase the speed of inflowing finances.

Day 8 is very good for healing.

Day 10 is special for visions of other realms and for gaining insights into old problems.

4 The waxing gibbous, days 12–14

The gibbous moon rises in the middle of the afternoon and sets before dawn the next day. It can be seen soon after rising and then until it sets. It is easily recognisable by the pregnant bulge on its left side.

Use its energies for increased personal power, commitment in love, fertility, promotion, travel and for a boost to finish a project and to make a good impression or sell yourself.

Day 13 and day 14 are good for starting healthy-eating plans and exercise regimes and for contacting old friends or people you would like to know better.

5 The full moon, days 15–17

You can experience the full moon energies most powerfully from moon rise to moon set on the day and night of the full moon. Within this time band, which is narrower than the full moon period described in the three-phase system, the hours immediately around the full moon rising and the following two days transmit these powerful energies.

The full moon rises before sunset and sets at sunrise so you can have a brief surge when both sun and full moon are in the sky together.

Use the energies of these days to initiate sudden or dramatic change, for all urgent or pressing matters concerning women and especially mothers, for the granting of small miracles, for artistic and creative success and for the swift and successful resolution of legal or official matters that have been dragging on.

Day 15 is good for an all-or-nothing leap and for confirmation that you are right to pursue a particular course.

6 The waning gibbous, days 18–21

The waning full moon (or disseminating moon) is shrinking and rises now in the mid evening, setting in the middle of the next morning, being visible for much of the time.

Use the decreasing full moon for focusing on the protection of home, self and loved ones, for banishing bad habits, phobias and fears, for ending a long-standing destructive or abusive relationship, for relieving acute pain and fighting viruses and for leaving behind past regrets that hold us back from happiness.

7 The last quarter, days 22–25

This moon rises at about midnight and sets around midday the next day. She is visible for the whole time she is in the sky.

Use for protection while travelling, especially at night, for getting rid of unfriendly ghosts, for concerns about older people, for mending quarrels, for avoiding intrusion of privacy, for peaceful divorce and for relieving stress.

Day 23 is an important time for healing and day 25 for women's needs.

8 The waning crescent, days 26–28 or 29

The waning crescent, or balsamic, moon rises before dawn (after the midnight of its day) and sets at mid afternoon of the following day. She is best seen in the eastern sky in the dawn and very early morning.

Use the waning crescent for quiet sleep if you are an insomniac, for peace of mind if you have been anxious or depressed, for protection from crime and violence, for the easing of addictions, for keeping secrets, for saying goodbye finally and for finding what is lost or has been stolen.

The moon void of course

This is not apparent in the sky, but is a brief time when meetings or projects tend to get stuck and travel plans can go haywire.

The void of course occurs as the moon leaves one astrological sign and travels to another. The moon spends about two and a half days each month in each zodiac sign. The void of course can last from a few minutes to almost a day.

You can check the timing of the moon void of course in any almanac, such as *Old Moore's*, or increasingly in newspaper horoscope pages. In an almanac, there will be 'v/c' or 'VOC' next to the moon symbol and the time this begins. The next entry will tell you the time the moon enters the new zodiac sign, marking the ending of the 'void of course' period.

Allow extra time for everything, double check travel plans or appointment details, especially venues, and if possible avoid trying to finalise anything during this brief stagnant period. This may sound weird, but monitor a few void-of-course times in your daily life and those of others, and you will find that the number of hitches or delays that occur is quite significant.

The significance of the full moon

Hunter-gatherers and, later, farmers created the earliest calendars by marking the full moons within the lunar cycle on rock, bone or wood. In indigenous traditions such as those of the Native North Americans and the Celts, the names of the different full moons reflected the annual observable migration and reproduction of the birds and animals and the growth of trees and food plants upon which human survival depended. By counting forward from any point, it could be calculated how many times the moon would be seen in the sky before the blossom appeared on the trees or the geese and ducks laid their eggs.

Full moons are still significant today, for example, in China where they determine the precise date of the Chinese New Year and indeed in Christianity, where Easter is marked by the first Sunday after the first full moon after the spring equinox (this usually falls around March 21 in the northern hemisphere).

A blue moon is when more than one full moon occurs in the same month, and these have always been regarded as especially lucky.

The Celtic lunar calendar

The pagan lunar calendar we know most about is the Celtic system, and the early first century CE Roman historian Pliny reported that the druids, the Celtic priesthood, calculated their months and years by lunar time. The Celtic calendar is more sophisticated than the remarkably similar Native North American moon calendar and noted the moon months when the roads would hopefully be sufficiently dry for travelling to markets, fairs or to seek justice, so that people could make plans to travel two or three moon months ahead.

The archaeological source of our knowledge of Celtic lunar calculations comes from the Coligny calendar which consists of surviving fragments of a huge bronze plate measuring, when it was intact, 1.5 m/5 ft by 1 m/3.5 ft. The calendar, named after the location where it was discovered in Eastern France in 1897, was engraved in Gaulish, but with Roman letters and numbers. It has 12 cyclical moon months and it seems, from the 62 consecutive months recorded, that an additional two months were included (one every two and half to three years, consisting of 30 days each). This extra magical bi-yearly month was called *Ciallos*, the month of no time.

The Coligny calendar ran from full moon to full moon. One theory suggests that the Romanised Gauls replaced an earlier Celtic calendar that was 13 lunar months long, the usual number of moons within a solar calculated year.

Making your own lunar calendar

If you are interested you can find many excellent online lunar calendars and calculators for the Coligny dates and some lunar almanacs include the Coligny and Native North American months. However, you may prefer, as I do, to adapt this and the Native North American-inspired calendars to your own everyday world.

Just as these peoples related the full moon in the sky to what was happening in their lives, over the coming year, beginning with the next full moon, create names for each of the moons to reflect the events in your world.

You may, if you wish, choose to name a full-moon month *Ciallos* or adapt the name to reflect a major change in your lifestyle. However, if you prefer, just keep the moons rolling one after the other. You can also use the spare month, which can be named as you wish, if a moon month name does not feel right for what is going on.

For me, for example, the full moon in January represents Reckoning Moon when my very chaotic tax accounts are due. Also, after Christmas, it really is a time for assessing what works and does not work financially, career wise and emotionally to plan the coming year's diary.

Wherever you live in the world you will probably find an older indigenous lunar calendar in existence that can act as your template. For example, among the Maori peoples of pre-European New Zealand, the lunar calendar was called *maramataka* and divided the year into 12 lunar months. *Ohua* was the night of the full moon when it was totally circular. The Maori months were calculated from the new moon, the night of *Whiro* before it was visible in the sky. For example, their *Pipiri* lunar month, its name in the east coastal areas, which began around early June, was also the Maori New Year. It was called the month when 'everything was shrunken by cold even humans', but it was regarded as a moon and a month of hope, as with the year turning, better weather and times were coming, a bit like my Reckoning Moon.

To make your own lunar calendar, follow these steps:

❀ Use a diary in which the full moons are marked, and start day 1 and your first lunar month from the nearest full moon (looking either forwards or backwards).

❀ Of course it does not matter how many full moons there are in the calendar year because once you have named your 12 full moons, you start again.

❀ Keep notes of how each full moon makes you feel and shape the name accordingly. You can use four or five words if you wish as the Native North Americans do.

❀ If you live mainly in town, you can follow the natural aspects by watching the changing leaves in the city squares and escaping to the countryside and coast at weekends.

❀ If your moon times are out of step with the solar clock, use a double date system in your diary. Continue to keep business and other appointments and remember birthdays by the modern solar date, but know that these occasions also occur on the third day of the Migrating Geese Moon, or whatever you call the moon in the sky at that time.

❀ If you have a chance, try to mark each moon month by standing under the full moon, breathing slowly and regularly and picturing yourself being filled with the moon glow.

❀ If you want to change the moon name in a year, do so, but make a note of the old name as this will reflect how far you have travelled on your moon journey.

❀ The following are a synthesis of lunar names I have gathered and used over the years from the Native North American and Celtic traditions and the energies they reflect. If you want to use some of these names and live in the southern hemisphere, you could move the moon names forward six moons.

Coligny name	Native North American name	Full moon date	Lunar energies of this moon are good for
Samnios Seed Fall	Hunter's, or Trading, Moon	October/ November	Making an end to what is not fruitful, drawing up realistic plans for the coming year, seeking rewards for past efforts made, storing resources such as money
Dumannios, the Coming of Deep Darkness	First Snows, or Frost on the Grass, Moon	November/ December	Bringing light into the darkness, seeking inner as well as outer illumination and inspiration, trusting in a better tomorrow, candle rituals for rebirth and new beginnings
Riuros, the Time of the Long Coldness	When Wolves Huddle Close Moon	December/ January	Material security, the home and family, rituals for older people and welcoming people back into your life, rituals for absent or estranged family
Angantios, Staying Home	Gnawing on Bones Moon	January/ February	Acceptance of life as it is, seeking joy in what one has, not fretting for what one has not, conserving strength, health and resources
Ogronios, the Time of Shining Ice	When the Geese First Lay Moon	February/ March	The stirring of new hope and trust, releasing potential that has been frozen, conception and planning new initiatives
Cutios, the Time of the Winds	Purification, or Eagle, Moon	March/April	Change, clearing away stagnation and inertia, banishing bad habits and negative influences

Coligny name	Native North American name	Full moon date	Lunar energies of this moon are good for
Glamonios, Growing Green Shoots	Frog, or Blossom, Moon	April/May	New horizons and opportunities, employment, fertility, love, speculation and creative ventures
Simiuisonnos, Bright Time or the Time of Dancing	Flowering, or Full Leaf, Moon	May/June	Joy, permanent relationships, maximising opportunities, potency and fertility
Equos, the Time of the Horse	Strawberry, or When the Buffalo are Calling, Moon	June/July	Travel, moves of all kinds (house or career), expansion
Elembiuos, Claim Time	Ripe Corn, or When the Young Geese Take Wing, Moon	July/August	Justice, promotion, recognition and financial gain, resolving official matters
Edrinios, the Time of Arbitration	Harvest, or Dark Butterfly, Moon	August/ September	Reaping what has been sown, abundance, assessing life and resources with a view to shedding what cannot be used
Cantios, Song Moon	Nut, or When The Birds Fly South, Moon	September/ October	Final burst of energy for tasks undone, salvaging relationships and missed opportunities

Working with the individual full moons

❈ When you see the full moon in the sky, name in your mind or aloud all the people who will be supportive or of concern to you in the month ahead. Mention also any who are ill or distressed and add a single white or pale yellow or pink flower to a vase for each one.

❈ Alternatively, plant a small appropriate herb in the garden by moonlight (see pages 46–48 for suitable herbs).

❈ If you wish, as you stand focusing on the full moon or the bright area behind a cloud, hold a silver charm or a favourite piece of silver jewellery (the metal of the moon) that can reflect your focus in the days ahead, between now and when you will see the next full moon; picture the lunar energies filling the charm.

❈ Leave the charm all night either on an indoor windowsill or outdoors in a sheltered space. Then carry it with you or wear it through the month ahead.

❈ Alternatively, choose a small round pure white stone or one of the moon crystals (see page 108) such as a small moonstone or a selenite. Using an incense stick, in one of the moon fragrances such as jasmine or myrrh, write your name over your crystal in incense smoke. Psychically or psychologically or both, this is a good way of saying you exist and are of worth. Then write in the air over the crystal, whatever it is you aim to achieve or get rid of (or both) by the next full moon.

❈ Leave the incense to burn out next to the crystal and keep the crystal somewhere safe as a luck bringer and protector against discouragement until the next moon when you can re-empower it or change the purpose.

❈ Make a special moon water to absorb the differing full moon strengths. Make enough to add a few drops to a drink, splash on pulse points or add to bath water to energise you and keep you on track (see page 114 for how to make moon water).

The zodiac and the moon

Pagans and non-pagans alike are usually aware of their birth signs and many can identify characteristics of these signs in themselves and friends and family. As the moon travels around the earth each month, in its orbit it passes through each of the sun or zodiac signs in turn and remains in each sign for about two and a half days. Each lunar sun sign period has its own specific energies that are especially potent for people born under that birth sign. It offers a mini birth-sign energy boost every month. However, it can also accentuate the basic characteristics of the sun-sign personality and so can bring out the worst as well as the best in the person born under the sign the moon is temporarily passing through.

People whose sign opposes the sign the moon is passing through may find the period challenging but stimulating. The opposing signs are:

* Aries – Libra
* Taurus – Scorpio
* Gemini – Sagittarius
* Cancer – Capricorn
* Leo – Aquarius
* Virgo – Pisces

Working with the moon within individual sun signs

The energies of the individual sun signs are favourable for particular purposes during the moon's presence in them each month. The emphasis will additionally vary according to whether the moon is waxing, waning or full, and more than one of these phases can occur within each two-and-a-half-day period. The full moon gives a burst of power to the waxing qualities but can also be used for change and to launch a waning venture. Use the lists that follow (pages 129–132) to choose the most suitable time for a particular energy or need, and look at whether the moon is waxing (to draw something to you) or waning (and therefore good for casting something away). As the moon enters a new sign and while it is right in the middle are the most potent times. Each sun sign the moon passes through has also been demonstrated in popular folk tradition to be especially helpful for particular conditions – something that seems to be amplified by the moon's presence in the sign.

To find out which sun sign the moon is in and what time it enters, consult a newspaper astrology column or an almanac or search online.

When you have identified the ideal time at which to deal with an issue that is important to you, you could carry out the following ritual:

- ❊ Choose the coloured candle, incense and crystal that relate to the relevant sun sign (see pages 129–132).
- ❊ When the moon is in the correct sun sign, light the candle and incense and hold the crystal between your hands in order to activate its powers.
- ❊ You could state your need or purpose as you light the candle and write it over the crystal in incense smoke to impregnate it with your own determination. This will be strengthened by the innate qualities of the chosen fragrance and the crystal.
- ❊ Then you could either leave the candle and incense to burn through or if you wanted an instant infusion of power, blow out the candle, saying,

    So may it be within (and name your time scale).

- ❊ You could end by stating what you will do in return for others if the blessing you seek is granted.

The waxing moon in a sign increases energy and self-healing and the waning aspect takes away pain and illness. Again, having identified the appropriate time at which to deal with a particular problem, you could try this healing ritual:

- ❊ Press the appropriate crystal gently near a point of pain or a relevant body part or hold it a short distance above.
- ❊ Circle it anticlockwise to remove pain or blockages and clockwise to energise. This symbolic action does seem to help stimulate the body's own regenerative abilities in ways we hardly understand but which has been a part of folk healing for many centuries.
- ❊ Afterwards, wash the crystal under running water and leave it in sunlight or natural light to dry naturally.

I am certainly not claiming any miraculous powers for crystals but do experiment, as it may be helpful, whether as a placebo effect or something more.

Moon in Aries

Waxing: For courage, independence, self-reliance, self-employment, action, health, assertiveness, launching major ventures or life changes, energy and passion

Waning: For anti-bullying and aggressiveness, to reduce hyperactivity

Use for healing: The face, head or brain

Candle colour: Red

Incense: Ginger or cinnamon

Crystal: Red jasper

Moon in Taurus

Waxing: For fertility, love, radiance, money, material security and to acquire beautiful things

Waning: For losing weight, overcoming possessiveness and emotional blackmail, anti-debt, to protect possessions

Use for healing: The throat, neck or ears

Candle colour: Pink

Incense: Apple blossom or rose

Crystal: Rose quartz

Moon in Gemini

Waxing: For speculation and games of chance, passing examinations and tests, healing using surgery or medical intervention, communication, travel and moves of all kinds, good luck

Waning: For protection against deceit, gossip and spite and to reverse bad luck

Use for healing: The shoulders, arms, hands or lungs

Candle colour: Yellow

Incense: Lavender or lemongrass

Crystal: Citrine

Moon in Cancer

Waxing: For happiness at home, family, children and fidelity, keeping secrets and all moon spells

Waning: For protection of the home, family and against accidents or hostile neighbours

Use for healing: The chest or stomach

Candle colour: Silver

Incense: Myrrh or poppy

Crystal: Moonstone

Moon in Leo

Waxing: For success, power, leadership, fame, prosperity, career and abundance, potency, childbirth and nobility of purpose

Waning: For reducing the negative effects of critical people, overcoming problems with bosses and financial shortages and losses

Use for healing: The upper back, spine and heart

Candle colour: Gold

Incense: Frankincense or orange

Crystal: Amber

Moon in Virgo

Waxing: For all health and healing matters, animals, striving for perfection, any detailed matters, employment, skill with hands, gardening and the environment and keeping to diets

Waning: For banishing illness and any form of addiction or compulsion, helping clumsy children or adults, overcoming unemployment, improving personal safety

Use for healing: The intestines or nervous system

Candle colour: Green

Incense: Fennel or patchouli

Crystal: Jade

Moon in Libra

Waxing: For marriage and partnerships, peace and harmony, justice, the successful outcome of court cases, charisma and compromise

Waning: For infidelity, laziness and inertia, to prevent lack of commitment, and in anti-war and conflict empowerments

Use for healing: The lower back or kidneys

Candle colour: Blue

Incense: Peach or vanilla

Crystal: Blue lace agate

Moon in Scorpio

Waxing: For transformation, wishes and passionate sex, to increase psychic powers and for any strongly felt desires or needs, for recovering what has been lost or stolen

Waning: For protection against physical, emotional or psychic attack, to guard against anyone seeking revenge, against vandalism, jealousy and being the victim of criminal activity

Use for healing: The reproductive organs

Candle colour: Indigo or burgundy

Incense: Sandalwood or mimosa

Crystal: Opal

Moon in Sagittarius

Waxing: For travel, adventures, house moves, horses, publishing and creative ventures, happiness and optimism, good ideas, sports and finding lost pets

Waning: For protection on journeys and against getting lost, preventing pets straying or being stolen, slowing or reversing money losses

Use for healing: The liver, thighs or hips

Candle colour: Orange

Incense: Hibiscus or sage

Crystal: Turquoise

Moon in Capricorn

Waxing: For commitment in love and business, financial security, all official matters, wise caution, steady promotion and career success, stable business ventures, perseverance and overcoming obstacles through persistent effort

Waning: For overcoming depression and self-doubt and releasing money that is tied up or disputed

Use for healing: The knees, bones, teeth or skin

Candle colour: Brown

Incense: Magnolia or vetivert

Crystal: Garnet

Moon in Aquarius

Waxing: For original ventures, the success of inventions and any intellectual matters, humanitarian issues, friendships and developing unique gifts and talents, alternative medicine

Waning: For overcoming intolerance, bad habits, prejudice and inequality, for banishing loneliness and isolation

Use for healing: The calves, ankles and blood and personality disorders

Candle colour: Purple

Incense: Benzoin or rosemary

Crystal: Amethyst

Moon in Pisces

Waxing: For new love or love after loss, music and the performing arts, balancing two commitments or having two careers, adaptability, merging two families and telepathic powers

Waning: For overcoming rivalries and people pulling you in different directions, reconciling quarrels and custody or divorce disputes and overcoming excesses or imbalances of any kind

Use for healing: The feet or lymph glands

Candle colour: White

Incense: Lemon or sweetgrass

Crystal: Clear quartz or clear fluorite

6 Rites of Passage

According to pagan belief, every day is a special day. Each new stage of life – birth, leaving home, entering a permanent love commitment, retirement – are all landmarks to be celebrated. Where there is loss, it should be mourned and so relinquished.

In the modern world, apart from weddings and 18th or 21st birthdays, the milestones of life largely pass publicly unmarked and those occasions that are celebrated can be overshadowed by their increasingly commercialised emphasis. Even children's birthday parties can become stressful because of the need to match other parents' party bag contents and elaborate entertainment in order to ensure a child's popularity with classmates. One answer I found to this problem was to invite only best friends, not the whole class, and go to a conservation park and have a picnic, or plan a beach barbecue or maybe overnight forest camping. Word spreads that you have exciting events and your child does not lose popularity, while at the same time other parents may feel more able to scale down their jamborees.

Weddings can put the couple marrying and their parents in debt for years and take many months of detailed planning. This can lead to the expectation of a day that must be perfect in every aspect, and the slightest deviation from the wedding plan or wet weather can then overshadow what should be a happy family celebration. Indeed the people involved can occasionally feel like bit players in an elaborately stage-managed performance. For example, I know of a bride whose wedding cost over £25,000 and who was told by her wedding planner she should not have her childhood friend as bridesmaid because an overweight and red-headed bridesmaid would ruin the pink-and-purple themed wedding photographs. Twenty years later it is the funny moments you remember and the fact that your best friend even now was your bridesmaid then.

Baby blessings pagan style

Baby-blessing ceremonies can offer a spiritual alternative for those who do not regularly attend church or want a formal christening where other unknown families may share the ceremony. You can organise a home-based indoor or garden baby-naming ceremony, to which you need invite only friends and family – there is no need for a priest or priestess, pagan or Christian.

At a family naming ceremony, you can either ask close friends or relatives to act as god or goddess parents or welcome the input of all those present in the life of your child. These equivalents of traditional godparents can be asked to make a promise to offer support to the growing child in whatever ways are most needed. If the god or goddess parents have or plan to have children, you can make promises towards their families too and this can be a wonderful way of creating an extended family in a world where blood relatives may be scattered.

The naming ceremony can of course be restricted to just immediate family, including grandparents or just parents and siblings. The informality also makes it easier to invite step siblings or step grandparents, as everyone can play a part in a ceremony that can be structured to fit the needs of the participants. Neither are there any limits on who can be god or goddess parents, so no one need feel left out. See page 136 for a sample baby-blessing ceremony.

Quaker baby blessings

An informal ceremony to welcome a baby into the world is not an exclusively pagan concept. My three younger children were born as Quakers, a religion that believes there is good in everyone and has no priesthood or organised services. People speak or do not speak, according to whether they feel moved to do so during a Quaker meeting, where everyone sits equally ranked in a circle. Even small children are encouraged to speak if they wish during the meeting hour, which is largely meditative.

When a new born baby is first taken to the meeting house, another Quaker member close to the family welcomes the new baby and everyone present at the meeting offers good wishes and blessings. There are no godparents as such but other Quakers promise to help with the new baby if possible and when needed. In fact, I was ill after the births of both of my youngest two children, Miranda and Bill, and Quakers offered babysitting, brought cakes and included my other children on outings when I was tired. They were always offering serviceable equipment and hand-on clothes for my growing family, a gesture that was reciprocated as my family grew out of toys and clothes.

Celtic baby blessings

Many modern Westernised baby-naming ceremonies are inspired or at least influenced by Celtic birth customs or what is popularly attributed to the ancient Celts of Scotland, Wales, Brittany and Ireland. The Celtic tradition is still largely oral, much of it pieced together from records made at a later date of old oral accounts and what people recall from their own family traditions. Some of the following ideas have been passed on to me by readers of Celtic origin or people I have met in my travels. As you adapt them and pass them on to people you know, the tradition will evolve whether or not you claim Celtic ancestry.

Even if you have a conventional christening for your baby or decide not to have a naming ceremony, you may like to follow some of the Celtic birth customs with your birth partner or a loving friend or family member as soon after the birth as is practical. You can adapt parts to a hospital setting or wait until you and your baby go home.

Immediately after the birth the Celtic midwife would put three drops of water on the infant's brow, blessing him or her in the name of the earth, sea and sky, the three sacred realms, saying in the version I heard from an old Irish druidess,

By earth and sea and sky be blest.

Even in hospital you could anoint the baby with water soon after the birth or ask the midwife to do so.

You can also ask friends and family to light candles for you when you go into labour and another one for your baby when he or she is born. The candles and the water are linked with St Bridget the Irish saint who was in legend, though not in fact, the midwife of Jesus and was supposed to have performed this rite on him. (There were four centuries between Jesus's mother Mary and Bridget, who was sometimes called Mary of the Gaels.) Deep in the magical forest of Broceliande in Brittany near Rennes, there is a natural spring called the Fountain of Youth. Here local legend tells that on the summer solstice the chief druidess blessed all the babies born during the previous year with the spring water and lit fires to keep them warm.

The baby's first bath doubled as a baptism. The bath water was warmed over the fire and traditionally run over iron to give the infant protection from any potential danger, earthly or paranormal. The Celts were very superstitious about spirits lurking as the dimensions parted for the child's birth. A gold and silver coin were added to the water to represent the power of the sun and the moon and to call prosperity to the child in future.

Holding the child over the bath, the midwife would fill her palm with water nine times and rub it over the child. With each handful of water she would endow a gift on the child, rather like the concept of the good fairies in the story of Sleeping Beauty. These gifts included gentle and wise speech, generosity of spirit, wealth, health and grace.

Then the child would be passed from the midwife to the father in front of the fire that was lit to keep the mother and infant warm and to keep away harmful spirits. The father would then carry the infant three times clockwise around the fire and promise that he would give the child a good home and protection from the dangers of the world. Finally it was the mother's turn to complete the ritual (sometimes at noon at a later date). She would touch the child's forehead to the ground thanking Mother Earth for a safe delivery and asking that Mother Earth would bless and care for the child throughout his or her life.

Finally the child was carried by the midwife to a higher level up a slope to ensure he or she would do well in the world. This continued as a superstition for hundreds of years, with newborns on coming home from hospital being carried upstairs.

The water ritual at birth has echoes in the Eastern European Slovakian bathing rites of a new baby that still prevail in remoter regions. When the baby was bathed by the midwife for the first time soon after the birth, small tools and coins were placed in the water in the hope that the infant would become a handyman or craftsman and become a wealthy person. Sugar and salt were also added to the water with the expectation that the child would grow to be good-tempered and healthy. In well-to-do families, a pen and pencil were given to the baby so that he or she would be scholarly. After this bath, the midwife gave the child to members of the household and relatives to be kissed as a sign of welcome, after which the mother was given the baby to nurse.

A sample baby-naming ceremony

You can have a baby-naming ceremony as soon as you feel ready after the birth and it can be a good way of combining all the visits by relatives and friends. Make it a 'bring and share' meal to reduce the practical strains, and enlist friends and family in the organisation. Ask a relative or friend to print out the order of ceremony with any chants or formal blessings you are using and a photograph of your baby on the front. Everyone can play a role and so no one need feel left out.

The ceremony can be held in the garden if fine or indoors.

- ❇ Everyone stands or sits in a circle except for the parent or parents and the infant, who stand or sit in the middle next to a table on which is set three large matching white candles and other items you will need.

* Whoever is leading the ceremony welcomes the baby, friends and relations and says that the occasion is to formally name and bless the infant. The mother, father or grandparents can lead the ceremony. If there are two sets of grandparents, they can get together beforehand to divide the roles. If there are no grandparents, older relatives or friends can fill this role (I will use grandparents as a generic term).

* The youngest person present makes a circle of rose petals round the outside of the guests. Alternatively, choose a young relative from both sides of the family to make the circle, moving in opposite directions at the same time. Use dried petals from the birth bouquets or fresh ones, and have them ready in a basket.

* The leader of the ceremony makes an opening blessing (see page 139 or the parents or grandparents can write their own). This gives thanks for the safe delivery of the little one and asks for future protection, health and happiness. It also names and welcomes any siblings.

* The first of the three white candles is lit for the infant by one of the grandparents or another older relative. He or she may say a few words about sending light to the infant and how the infant's arrival has lit up the family with joy. The same person may also ask for blessings on the candle and the infant.

* If there are other brothers and sisters present, whether step or birth, they can now each light a small candle on the table.

* A grandparent who did not light the candle passes round a small basket, into which each person in the circle puts a crystal that he or she has been asked to bring. (Have spare crystals in case anyone forgets.) The same grandparent makes a blessing for the baby as the basket is passed round the circle. Blessings may include health, joy and a happy home and can be impromptu.

* The basket is set in front of the candle by the family members who scattered the petals.

* The naming ceremony now begins. One of the parents or both together name the child for the first time aloud, welcome the child to the family and ask that all who speak the name in future may be blessed by the love and life of the child as he or she grows to adulthood. They may each anoint the infant's brow with a drop of water from a sacred well or sparkling mineral water and say,

By earth and sea and sky be blest.

They may also ask the child's guardian angels to protect him or her.

✿ A grandparent or parent asks any who have agreed in advance to be god or goddess parents to come into the centre of the circle. Each in turn touches the brow of the infant with a single drop of water.

✿ Each god or goddess parent repeats the name of the child and makes a promise to care for the named infant, listing any special spiritual gifts or talents they are offering as god or goddess parents.

✿ The god or goddess parents return to their places.

✿ Two of the grandparents light the two remaining candles from the first, saying that the new candles represent the light and potential of the child's future and adulthood. They return to the circle.

✿ Each person in the circle is invited to offer a wish for the infant's future, for example, that he or she may love animals and nature.

✿ The two candles of the future are extinguished with a candle snuffer by the person who lit each one (you can double up roles if only a few people are present). These candles can be saved and relit at future milestones in the child's life, such as going to school or leaving home to go to college.

✿ The birth candle remains burning.

✿ A grandparent makes a final blessing (see page 139 or write your own) on the occasion and repeats the child's name.

✿ The parent or parents lead the guests to plant a small tree in the garden for the child (if indoors, a miniature one can be used) and everyone throws a little earth into the hole saying,

May the blessings of the earth and angels grow within this child as the tree grows.

✿ Alternatively, if you are indoors, you can throw petals.

✿ Finally the parent or parents lead the way to the meal.

✿ Informal contributions of songs and so on can be combined with the meal.

✿ The candle is left to burn down in a safe place.

✿ The crystals are kept in the child's room and god or goddess parents can add a new one every year, possibly in a mini re-dedication ceremony of the child's life on special birthdays.

A traditional opening blessing

> May the blessing of light be with you – light outside and within.
> May the sunlight shine upon you and warm your heart 'til it glows like a great peat fire, so that the stranger may come and warm himself by it.
> May a blessed light shine out of your two eyes like a candle set in two windows of a house bidding the wanderer to come in out of the storm.
> May you ever give a kindly greeting to those whom you pass as you go along the roads.
> May the blessing of rain – the sweet, soft rain – fall upon you so that little flowers may spring up to shed their sweetness in the air.
> May the blessings of the earth – the good, rich earth – be with you and all who meet here on (name child's) special day.

A closing blessing

> May the road rise up to meet you.
> May the wind be always at your back.
> May the sun shine warm upon your face,
> The rain fall soft upon the fields, and until we meet again
> May God/the Goddess hold you in the palm of his/her hand.
> And until we meet again may Mother Earth protect and bless you.

All customarily reply,

> Blessings be.

Welcoming new members into the family

In the modern world with remarriage and single parenting much more common, we can acquire all kinds of step relations, of all ages, who become grafted on to the family. Existing family members may find it hard to welcome people who inevitably still have loyalties elsewhere and new members of the family may not immediately feel comfortable with their new relations.

In earlier societies such as the Native North American and those in the pre-Christian Scandinavian world, where children were frequently orphaned through war or disease, there were formal welcoming ceremonies. At these occasions, called 'making of relations' ceremonies by the Native North Americans, families would adopt the orphaned children. At the end of many ceremonies, Native North Americans still use the phrase 'we are all related', or a similar expression to emphasise the link between all people, past and present.

In these ceremonies, the person to be adopted sat on a carpet of sage and was covered with a blanket. An eagle's feather was tied in their hair, hair being a symbol of a person's life because it is constantly growing and being replaced. It is also believed to contain a person's wisdom, and their connection to the past and the path still to be trodden. Attached to the feather was a medicine (power) wheel made of rawhide and painted or created out of porcupine quills. In the modern Westernised world these symbols have less meaning, but the concept remains valid.

A sample 'making of relations' ceremony

You can, of course, alter the details of this sample ceremony to suit your family's needs.

- ❀ Before the new relations arrive, choose a herb, flower or small bush for each existing family member, and plant these in a circle with wide spaces between them. This can either be done in the family garden or in pots in an indoor plant area. As you put each plant into the soil, make a private blessing for the family member, even if you find him or her difficult or do not approve of a relationship. Label each plant with the name of the family member it is dedicated to.

- ❀ You will also need to choose a herb, flower or small bush for the new family members, but this will not be planted until the day of the ceremony.

- ❀ Choose also a small plant or crystal for each person that you have invited to the ceremony.

- ❀ Place photographs of existing family members on a small table.

- ❀ Prepare a family tree of your existing family, and include the new family members, leaving space so that they can add their families too. You may well need a huge piece of paper.

- ❀ When the time is right, hold a small informal party and invite the new members of your family, for example, a new partner's children and relatives.

- ❀ Ask each person to bring a small photo to put in your special photo area and at the end of the party give them a small picture of your family. (Even if they do not choose to display it, you have at least made the gesture.)

- ❀ You can ask children to bring pictures of their other parent, even if the absent parent is causing difficulties.

- ❀ At some point during the party, you can ask your visitors to add their families and ancestors to your family tree and maybe tell you some of their family legends.

- ❀ Invite each new member of the family to plant their herb, flower or bush. They should be positioned between the existing plants and labelled with the person's name. The idea is to plant them all close together so that they will grow together.

- ❀ As each person plants their herb, flower or bush, say out loud or in your head if it is more appropriate,

    We are one family and we welcome you in love.

- ❀ Before the meal, give everyone a tea light and invite them to sit around a circular table or in a circle on the ground. Light your own tea light and, from this, light the tea lights of those sitting either side of you. This continues around the circle, with each person greeting the person to their immediate left and right with words of welcome and a few fun words about themselves.

- ❀ Leave the candles to burn through. If small children are present, move the candle circle to a safe place.

- ❀ Give everyone a small plant or crystal to take home to carry the energies of the new family with them.

If someone leaves the family permanently, perhaps because of divorce, transplant their plant a little way off, so that they are separate but still come under your care. Add new plants, pictures and names on the family tree for each family addition, even if it is a birth of a sibling for one of your step children with the absent parent's new partner. This can take an immense amount of goodwill on your part but pays dividends if only for your own peace of mind.

A rites of passage for those involved in adoption

If you are adopted and do not know where your birth mother and father are or if you were separated from your child when they were born and cannot trace them, an anniversary or birthday can be a very sad time when you will naturally be thinking about each other.

The following ritual may help to mark the occasion as significant without overshadowing the day.

- ❦ Find a personal item linking the two of you, for example, a baby photograph, a birth or adoption certificate or a small shoe or toy.

- ❦ Go quietly into the garden or some other open space. Hold the personal item in your cupped hands and speak the following words softly into the breeze,

    *Mother/Father/Son/Daughter of mine, though far away,
    I call to you in love this day.
    I send this message on the wind to wherever you may be.
    Wherever you are, I ask that you will try to find me.
    If this cannot be, I send you love and peace and carry you in my
    heart as a precious part of me.*

- ❦ Walk or stand for a while and then go indoors and, if appropriate, leave the item where the air can circulate round it all day or alternatively wrap it in soft fabric and put it in a drawer.

This may help you to open the channels of communication and love or will give you some peace of mind as you acknowledge what is a part of you, even if you never talk about it.

Marriages pagan style

Pagan marriage is called handfasting, from the old custom of a couple tying their hands together to symbolise unity and fidelity. Formal marriage is still sometimes called tying the knot, which recalls this old form of wedding.

Those who unite in a handfasting, usually do so with the intention of staying together for life, or some indeterminate long period such as the Ancient Egyptian phrase 'so long as the sun shines and the waters flow'. Couples who are not ready for a forever commitment but feel seriously about each other have the option of following the old custom of dedicating their union for a year and a day, after which they may then decide to commit formally to settling down and bringing up a family. Others believe that an ongoing year-and-a-day renewal ensures that the couple choose to stay together and so offers a more whole-hearted commitment through the years than a single lifetime dedication.

Modern handfasters may have a civil ceremony beforehand to make the marriage legal or may wish to keep the union one of the heart and mind. In an age of frequent divorces, handfasting offers a thoughtful alternative or prelude to marriage, a substitute for rushing into a legal commitment with all the stresses and expense of a modern wedding. It also provides a form of dedication if for whatever reason a couple cannot legally be married.

Even if you are having a formal ceremony you could adapt parts of the ritual, and use these together in the week before the wedding to remind yourselves why you are getting married.

A sample handfasting

- ❦ Traditionally held around the full moon, May Day or the first of August, you do not need anyone to conduct your ceremony though it can be very moving if the parents or godparents or friends who brought the couple together lead the ceremony.

- ❦ Handfastings are usually held outdoors either on a beach, in a forest clearing, at an old stone circle or near an ancient sacred site. If the place is publicly owned it is as well to ask in advance and find out about any restrictions and help or facilities on offer. Some sacred sites like the Rollright stone circle in Oxfordshire can be reserved and you will be provided with a fire dish. Choose a quiet time when you know there will not be too many people walking through.

- ❋ If your own or a friend's or family member's garden is large enough, you can have the ceremony there and hire a large gazebo or marquee in case it is wet. If you are getting legally married first, then allow time to get between the sites and have refreshments.

- ❋ In the US you can get legal certification for a handfasting but would need someone to officiate.

Preparations

- ❋ The homeliness of a handfasting is to me its strength and the couple usually do not hide from each other before the ceremony but share the preparations, though of course with some delegation.

- ❋ There are plenty of presiding roles so parents, grandparents and even step parents can be part of the ceremony. A best man, bride's attendants and flower children are usually required. These roles will have to be shared out beforehand.

- ❋ The couple often choose to plait their own cords before the ceremony. These cords can be made from lengths of coloured curtain cord or thick wool.

- ❋ Red or purple is a usual colour for a bride but any favourite clothes can be worn.

- ❋ The circle around which everyone stands is made of flowers and is usually set up before the ceremony. However, as with a baby blessing, flower children can make or add to the petal circle enclosing the circle of guests. If pre-setting the circle, leave a small gateway that can be closed by the flower children when the circle has been blessed, and note that you will need plenty of space to move around inside the circle.

- ❋ Some bridegrooms, with the help of the best man, make an arch of flowers and branches to set near the centre of the circle. This is done the night before the wedding. In older-type ceremonies a broomstick is set in front of the rock or table, or in front of the flower arch.

- ❋ A fire dish or some kind of small fire container or a large candle embedded in sand is positioned near the centre of the circle. This will be used for burning herbs. The fire is lit before the ceremony by the groom and a helper, who can keep an eye on the fire during the ceremony.

- In the centre of the circle you will need a table or flat rock for three white candles, two small and one larger. The two candles represent the bride and groom and the larger one, the unity of the marriage. Also on the table or rock, there will be the two rings on a cushion, a dish of herbs (such as lavender, sage or thyme), a dish of salt and a dish of water, a bell and the two cords. You can light incense if you wish. The bride and her attendants prepare the central table while the bridegroom is sorting out the fire.
- Put candles or garden torches at the four cardinal directions of the circle. These directions can either be measured with an ordinary compass or just guessed from known directions. If it is an open site, glass holders should be used to enclose the candles.
- If the couple or guests have not attended a handfasting before, a dress rehearsal for the main players can be useful. One or two trusted people can then be asked to keep an eye that everyone is in roughly the right place and knows what is happening.
- A printed order of service can be prepared, but if things become chaotic that is often part of the joy of it.
- Gifts of wildflower seeds or crystals are often given to the guests and so need to be prepared before the ceremony.

The ceremony

- The couple lead their guests in pairs or small groups to stand around the circle and then walk once round the completed circle clockwise outside and then inside.
- The bridegroom's father or mother or a senior relative comes into the centre, rings a bell three times to open the ceremony and welcomes everyone to the occasion.
- At the request of one of the bride's parents, the four candles at the cardinal directions are lit, one after the other, by four younger guests, two from each side of the family. They can stand near the candle they light.
- The bride takes the dish of salt and tips a little into the dish of water, which the bridegroom holds. The bridegroom swirls the water and then each sprinkles a little on the other's cords. They then tie the cords together, each saying something about what the handfasting means to them.
- The circle is blessed by a chosen person entering the circle via the doorway, taking the salt water and walking round the outside of the circle, asking for blessings on all present one after the other.

- ✤ Some more formal handfasting ceremonies bless the circle also with incense and the candle of the south.

- ✤ The couple visit each candle around the circle in turn, while carrying the dish of herbs. In the north, they ask for the stability and lasting unity of the earth for their relationship, in the east, for happiness and a willingness to adapt, in the south, for passion and commitment and in the west, for love and gentleness. In each flame they drop a pinch of herbs.

- ✤ They tip the rest of the herbs on the central fire.

- ✤ The person who rang the bell calls the couple and asks what it is that they seek. The couple then ask for the handfasting, saying they come of their own free will 'in perfect love and perfect trust' to seek union of heart, soul, body and mind with each other.

- ✤ The father or mother of the bride asks who supports the couple and a chosen number of bridesmaids and ushers will come forward and say they support the handfasting on behalf of everyone. Alternatively, everyone can shout that they do and just a chosen attendant can come forward.

- ✤ The rings are then blessed by the bride's and bridegroom's parents or senior relatives who each sprinkle a few drops of salt water over each ring and say a few words.

- ✤ One of the parents asks the couple to make their vows to each other and to exchange rings.

- ✤ The bride lights her small white candle and the bridegroom his. They then join their separate candle flames in the larger unity candle to represent the marriage, saying,

    Now we are one

    plus anything else they wish to add.

- ✤ The single candles are left burning unless the couple wish to extinguish them.

- ✤ The bride's mother and the bridegroom's father, or the attendants if preferred, take the cords and join the couple, right hand to right hand, naming the couple and saying,

    May no one part those whom the God/Goddess or Mother Earth has joined together except by the couple's own free will.

- ✤ The couple kiss each other and then leave the circle through the gateway, jumping over the broom (which symbolises domestic bliss) and running through the flower arch if these have been used.

❋ The candle lighters blow out the four candles but the unity candle and the others on the table are left burning.

❋ The flower children or the couple take round gifts of wildflower seeds or crystals for the guests.

❋ Finally the bridegroom's mother or the bride's father rings the bell and the other declares that though the ritual is ended the loves remain unbroken. He or she then either reads a final prepared blessing or speaks directly from the heart.

❋ The bride and groom slip out of the cord and put it on the table. This will later be hung over the honeymoon bed and be kept to be re-dedicated annually.

❋ If in a private garden, the couple can plant seeds in the centre of the circle.

❋ The couple blow out any remaining candles and run round the inside of the circle as the guests throw flowers and petals.

❋ The bride tosses her bouquet unless she wishes to keep it.

❋ A feast traditionally follows, often 'bring and share'.

Marking the family rites of passage

Four or five generations ago, an older member of the family would have kept a family Bible or a scroll in which family births, marriages and deaths were carefully recorded in copper plate handwriting. You don't have to be the most senior member of the family to take on the task of record keeper; you just need to be persevering enough to track down past generations and set up a family tree. This can be done by questioning family members and searching through official records (in the UK, these have only been kept since the 1830s, but church registers go back hundreds of years). Having created a family tree, you can add more recent events – births, marriages, re-marriages, permanent unions, deaths and adoptions. Once your record is as complete as you can make it, take it along to family occasions where family members may help to fill the gaps. In creating a book, you are symbolically creating the heart of a family, perhaps one that is geographically separated.

You could also start a family treasure box. Collect mementoes of shared occasions such as jubilee celebrations, the location you live in and events in individuals' lives. These can be passed down through the family or, if you have no surviving relatives, you can bequeath them, along with video film or photographs saved on CD, to archives or schools. This will ensure that the collection survives and becomes a resource for future generations.

Death and burial in the modern world

Modern funeral services, conducted one after the other in regimented graveyards and crematoria, can make the loss of a loved one even harder to bear as you try to link the fun-loving person you knew with rows of orderly marble urns and stone crosses, especially if he or she was not a Christian. The expensive decaying cut flower wreaths in the days after the funeral may seem a symbol of waste and not regrowth.

In contrast, a natural burial in a woodland site offers the blessings of Mother Nature, and a growing tree as a memorial is a reminder that there is rebirth and renewal – whatever you may believe about the afterlife. In Montana, a fruit tree is often planted over a grave. Some non-conformist priests will bless a natural burial spot or you may choose to carry out your own ceremony and either employ gravediggers and undertakers or even organise your own transport. Eco-friendly coffins are made of wicker, bamboo, local woods or cardboard and the site will become a haven for wildflowers and wildlife as well as a source of oxygen for the planet. One wildlife burial place I encountered even had little frog shelters on the graves.

Your body can be buried by friends and relatives in a garden or farm with the permission of the landowner. Subject to certain regulations, you do not require permission from the council planning department or the environmental health department. Unless you have a huge garden, however, you may prefer a woodland burial. See page 250 for details of an excellent book published by the Natural Death Centre that gives websites, natural burial grounds and absolutely everything you need to know about natural burial including information about home burials and burials at sea. By 2010, the Natural Death Centre estimates that 12 per cent of UK burials will be natural ones. Some natural cemeteries allow pets to be buried close to their owners. At the time of writing this book, the Church of England has consecrated its first natural burial ground in Barton, Cambridgeshire.

Burials can occur very fast after death and this can make mourning hard. Increasingly, people are returning to the old ways and having their relative's body at home for a day or two before the funeral so that family members can spend time letting the person go. This can also help children who may fear that they too may disappear.

Candlelit vigils before the funeral were traditionally held at home, and a wake, during which photographs, tools of the deceased's trade and mementoes were displayed, was held on the night or two before the funeral. Visitors would come to share food and drink at the kitchen table and pay their respects and write memories of the deceased person in a special book. Traditionally, clocks were stopped and the body was never left alone. However, in the modern world, unless you have your relative home for the day or two before the funeral, it may not be practical to have the two traditional companions day and night.

The vigil still occurs with royalty and great people but it was common in Ireland in ordinary homes until the 1970s. During my childhood a local woman in my street always prepared a body after death. I myself did this for my own mother, who died at home.

If you can see a relative before the funeral and it will not offend anybody, put three drops of water on the brow and say,

> *By Earth and sea and sky be blest.*

This reverses the birth custom, and returns the soul to spirit.

The souls of the dead

Even in an impersonal hospital and certainly in a hospice, there can be special moments with the deceased person. Kasja, a Swedish ex-nurse, told me of her experience:

> *I was nursing very ill patients and one old man had very bad gangrene. When he died all the windows in the ward were opened and the ward was closed for cleaning. Since I had nursed the patient, I volunteered to get everything ready. Suddenly a small brown bird flew in through the window and perched on the end of the old man's bed. It showed no fear of me and sang beautifully for several minutes and at last flew away. For me it made what seemed a sad painful dying very beautiful.*

I told Kasja about the belief that souls could take the form of birds. This dates from the Ancient Egyptian Ba or hawk-headed part of the human spirit that was said to fly from the mummy after death. In European folk custom, a bird entering a house or tapping at a window when someone was dying was thought to be the spirit of a deceased relative come to fetch the soul of the dying person. In Finnish mythology, it was believed that birds were servants of Sielulintu, the Soul-Bird. On his behalf, they carried human souls into their bodies at birth and took them back when the person died.

Making a funeral special

✤ If you are having a more formal funeral service you might like to book a double session in the chapel or church. This then allows plenty of time for arranging photographs and other mementoes around the building and gives everyone who wants to speak the chance to do so.

✤ Have a book for people who prefer to write down their memories.

✤ Before the service, create a memory box for the deceased person containing a favourite item of jewellery, a medal, a school or trades certificate, poems or sketches he or she made, photographs of the person's life, holiday postcards, a wartime ration book, a passport, a pressed dried flower from the wedding bouquet, a button from a well-worn coat or any newspaper cuttings in which he or she featured. Add a small sachet or purse filled with dried lavender or rose petals, fragranced on the outside with a favourite perfume, cologne or aftershave. This will not only remind you of the deceased person but is also an heirloom – a memento of the person's unique life for future generations.

✤ Ask mourners to bring any small personal reminders of the person to add to the box during the service. This box can be of great comfort to relatives and can be opened and read on anniversaries.

✤ Ask people to bring wildflower bulbs to plant around the grave if allowed (ask the relevant authority in advance) instead of wreaths or to bring plants and small trees to be planted back at the family home or in a suitable place as a little memorial garden. This garden of remembrance can be created during the funeral meal and may be particularly helpful for children.

✤ If it is a dark day, adorn the service place with small tea lights. Light the first tea light and then ask the people present to pass the flame on from one tea light to the next. This could also be done around the graveside, with each person saying a few words as they light their neighbour's tea light.

✤ Personalise the coffin by placing a favourite hat or some fun memento on top.

✤ Ask everyone to bring a single flower or a small bunch of herbs from their garden to throw into the grave before the earth is filled in.

* Though coffins are heavy there is something very homely about relatives and friends carrying the coffin. Alternatively, use a horse and cart rather than a car and walk alongside.

* The more laughter the better and if there is someone who can play music as you walk along or during the service, that is worth more than listening to a thousand tape recordings.

* Choose words that express your feelings. It is better to speak from the heart than to read the finest poetry or passage from the Bible unless, of course, they have personal meaning for you or the deceased person.

* Be as imaginative as you wish with the grave goods to put inside the coffin at a burial, a custom going back thousands of years. You could wrap the body in a favourite blanket or throw or a beloved coat for the journey. Think about what the person loved most and what typified their life. I would want as grave goods my best spectacles that my children call my moon glasses because the lenses are so thick, my special crystals, some dried lavender, ears of corn for fertility in the afterlife, some bread and honey and some expensive chocolate in a little wicker hamper for the journey, the traditional coin to pay the ferrywoman to carry me to the Isles of the Blest and a twist of salt (a pinch of salt wrapped in a piece of silver foil) – the symbol of immortality.

* Maybe you could release some white petals at the service or get people to blow bubbles, made from a non-chemical soap.

* Bring some birdseed to feed the birds after the service. You may not be allowed to do this at the graveside even in a natural setting, so do check first. If this is not possible, stop on the way back to the house to call the soul birds or to feed the ducks.

* If the weather is nice, have a remembrance picnic in a favourite spot or in the garden.

* 'Bring and share' post-funeral meals make the occasion much more personal than caterers. Try to include the deceased person's favourite foods.

* If people are gathered in a circle round the graveside, a young relative could scatter a circle of dried sage and rosemary for immortality and remembrance around the outside of the mourners.

* As with the naming ceremony (see page 136), each person at the service could put a crystal in a basket and make a blessing to the deceased person or recall a gift, for example, 'May your laughter and good humour sound across time and space'. These could be

given to the family or set in the home memorial garden or put in the grave before it is closed.

* If it is not too windy, light tea lights, one by each person, or a single white candle at the graveside. As the grave is finally covered over, blow out the flames and say,

> Go on in peace and in blessing but know you are always welcome at our table and in our hearts.

* As everyone leaves, after (if permitted) planting a few bulbs on top of the grave, the closest relative or someone they choose could scatter a little earth over the grave and say,

> Return to the arms of the Mother. So long as your name is spoken so shall your light remain with us, which is forever.

A private bereavement ritual

After the funeral it can be hard when everyone has gone home, or you have gone home alone with your thoughts, to link with the essential person who has been buried or cremated. Sometimes too because of the physical distance to the place where the funeral is held, because of some family estrangement or if your love for the person must remain secret, you may not have been able to say goodbye publicly.

Some people dream of the deceased person soon after the funeral or sense their presence in the home, but this does not happen to everybody – and, indeed, some would not wish it to.

You may find this ritual helpful in the days after the funeral or on an anniversary, not necessarily of the death but perhaps of some personal shared date.

You will need: A small memento, perhaps a gift bought by one for the other of you, an item bought on a shared holiday that evokes happy or humorous memories or anything that for you sums up the deceased person at their most vibrant; a rose- or lavender-scented candle

* Go to a favourite place in your garden or a local park or square, taking the memento with you.

* Sit quietly in the place and let happy memories, conversations and jokes flow through your mind. Recall the familiar voice of the person who is no longer physically with you, together with any fragrances – wood smoke, tobacco, aftershave, perfume or soap – that remind you of him or her.

* When you are ready, go indoors and, even if it is not dark, light the scented candle.

- ❋ Look into the candle flame and speak words of love, together with any of regret.

- ❋ When you have finished, blow out the candle and let the light be a link of love with the essential person who lives on in their descendants and in all the kind deeds they performed and wise words they spoke.

- ❋ You may be rewarded by a sense of peace, as well as perhaps by a fleeting shadow, a touch as light as gossamer or a momentary smell that you associate with your loved one. Even if you do not believe in the afterlife, you can still connect with the essential love that never dies.

Other rites of passage

Each time you come to a change point, whether it is your children leaving home, a new job or a change of location, take time to mark the occasion with a simple candle-lighting ceremony or by planting flowers, casting petals off a bridge or burying a stone or dark crystal to help ease a transition you find hard. Even if you are alone, try to mark birthdays and anniversaries with a special meal or outing and by buying yourself a small memento of the occasion. Make your plans for the year ahead, including something you have always wanted to do, however modest, and try to build your life around that, rather than fitting your plans in around life as it happens.

Rites of ending

There are many small deaths in everyday life: opportunities that do not work out, paths that seem promising and yet go nowhere, an unfair dismissal from a job you do well or a betrayal in love. Some people are held back for years by being unable to let a faithless or unkind love go in their minds or accept that a money loss was unfair and will therefore never be repaid.

These endings often coincide with the twilight and waning moon periods (see Chapter 5) and the natural seasonal down turns (see Chapters 7 and 8), but for a specific injustice, loss or act of unkindness we may need to mark closure with a small ceremony if we are to move naturally from one stage to another and open ourselves to new experiences.

About 40 per cent of people who contact me for advice feel trapped in a negative situation where bitterness, anger and resentment, which are ultimately self-destructive, may linger from childhood abuse or cruelty. Early negative patterns can result in lack of self-belief and can be repeated in subsequent relationships.

I am not talking about forgiving and forgetting, for to do so may not be possible if the wrong was grievous. Rather, rites of ending focus on drawing a line under the past, cutting off communication with the source of destruction if possible or limiting it to necessary, polite, non-confrontational contact and establishing a personal way forward (the other person has to make their own destiny). I have focused on the most common situation: divorce or a major relationship break up. However, you can adapt the same methods to mourn other losses and to separate yourself from sorrow or injustice so you can move forward.

If your ex-partner is still alive and you are forced to see or hear of him or her – or must meet because of children or for business reasons – it can be very hard to grieve or heal. Rituals can be very helpful in enabling you to walk away emotionally with dignity and without bitterness and to draw boundaries.

What is more, the power generated by a rite of ending can give you the strength to leave a destructive relationship or an affair that is going nowhere because you know the person you love will never leave their marital partner.

The following is the single most effective ending rite I have found. It is suitable for everything from letting go of abuse in childhood or accepting that short of a miracle (and they do happen) you may never have a child of your own to leaving a lover who will never commit.

Breaking the cord

If a couple who are handfasted end the relationship they may untie the cords that have been knotted over their bed. Each then takes their own cord back, with the option of burning or burying it or keeping it as a reminder of the good times and the intention of finding future love.

In other relationships too, or where there is bitterness or regret associated with a situation rather than a person, cutting the cord is a powerful outward expression of an inward intention. If you are bound tightly to the person or situation, you may need to repeat this action many times with different cords, but each time it gets easier. I have a cord graveyard under my olive tree. This is a very old ritual and I have described a similar one in my *Complete Book of Spells*, but like all magic it is actually based on sound psychology.

You will need: A deep blue large candle in a holder; a metal tray or flat metal holder to put beneath the candle; small dish of salt; 25 cm/10 in of thin dark blue curtain cord; a deep pot of earth

- ❧ If possible, work during the waning moon period and after twilight as the energies at this time will work in your favour to lessen the pain. You can, however, carry out the ritual whenever it is needed.

- ❧ Light the candle and put a pinch of salt in the flame to signify your moving back into life. Begin by saying 'I' – this symbolically says 'I exist and I have the right to ask whatever it is I am asking'. Then say your name, again to create the idea in your own mind that you matter (which some people find hard to believe) and to establish your separate existence and your right to happiness. Then name the person or the situation you wish to separate yourself from without blame and without anger.

✤ Being careful not to burn yourself, hold the cord taut in both hands over the flame, so that the centre of the cord is just in the flame. As you do so, say,

> *The cord between us is long.*
> *The bonds between us were strong,*
> *But now they are decaying, fraying,*
> *Burning, breaking*
> *And so it must be.*

✤ When the cord has broken in the flame, drop both halves into the pot of earth and let the flames die out, saying,

> *The cord is broken and with it the power to hold me back.*

✤ When the cords are cool push them down into the earth and tip the earth away under a tree or bush in the darkness.

A ritual to end a marriage or committed relationship

This gentle candle ritual is particularly useful if there are children involved in the end of the relationship or if for whatever reason you have to stay in contact with your ex-partner. It is also good if you have to leave a business partnership, a workplace or a home that you love. It will act as a reminder that you can and will go on alone.

In America, and increasingly in other parts of the world, divorce and separation ceremonies are being held to mark the end of a relationship. This ritual, however, can be carried out less formally alone or with your ex-partner perhaps on the day the divorce goes through or when joint property is being sold.

While it may be difficult to perform the ritual if your ex-partner has acted callously or deserted you, or if he or she is making matters hard financially or manipulating the children, it will help to heal your own negative feelings. Even if the other person continues to behave destructively, you and any children involved will benefit from your positive intent.

You will need: A large beeswax or white candle; two smaller beeswax or white candles representing the two separated/divorced people or you and the situation, business venture or property you are leaving behind or being forced out of

✤ In silence, light the large beeswax or white candle (to represent the marriage, relationship or other link).

✤ From the large candle, light the two smaller ones, the first to represent your ex-partner or the situation or location you are leaving behind, and the second to represent yourself. Set them one on either side of the large candle.

✤ When you feel able, extinguish the central candle while saying appropriate words, such as,

> *The flame of love grows dim, and so we go our separate ways, with regret, in peace and with thanks for the happy times we shared.*

You can adapt the words for the situation.

✤ Let the separate candles burn down in a safe place and make the rest of the day special, no matter how bad you feel.

7 The Wheel of the Year – Old Festivals in a Modern World

Although many of us are no longer personally involved in hunting for food, farming or the sowing and harvesting of crops, the changing seasons remain part of our genetic heritage whatever part of the world we live in. The seasons are by far the broadest energy bands and mirror those of the sun and moon, but offer longer periods of opportunity.

Each season brings benefits if we work with it instead of regretting its limitations. In winter, for example, we can withdraw spiritually and grow stronger inwardly as the earth rests under the winter snows. We can light candles, cook warming foods and enjoy early nights and weekends by the fire reading a good book instead of complaining about how cold and dark it is outside.

The annual cycle of the seasons, sometimes referred to as the Wheel of the Year, is central to modern paganism. Focusing on the eight spokes or festivals that make up the Wheel of the Year can help to heighten your awareness of the changes that occur as the seasons pass. This chapter covers four festivals, starting with Imbolc, and the other four come in Chapter 8.

The origins of the festivals

The cyclical seasonal light patterns are still central to modern pagan festivals, such as the midwinter solstice, which comes just before the present Christmas when the sun reaches its lowest point in the sky and the trees are stripped of their leaves. This celebration began long before written records when early peoples feared the sun might die. They may have lit fires and decorated evergreen branches with small fire torches to give power to the sun and to cause new life to stir within the bare trees (there was believed to be a magical transference of energy from the evergreens).

Once the hunter-gatherer way of life had been replaced in more temperate regions by the farmers of the Neolithic period from around 8000 BCE, the ritual year became inextricably linked with the annual sowing and reaping cycle. Blessings were given at the time of sowing and at high summer to ask for plentiful sun and rain, which would ensure an abundant harvest.

Because these celebrations seemed generally to work, they became entrenched as annual rituals and ordinary people felt that their personal actions and celebrations at these change points assisted with the turning of the year. They believed they were joining their personal energies with those of the seasons to their mutual advantage. Although we no longer literally think that our fertility is linked with the crops and the animals, psychologically and spiritually these celebrations can be modified to enrich the modern faster and more urbanised world and to awaken our own inner potential.

The gift of abundance

The turning year depends upon the circle of planting, caring for crops and animals and harvesting, upon the need to generate and share abundance. This teaches the valuable lesson that good things come from hard work and willingness to give, which should be passed on to our children. From an early age, they should be encouraged to offer, ask for and receive help from relatives, partners and friends. Naturally loving, generous people sometimes find it hard to ask others to share their abundance, which can lead to thoughtlessness and selfishness and a feeling of being overburdened and disregarded. This balancing of giving and receiving is part of paganism and its changing seasonal patterns.

Abundance is very different from materialism and the acquisition of consumer goods, and can be expressed as generosity with time and efforts, resources and talents.

By sharing abundance, we can generate a sense of well-being and contentment. Make a start by cooking a meal for friends and family; inviting friends, colleagues and neighbours to a 'bring and share' barbecue or indoor meal; or setting up a local baby- or pet-sitting service or practical talent exchange in which money does not change hands. Fix someone's dripping tap or help them decorate a room and they may help with your accounts or invite your children on their next family outing.

Making your own village community

Generally, within a family and a community or workplace there is an abundance of talents (especially among retired people) and also unwanted serviceable items and information about local services. With the help of computers and mobiles, information and resources can easily be advertised and exchanged.

Instead of holding a private garage sale, organise an event in your street, where everyone brings along their unwanted items. These items can then be exchanged (what you no longer need may be just what someone else was looking for) or paid for with time, homemade food, plants or flowers. Next time you go to the dump, look at the old computer that would have suited a struggling student or the perfectly good sofa that has been replaced and would be ideal for someone who is setting up a first home.

Recreating a village atmosphere on your housing estate is not hard, and even difficult neighbours may turn out to be a mine of information or make wonderful jam or chutneys or have sewing skills but have no family to use them for.

Abundance is not like a cake that the more people share it, the smaller the slice, but like a stew that becomes more nourishing and richer the more ingredients are added to the pot and that can be used to feed an infinite number of people. The more welcoming and hospitable we are and the more we encourage others to contribute time and effort and to be aware of the satisfaction of giving, the wider we can spread the pleasures of a better lifestyle rather than clutching them to us.

The eight-spoke Wheel of the Year

In modern Wicca and druidry, as well as other forms of neopaganism, the Wheel of the Year with its eight divisions is one of the most natural ways to get back in touch with the ebbs and flows of the year. I use the old Celtic-influenced names since the Wheel of the Year is associated with Celtic wisdom but you can give each festival its own name according to what is happening in your life.

Although each actual festival celebration point is regarded as three days, its ongoing energies span the whole six-week period. Generally, the festival energies were considered to begin at sunset on the evening of the festival (the beginning of the day in the old northern tradition). If you live in the southern hemisphere, just move the festivals round by six months or adapt them as appropriate to your local seasons.

Of course, each year follows the same patterns and you may like to note from year to year whether, at the end of 12 months, you are where you hoped to be or if the alternative path you followed proved better than the anticipated one.

Wheel of the Year diagram:
- **North** – Alban Arthuran, around December 21
- **North East** – Oimelc, January 31 – February 2
- **East** – Alban Eiler, around March 21
- **South East** – Beltane, April 30 – May 2
- **South** – Alban Heruin, around June 21
- **South West** – Lughnassadh, July 31 – August 2
- **West** – Alban Elued, around September 21
- **North West** – Samhain, October 31 – November 2

Celebrating the changing season

Celebrations are by their nature spontaneous and adaptable. Take May Day. One year when you are busy you may light a red candle on May Eve just before going to bed as a substitute for the traditional twin bonfires, to make your life flower and light up in the way most needed. Another time you may go along to a local May Day celebration that is not necessarily openly pagan, for example, one that involves Morris dancers, an important feature of May morn celebrations both in America and England. In cities and suburbs everywhere there are May Queen carnival processions (a symbol of the pre-Christian maiden flower goddess).

Other people may go to a more openly focused Beltane, May Eve or May morning neopagan celebration at an old stone circle or other pre-Christian pagan place to welcome in the summer and to join their energies to the land and animals to make the crops grow (or your online business expand) and to make people and animals everywhere healthy and fertile.

Old festivals in a modern world

Why bother? Even if you just stop and greet, for example, the May morning with an empowerment of what you intend to create in the months ahead, it is like taking a huge inrush of pure earth and natural energy. When you feel yourself losing enthusiasm, you can tap into the summer solstice about six weeks later to revive your impetus. You will also draw strength from people who have carried out rituals, maybe on the same land, for hundreds or even thousands of years.

The seasonal energies are not something whirling overhead like the stars or the moon but are pure, beneath-the-feet earth energies that you can access when you smell or touch flowers, lean against a tree in a city park, grow herbs in your kitchen or walk across sand, grass or earth. Because they accumulate, your actions and thoughts do, in a symbolic sense, help the wheel to turn and will add to the store of power available to future generations.

In the world today there are remnants of these old festivals beneath more modern and often commercialised festivals and even if you live in a very conservative community, have strict religious beliefs or encounter family opposition, you can apply the principles and nature-based aspects of the older festivals to make modern commercialised festivals like Christmas more spiritual. The fact that people have celebrated the rebirth of the sun or the Sun God or Goddess for thousands of years around the shortest day of the year in December means that the symbolic birthday of Jesus on 25 December is entrenched in human consciousness on a very deep, instinctive and meaningful level. What is more, alternative celebrations such as midwinter can be very helpful if, for example, you share custody of children and have to miss part or one of the main festivals with them.

The two myth cycles

In the neopagan tradition, the eight festival energies are expressed through two intertwining myths, the story of the God and Goddess's relationship through a single year and the battle between the twin of the dark times of the year and the twin of the light or bright times of the year.

Sometimes the two myth cycles merge together but at other times they are quite separate. The light and dark twins are not even really twins since they are born six months apart and grow up incredibly quickly as their whole life cycle takes place within the single year. Although many neopagans do use the old symbolism, you can create your own wheel-of-the-year myth based on a more modern relationship saga between a couple and/or female or male twins.

Imbolc or Oimelc (31 January–2 February)

Focus of the period: New ideas; the promise that winter (actual or emotional) will end; planning the future and putting out the first shoots of new love; the growth or regrowth of trust; for taking the first steps to launch any projects that start in a small way; for melting rigid attitudes or prejudice that may have led to conflicts between families and work colleagues; for newborn infants, babies and young animals

Key words: Trust, germination

Emphasis of festival: Light, candles

Energies of the season: Rising. Its alter ego festival is Lughnassadh

Symbols: Milk, honey, seeds, early budding flowers and early greenery

Tree: Willow. With her willow wand, the Goddess was said to melt the snows of winter

Incenses, flowers and herbs: Angelica, basil, benzoin, celandine, crocus, heather, myrrh, snowdrops, violets

Candle colours: Pale pink, green, blue and white

Crystals: Dark gemstones such as the garnet and bloodstone/heliotrope, also amethyst, moonstone and rose quartz

Festival foods: Seed bread, milk, honey, any seeds, hot milky drinks, cheese and butter

Angel: Raguel, archangel of ice and snow, who melts the winter snows with his fiery sword. He is often pictured wearing dark grey and silver robes with a halo gleaming with icicles

Goddess: Bridget, first in the form of the goddess Brighid and then the Irish sixth-century saint, who were both associated with milk, nourishment, midwifery, healing, blacksmiths, inspiration, poetry, fire and the sun and who brought life back to the frozen winter land

The place on the wheel

Imbolc means 'in the belly of the mother' and refers to the potential for growth in whatever way is most relevant in your life.

The first festival of spring often takes place when the land is still frozen, and is thus a reminder that new life stirs within the earth and within people long before the effects are seen or felt externally.

In early agricultural societies, this was the all-important time when sheep and cattle gave birth to their young and so fresh milk and dairy products were first available to the community after the long winter.

In a number of pre-Christian traditions, this was the festival of the young maiden goddess, but it is also linked with the story of the newly delivered mother of the sun king whose milk is mirrored by the milk of the ewes who gave this festival its name of Oimelc, or ewe's milk.

The dark twin is still powerful as reflected in the cold weather and dark days but the young god of light is growing in power as he is nursed by the Goddess.

The Christian Candlemas, the festival of candles, takes place on 2 February, the day of the Purification of the Virgin Mary, on which she took baby Jesus to the temple for the first time.

Marking the festival in the modern world

- Carry out a personal and home purification, by burning smudge sticks in sagebrush or cedar and spiralling the smudge around your home, your possessions and yourself before taking the smoke stick outdoors to burn away or go out.

- Begin a fitness and healthy eating regime with a personal detox to maximise your energy and increase your resistance to winter ills and chills.

- Try some candle meditation or just take some quiet time to sit by candlelight talking to your family or friends. If you are alone, hold a clear crystal between your hands and ask your guardian angel and spirit guides if they have any messages for you. These may be expressed through words that come into your mind or images and sudden good ideas.

- Create a candle web with friends or relatives for healing or peace. Choose an evening when you are all at home and agree beforehand a time when you will light a white or beeswax candle and all focus on the same person, animal or place and send healing through the candle. You can adapt the web for people who live in nearby time zones. Leave the candle to burn through.

- Unless you live in a warm land, plant seeds indoors or under glass, naming for each handful of seeds what you wish to bring into your life in the months ahead. You can plant the germinated seeds outdoors on the spring equinox if it is warm enough.

- In age-old tradition, pour a little fresh milk on to the earth as a tribute to the Earth Mother and, as you do so, ask for fertility in any aspect of your life where you need it. Drink the rest of the milk or use it in cooking.

✤ On the night of 1 February, place nightlights safely at every window of your home to welcome in the new energies. Once candles were lit to welcome Brighid the maiden goddess on her day, 1 February, and later St Bridget on the Christian festival of Candlemas, 2 February, when the candles are blessed for the year ahead in a special church service.

✤ Take a ceramic heatproof bowl of milk and in it drop ice cubes to represent the cold of winter. Gently melt the ice with a small candle or burner beneath the bowl, stirring it and naming any quarrels or coldness you wish to resolve or remove from your life and any positive energies you would like to replace them with.

✤ This is a time for career renewal. In the old tradition, a local girl dressed in white as the maiden goddess and later as St Bridget would appear at the door of important houses and farms. Indoors would be a straw bed by the fire where she would be given milk, seed bread and honey and would bless the local workers. To focus on the way you wish your career to develop, on the evening of 31 January make a tiny straw bed or one of dried rose petals and in it place a small doll dressed in white. Surround it with the first greenery or buds of spring. Place in the straw symbols of the blessings you would like in your life, whether tiny charms related to your craft or ideal career. Drink a little milk sweetened with honey and put three drops on the head of the doll. Keep the doll and bed in position until dusk on 2 February and then scatter the straw or petals to the wind, give the doll to a child and carry any charms in a small drawstring bag to bring you luck. Send off an application, start learning some new skill that will further your career or apply for a course or extra training.

✤ Give packets of seeds to friends or friends' children to plant indoors and take along a green plant or two to refresh the workplace and to act as a reminder of the coming spring.

✤ Write some poetry or a story or start your novel, whether for pleasure or publication.

Alban Eiler, Ostara or the spring equinox (20 March–22 March)

Focus of the period: Fertility and positive life changes; new beginnings and opportunities; new flowering love; for initiating creative ventures, travel, house moves and clearing what is no longer needed in your life; anything to do with conception and pregnancy, children and young people, mothers, healing, helping family members to believe in themselves; for welcoming the winds of change into your life in the way most appropriate

Key words: Initiation, signs of growth

Emphasis of festival: Rebirth, hatching (as of eggs or plans)

Energies of the season: Balanced, as day and night are equal on the equinox day. Its alter ego festival is the autumn equinox around 21 September

Symbols: Eggs, especially painted ones, feathers, spring flowers or leaves, a sprouting pot of seeds, pottery rabbits and birds and anything made of dough or clay

Tree: Birch

Incenses, flowers and herbs: Celandine, cinquefoil, crocus, daffodil, honeysuckle, hyacinth, lemon, primroses, sage, tansy, thyme, violets

Candle colours: Yellow and green

Crystals: Sparkling yellow crystals, such as citrine, golden beryl and rutilated quartz, also lemon and apple green chrysoprase and aventurine

Festival foods: Decorated boiled eggs, chocolate eggs and rabbits, hot cross buns or small cakes with pastry crosses on for the old astrological sign of the Earth Mother, lamb, simnel (marzipan-topped cakes)

Angel: Raphael, archangel of the dawn, the east, the spring and of healing. He carries a golden vial of medicine, with a traveller's staff, food to nourish travellers and is dressed in the colours of early morning sunlight, with a beautiful green healing ray emanating from his halo

Goddess: The Norse goddess Ostara who opened the gates of spring on equinox morning and whose magical animal, the white hare, dashed across the lingering snow in northern climes, promising Ostara was on her way. In the Christian tradition, 25 March is the festival of the Annunciation of the Virgin Mary when Gabriel appeared telling her she would bear Christ

The place on the wheel

Alban Eiler is Gaelic and means 'the light of the earth'. This refers to the light that returns after the winter at the time when sowing begins in earnest, young animals are thriving and the early spring flowers are finally in bloom.

The maiden goddess in pre-Christian tradition mates with the young virile sun god to conceive the new child of light who will be born on the midwinter solstice the following December so that the wheel may continue turning.

The light and dark brothers fight and the light twin kills his brother, so henceforward the days will be longer than the night. The dark twin descends to the earth or the underworld or the womb of the mother, like the seeds planted in the earth, to await rebirth at the summer solstice.

The spring equinox festival is also associated with the resurrection of light and of Christ and, in the pre-Christian tradition, gods such as the Greek Attis. Indeed, in some myths, this is the birth of the sun king. It is said that on the spring equinox morning the sun dances in the water at sunrise, an association transferred to angels.

Marking the festival in the modern world

Work either during the spring equinox or on Easter Sunday, which is the first Sunday after the first full moon after the spring equinox, the only surviving Christian lunar-related festival.

- ✤ Boil eggs in pastel-coloured vegetable food colouring or after boiling decorate them using non-toxic marker pens, with flowers, mother goddess spirals, birds and bees and offer them on a basket of spring flowers and leaves on the breakfast table. The family can help but, especially with young children, make sure the decorated eggs are peeled and well washed before eating.

- ✤ Hide small chocolate eggs for an Easter egg hunt for friends and family of all ages. If it is warm enough, go for a picnic and hide them around the picnic place. This is more fun than buying expensive chocolate eggs that overload people with sugar and make them irritable.

- ✤ This is a time for increasing your personal fertility if you wish to conceive a child or to re-establish the natural rhythms of your life or to launch a creative venture such as selling paintings, crafts or getting a book published. On the equinox or Easter morning, prick an egg with a needle or large silver pin and take out all the white and yellow. Then carefully cut the shell in half and leave the halves open for the sun or light to shine on them.

Leave the eggshell on an indoor window ledge until the first night of the crescent moon after the spring equinox or the first crescent after Easter Sunday.

Then place a tiny moonstone or worry doll in one half, leaving it on the same indoor window ledge until the next full moon. Place the silver pin or needle in or on top of the other half and also leave it on the window ledge.

On the night of the full moon, prick the moonstone very gently with the silver pin and rest the pin on top of the moonstone in one half of the egg. Name what it is you need. If you are trying for a child, make love unless some ongoing medical treatment will not allow this.

The next morning close the egg and wrap up egg, pin and moonstone in a fabric scarf until the moon can be seen no more in the sky even as a waning crescent. Then bury the eggshell and repeat the ritual with a new egg and the same moonstone and pin. We used a similar ritual with just lunar energies, but the spring festival gives an added impetus.

- Spring clean your life as well as your home (see page 65). Answer any correspondence that is piling up. Deal with unavoidable issues. Change your routine so that you rise half an hour earlier and can enjoy the growing light, perhaps walking to work or sitting in the spring sunshine on your balcony or in your garden.

- Initiate those projects you always meant to get around to by first clearing out the clutter of old commitments or activities that you no longer enjoy.

- Visit a clear river or lake on equinox morning or Easter Sunday and look at any light dancing or moving on the surface of the water. Throw a tiny crystal or white stone into the light area in the water. As it splashes, blink and you will see externally or in your mind's eye a momentary image framed in light that will help you to plan your future path.

- Make some spring equinox or Easter morning energising and healing water by leaving still mineral water in a clear dish from dawn or from when you wake until noon or when you break for lunch. Use this for revitalising office plants or sickly house plants and for splashing on your inner wrists and brow to give you enthusiasm and optimism whenever other people are being negative or discouraging. Put a small sealed bottle of the water near the front door if you are trying to sell your house or on top of job applications or manuscripts, legal or tax papers you are sending. Do this for just a few minutes, to create a positive response.

❀ Plant in the ground the seeds you germinated at Imbolc, naming the results you hope for within six months. If they did not thrive, plant new seedlings rather than seeds, naming again or adapting the earlier plans.

❀ Burn an ear of dried grass or corn in a candle set in a bucket of soil to symbolise the ancient spring equinox corn figure that was woven from the previous year's harvest or the straw effigy of Judas in Christian times. These ashes were scattered on the fields to ensure the successful growth of the seeds. You can scatter your soil containing the burned corn or grass on to your garden or use it for planting an indoor flower display to ensure that what you gained practically, financially and emotionally from the previous year grows even more in the year ahead.

❀ As close to the equinox or Easter Sunday as possible visit a place near your home that you have always wanted to go to – perhaps you always drive past and say 'We must go there.'

❀ Make a cake and mark it with a diagonal cross for Mother Earth. Invite for coffee or tea people you have been meaning to ask round for ages or who you know would welcome an invitation because they are lonely or feeling sad.

❀ Buy a new small colourful item of clothing or some flowers (to represent the traditional Easter bonnet) or organise a clothes exchange with friends.

Beltane or Beltaine, the beginning of the Celtic summer (30 April–2 May)

Focus of the period: Fertility, whether for initiating a creative venture or conceiving a child (even stronger energies than the spring equinox); for improvement in career, business or financial matters; for increasing commitment in love; for passion and the consummation of love; for creative inspiration; for improving health and increasing energy; for optimism and self-confidence; for abundance in every way and for generosity; for people in their twenties and thirties; for speaking your mind honestly but with tact

Key words: Passion, fertility

Emphasis of the festival: Fire, flowers

Energies of the season: Rising. Its alter ego festival is Samhain or Halloween on 31 October, the beginning of the Celtic winter

Symbols: Fresh greenery and blossoms, especially hawthorn (indoors only on 1 May), ribbons, staffs or staves decorated with flowers and ribbons, bells

Tree: Hawthorn, elder

Incenses, flowers and herbs: Almond, angelica, ash, bluebells, cowslip, frankincense, hawthorn, lilac, marigolds and roses for love; also any floral fragrance

Candle colours: Dark green, scarlet and silver

Crystals: Amber, clear crystal quartz, golden tiger's eye, Herkimer diamond, red tiger's eye, topaz

Festival foods: Any roasted meat, traditional oatmeal cake cut into 13 portions (or one piece for each person present – the person drawing a piece marked beforehand with a cross traditionally has to pay a forfeit or entertain those present with a song), egg custard dishes, mead (fermented honey drink), any miniature delicacies said to be left by the fairies (whose festival it is), elderflower and berry jams

Angel: Camael or Chamuel, archangel of courage, divine love and justice who wears a deep red tunic with dark green armour, and has a halo of dark ruby flames and rich green wings

God and goddess: The Green man, god of vegetation who as Jack of the Green, a kind of Robin Hood figure, married the flower goddess whom he crowned as the May Queen with garlands of flowers; also the Anglo Saxon goddess Walpurga of spring who was Christianised as St Walpurga

The place on the wheel

Beltane or Beltaine is named after the Irish god of light, in whose honour fires were kindled at this time by rubbing wood together.

Sundown on May Eve heralded the signal for the Celtic druids to kindle the great Belfires from nine different kinds of wood. At this time, cattle were released from the winter barns and were driven between twin fires to cleanse them and to invoke fertility as they were released into the fields.

The light god becomes stronger as light and warmth increase and the two myths merge for a while in the woodland wedding of the god and goddess. This is the last appearance of the maiden goddess.

Winter is finally dead as at midnight on May Eve Caillieach Bhuer, the old hag of winter, casts her staff under a holly bush and turns to stone until six months later on Halloween.

A time of great fairy activity, especially around standing stones and stone circles.

Sacred wells are very potent on 1 May both for healing and fertility.

Marking the festival in the modern world

- Light your own Bel bonfire, burning as many different kinds of wood as you can find. When the fire is burned through, scatter a few of the ashes to the four winds from a hilltop, sending your wishes for the future with them. Bury the rest.

- Alternatively, light a huge scarlet candle embedded in sand or earth and drop dried rosemary, lavender or rose petals into the flame, asking the cosmos to send what you most need, which may be different from what you think you want.

- Trade plants with friends and save any fragrant flowers or herbs you pick or are given over the coming weeks to dry and make into pot pourri or homemade incense to burn on charcoal or an outdoor fire.

- Make a garland on a circle of wire or fill a vase with nine different flowers or different-coloured flowers. For each flower make a wish, some of which will need all your power and optimism to fulfil. According to legend, Blodeuwedd, the Welsh maiden goddess and bride of Llew the young Welsh god of light, was made on 1 May from nine different flowers.

- Rise at dawn on May morning and wash your face in water to which you have added a few drops of the morning dew (you can collect it with an eye dropper). May morning dawn is said to make you radiant and bring health and fertility.

- Fill small baskets with garden flowers or greenery and leave them on the doorsteps of anyone who is sick or lonely to spread the abundance of the season.

- In accordance with tradition, visit a sacred well or a small lake or pool just before sunrise and walk round it three times sunwise (clockwise), asking for healing for yourself or loved ones. Tie a ribbon to a nearby tree as a traditional way of saying thank you to Mother Nature.

- Run, cycle, dance, swim, roller blade or jump and stir up the energies as a way of building up your inner power. If on a bike, cycle up hill and then freewheel down.

- Go along to one of the traditional May morning celebrations in your area or invite a group of friends for a flower party and ask them all to bring along a few flowers or plants to exchange.

- Decorate a tree or a branch from a tree with flowers, ribbons and bells and your May-time symbols and spiral round it, allowing your feet to trace and amplify the energies of the earth, as if you were maypole dancing.

Alban Heruin, Litha, midsummer or summer solstice (20–22 June)

Focus of the period: Power, joy and courage; male potency; success; marriage; fertility of all kinds, especially for older women; for health, happiness, strength, energy, self-confidence and identity; for fulfilling personal and career ambitions and maximising opportunities; for all matters concerning people approaching middle age; for seizing chances and enjoying the present rather than worrying about the past or future; summer solstice power can be harnessed for tackling seemingly insoluble problems

Key words: Power, leadership, authority

Emphasis of the festival: Sun, gold

Energies of the season: The turning point as full power begins to wane from this day. Its alter ego festival is the midwinter solstice, the shortest day around 21 December

Symbols: Brightly coloured flowers; oak boughs; scarlet, orange and yellow ribbons; gold-coloured coins and any gold jewellery that can be empowered at the festival and worn afterwards to give strength and confidence; any golden fruit or vegetables

Tree: Oak

Incenses, flowers and herbs: Benzoin, chamomile, dill, elder, fennel, frankincense, juniper, lavender, lemon verbena, marigolds, orange, rosemary, sage and sagebrush, St John's Wort, vervain, any golden, red or orange flowers

Candle colours: Red, orange, gold

Crystals: Amber, carnelian, red jasper, sun stone, any sparkling crystal quartz spheres

Festival foods: Red and yellow fruits and vegetables, spices, honey, ham and fatty meats, butter and cheese, mead and red wine

Angel: Michael, archangel of the sun, noon, fire and the summer; dressed in red and gold, carrying a golden sword and the scales of justice and with a golden halo and shining wings

God and goddess: Llew or Lugh the sun god in his earth god role, as king, wise farmer and protector of the homestead, land and flocks. His goddess in the Celtic tradition whom he crowned with gold at their formal wedding was Macha, a beautiful solar goddess who welcomed Llew as her equal

The place on the wheel

Alban Heruin is Gaelic for 'the light of the shore' and is the height of the light year and so the festival of power and triumph.

Druid ceremonies are still held at sundown on the solstice eve, and at dawn and noon on the summer solstice itself at sacred stone circles such as Stonehenge.

This is the sacred marriage of the earth and sky or the land/king and the Goddess/priestess, in which the Goddess, or her representative, in later times a married woman of rank from the local settlement, casts the wedding bouquet, made of brilliantly coloured flowers and fragrant flowering herbs on a hilltop fire to add her power to the sun.

The God reaches his full power and maturity, but knows that after the festival he will begin to lose this vitality. Even at the height of his joy, there is an awareness that even he is subject to the powers of the changing seasons.

Because the Goddess loved him so deeply, bonfires were lit and sun wheels thrown down the hillsides to delay the moment when his power must wane – and he must leave her.

In the light god cycle, the dark twin is reborn, but cannot yet challenge the light god though the power is starting to drain from him.

Marking the festival in the modern world

* Watch the sunset on the evening before the summer solstice and set your alarm just before dawn so you can greet the sun on this most powerful of days.

* Plan to do five courageous actions or make five powerful assertions during the day.

- ❋ Say goodbye to the sun as it sets on the day of the solstice, if possible having enjoyed the day outdoors. Light a gold candle and make a final solstice empowerment. Blow out the candle and welcome whatever the future brings.

- ❋ Go to an old stone circle such as Stonehenge in Wiltshire and watch the sun rise over the marker stone. Join in the celebrations of tourists and pagans alike. If you are lucky enough to see the sun shining at noon on the solstice day either on one of the stones in the stone circle or on the space between two oak trees, it is believed you can enter into other dimensions.

- ❋ Cast golden petals into the air a handful at a time on the solstice evening before dark, picturing your talents and ventures succeeding and abundance coming to you. Where they land represents in the old tradition places of buried treasure and symbolises new or buried talents you can develop to realise your hidden potential over the next six weeks.

- ❋ Set any small items of gold jewellery in the summer solstice morning sunlight for a few hours to transfer the power of the sun into your life as you wear the jewellery. If it is a dull day, use a lighted gold candle.

- ❋ Make summer solstice water, the most potent sun water of the year, by leaving water in a gold-coloured dish surrounded by yellow flowers from dusk on the solstice eve until noon on the longest day. This is especially healing and empowering and you can keep it in clear glass bottles to drink or add to bath water to give you energy and confidence.

- ❋ Have a jewellery party and bring along all the pieces you no longer want to exchange with friends.

- ❋ Make a small solstice sun garden, either indoors or outside, using the flowering herbs of midsummer such as vervain and St John's Wort, sun herbs such as rosemary and chamomile and small yellow or golden flowers. Plant them in the form of a wheel and fill in the centre with tiny golden crystals or glass nuggets. You can breathe in the golden light from your living sun wheel whenever you feel tired or anxious.

* Light sun oils (frankincense, juniper, rosemary, orange or benzoin) or burn them as incense to bring the power of the sun into your home or workplace.

* At any opportunity on the solstice days, open your arms and legs wide, palms outstretched and uppermost. Raise your face upwards to the light and breathe it in. Picture the light flowing around your body and filling it with sunshine gold. On your out breath, sigh out through your mouth any darkness, sorrow or fear. When you feel full of sunshine, say nine times slowly,

> *I am filled with the light. I am pure light.*

Recall the feeling at other times when you are exhausted and call back the solstice light into yourself.

8 The Wheel of the Year – from Darkness Back to Light

The final four points on the Wheel of the Year take us on the slow descent into the darker, colder days and eventually back to light. This descending part of the wheel belongs to the ancestors and to reconciliation and integration of the past with the present so that we can face the future and the lighter times feeling both rested and restored.

The wise ancestors

The ancestors are an essential part of the Samhain or Halloween festival, not as spooks but as wise and beloved family members who are deceased but still welcome. Yet even in the festivals of the ascending or growing light, the ancestors were invited and asked for blessings as a continuing part of the family. This is very different from the modern concept of deceased relatives as ghosts only to be contacted through mediums for messages.

Whatever point of the wheel's turning you are celebrating or indeed on any family occasions, I believe it is important to remember your personal ancestors who once gathered in the harvest or danced round the maypole in the sunshine or picked a few flowers from the soot-covered hedgerows on the way to the factory at the beginning of spring.

I believe also that as we celebrate the festivals in the present we make psychic and not just genetic markers as the future ancestors of our descendants. In this way, hundreds of years from now people who will still notice the nights getting darker, can tune into our feelings in the places where we are dancing or lighting our fires.

The essential personalities of the more recently deceased were still regarded as part of the living family as recently as early Victorian times. It is only in the modern world that the idea of the family ghosts celebrating the passing of the year with you is sometimes thought strange. In earlier times, what could have been more natural, as the herds were brought down from the hills and the fields for the winter, and the herdsmen and women huddled close to the hearth, than the family ancestors also moving close to the fire for warmth? It would not have seemed strange to our forebears that deceased great grandparents would want to be present at the birth of a new family member, or at a christening or a wedding. Even in today's world, a number of people have told me how a friend or newcomer at a family christening or wedding has asked about an older man or woman who was peeping into the infant's cradle or watching the bride throw her bouquet, with a proud smile. Invariably the description of the older relative matches a deceased relative who has returned to share the occasion.

The ancestors in societies ancient and modern

Norse neopaganism echoes the early forms of the Viking ceremonies described in the sagas such as the *Prose Edda* recorded by the Icelandic Christian historian and statesman Snorri Sturluson (1179–1241). He portrayed the Viking ancestors as an integral part of the interwoven web of every person's fate and so they were routinely welcomed and honoured at the harrow or family or tribal outdoor stone altar. The same is true in modern druidry and Wicca where the ancestors are invited as guests to all seasonal celebrations and to special rituals. Indeed, at a Wiccan funeral the priest or priestess officiating ends by telling the deceased person that they always have a place in the circle and in the hearts of those present.

In indigenous societies the ancestors are still regularly consulted in divination about the growth of the crops, the welfare of the animals and other matters of daily life. For example, among the Maoris of New Zealand, it is believed ancestors appear in the form of animals or particular birds, whose presence and behaviour indicates, for example, that a new home is blessed or that it is unsafe to travel. In other societies, too, from Africa to the Orient, wrongdoing by a family member is seen as offensive to the ancestors. Indeed the societies where the ancestors still play a significant role are usually those where the living elderly are well cared for and respected by younger members of the family.

According to evidence pieced together from archaeological artefacts and by studying contemporary societies who practise the older ways, the wise ancestors featured strongly in many of the old seasonal celebrations, since it was thought that they would send help to make the crops grow and to bring a good harvest.

From about 3500 BCE it seems a number of these agricultural rituals centred on long barrows and passage graves. You can still visit some of these old sites, for example, West Kennet Long Barrow tomb near Marlborough in Wiltshire. This is the largest chambered long barrow in Britain and was built about 3600 BCE. In Neolithic times, the grave was used for ceremonies in which the bones of the ancestors were carried with great reverence from the long barrow, where they were carefully preserved, to nearby Windmill Hill. These rituals were carried out especially at Samhain (Halloween) and in the springtime to ask favour on the sowing. It was thought that the ancestors could intervene directly with the deities on behalf of the living and so the burial mounds had doors in them, a kind of halfway house where the ancestors could be visited and asked for advice. You can still follow the route on foot today and picture how the tribes must have felt as they walked along the windswept tracks.

The wise ancestors and the changing year

As you travel through your personal wheel of the year, recalling your personal ancestors and perhaps people from past times in cultures to which you feel an instinctive connection, you can draw on their experiences and strengths in your imagination. For the seasonal connection with the past is not only through your genes, but spiritually as you use the same herbs and flowers that people have worked with through centuries at the same time of the year. Within the eight spokes of the wheel there is a more detailed interconnected web of experiences past and present that is at the heart of both older and modern paganism and is an antidote to the isolation and impersonal nature of both rural and urban living.

There may be a particular relative you associate with each festival. For example, for me, Lughnassadh, the first corn harvest at the beginning of August is the festival of my late father Jack. Jack worked in a factory in the centre of industrial Birmingham. Every year at the beginning of August we went to Wales for two weeks to stay in a caravan. Rain or shine, and wearing his cap to hide his bald patch, my father would pick his way over the stony beach every morning and paddle in the sea. Then, for Lughnassadh holiday feast we would go in the afternoon to what I thought was an amazingly posh hotel on the seafront in the nearby town for what was called a plain tea (I think basically bread and jam) with the tea in a silver teapot. So bread and jam is always part of my Lughnassadh feast, plus a trip on 1 August when possible to paddle in the sea in honour of Jack, for whom the harvest of a year's work was being able to pay for the holiday.

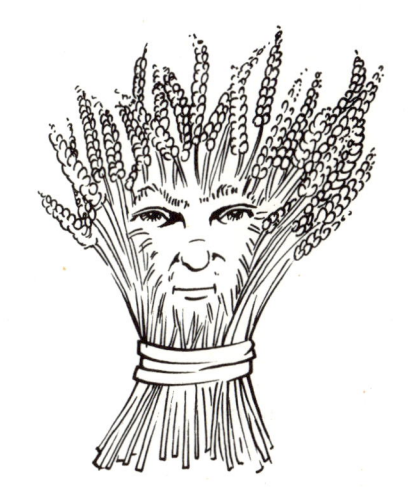

Lughnassadh or Lammas (31 July–2 August)

Focus of the period: Justice and natural justice or karma; human and personal rights issues; freedom from abuse of any kind; for partnerships, both personal and legal or business; for signing contracts or property matters; promotion and career advancement and the regularising of personal finances; for holidays and journeys to see friends and family or on business; for the renewal of promises, loyalty and fidelity; for willing sacrifice for a long-term gain or made in love, trusting the cosmos to provide by giving without seeking immediate return; also for all matters concerning people in their forties and fifties

Key words: Justice, fulfilment, sacrifice

Emphasis of the festival: Transformation, bread

Energies of the season: Waning

Symbols: Any straw object such as a corn dolly, a corn knot, a straw hat or a straw animal tied with red ribbon; harvest flowers such as poppies or cornflowers (they can be silk or dried); a container of mixed cereals; dried grasses or long ears of grain; stones with natural holes; bread and dough

Tree: Alder

Incense, flower and herbs: Cedarwood, cinnamon, fenugreek, ginger and heather, myrtle, poppies and sunflowers, any dark yellow, deep blue or brown-gold flowers

Candle colours: Golden brown or dark yellow

Crystals: Banded agates, dark yellow and any brown jasper, fossils, fossilised wood, titanium aura

Festival foods: Homemade bread, milk, cereal products, elderberry and fruit wines, strawberries, berry pies, fruit juices, potato soup, popcorn, chicken

Angel: Sachiel, archangel of the grain harvest and of abundance. He wears robes of deep blue and purple, carries sheaves of corn and baskets of food, and has a rich purple and golden halo and blue and purple wings

God and goddess: Eriu/Macha as Irish goddess of the land. As Lugh or Llew (sun and grain god) was dying, the earth goddess symbolically accepted his power and so ensured that the sun would continue to shine even after he had died

The place on the wheel

This is the festival of the first grain harvest.

The god promises to defend and die for the land. The sun or grain god agrees to be cut down in the form of the last sheaf of grain to be harvested and his spirit descends into the earth, back into the mother's womb, to be reborn on the midwinter celebration as the infant sun king.

The decisive battle of the light and dark twin cannot take place until the autumn equinox six weeks later and so the myths divide again. Some versions say the fatal blow to the light twin is delivered at Lughnassadh but the light twin lingers wounded for another six weeks until the autumn equinox.

In both the pre-Christian and Christian tradition called Lammas or loaf mass, a loaf baked from the first harvested sheaf was offered on the altar.

In Celtic-influenced lands on 15 August, at the feast of the Assumption of the Virgin Mary into heaven, a bannock was made from bread and milk to be broken by the father of the household and given to the family to ensure sufficient bread throughout the year on the family table (and his willingness to work to provide it).

Marking the festival in the modern world

- ✤ Bake your own bread on Lughnassadh Eve, forming the loaf in the shape of a figure who can either represent the grain or corn spirit or the grain mother. Add milk to the mix and as you stir it in turn with friends and family or alone, make wishes for abundance and the harvest you wish to reap during the coming months. Ask also, if appropriate, for suitable employment. When your bread is cooked, eat or share it and name the transformations you seek in your life or the world. At dawn put out any remaining crumbs for the wild birds to eat.

- ✤ Bake extra bread or fruit pies to give to neighbours and colleagues who live alone and may not often cook for themselves.

- ✤ Cut down an area of weeds or overgrown grass in your garden or tidy up indoor plants. Alternatively, spend a day on an organised project clearing a local wilderness. This symbolically generates the energies to clear the way ahead in your life and relationships.

- ✤ Light an orange candle every evening for a week around the festival. Sprinkle a pinch of salt in the flame to let go of any injustice that cannot be put right but which needs to be released from your mind in order to set you free. Then add a small pinch of dried sage to the flame and name a blessing, however small, or an unexpected kindness you have received in the previous few months. At the end of the week, make a practical gesture or spoken small blessing to someone who does not merit it.

❋ Alternatively, if you feel you have been unjustly treated and cannot put matters right, knot dried grasses or pluck the petals of a dying flower, one for each injustice, and cast them into running water or bury them when planting late-flowering seeds or autumn flowers.

❋ Use corn or dried grasses to create corn knots and corn mother figures (with featureless head, arms, body and legs) tied with red and blue threads. Hang them in the home through the winter to bring protection and burn them on the first Monday after Twelfth Night (6 January) or on next year's spring equinox fires.

❋ Make a corn spirit by creating an abstract shape from ears of corn tied together. Burn him on the last day of Lughnassadh, just before dusk on 2 August, and scatter some of the ashes in your garden or on indoor plants to bring abundance to the home during the winter.

❋ Arrange journeys to see friends and relations or write or telephone, making definite plans to meet, as this is a time when tribes would get together before the long winter. Try to take an impromptu weekend away to fill you with energy for the coming months.

❋ Make a final effort to resolve an unfair official or neighbourhood dispute or a disagreement over an inheritance or property matter, if necessary by changing tactic or the person representing you.

Alban Elued or autumn equinox (21–23 September)

Focus of the period: The completion of tasks; the fruition of long-term goals; for mending quarrels and forgiving yourself for past mistakes; for recovering money owed and overcoming debt problems; for assessing gain and loss; for family relationships and friendships; for material security for the months ahead; for abundance in all aspects of your life; for issues of job security or the need to consolidate finances; for all matters concerning retirement and older people; for the resolution or management of chronic heath problems

Key words: Reconciliation, assessment, storing assets

Emphasis of the festival: Reconciliation, fruit and nuts

Energies of the season: Balanced

Symbols: Copper-coloured, yellow or orange leaves, willow boughs, harvest fruits such as apples, berries, nuts, copper or bronze coins, pottery geese

Tree: Apple

Incenses, flower and herbs: Ferns, geranium, Michaelmas daisies, myrrh, pine, sandalwood, Solomon's seal, all small-petalled purple and blue flowers

Candle colours: Blue and green

Crystals: Aqua aura, blue lace agate, all calcites, chalcedony, rose quartz

Festival foods: The finest of the harvest, fruits, vegetables, jam, nuts, apple pies, geese (sacred to St Michael whose festival falls on 29 September), game, cider, barley wine and ale

Angel: Rismuch, angel of agriculture and cultivated land, wearing every imaginable shade of brown, carrying a scythe and a hoe as symbol that he is conserver of the land and the crops. His symbols are sheaves of wheat and ears of corn, and dishes of seeds and nuts

God and goddess: A sad pairing. The twin god myth blames Llew the Welsh god of light's faithless wife Blodeuwedd or Arthur the Sun King's Queen Guinevere for the king's demise. This was because the queen transferred her love to the dark twin, called here Goronwy or Lancelot. She is said to have given the dark twin the secret of the light twin's fatal weakness and so brought about his destruction.

But even these treachery myths reflect the need for the earth goddess to mate with the dark twin at the autumn equinox so the new dark twin can be born at the summer solstice and the wheel continue to turn. The wounded Llew is left waiting in the body of a dying eagle to be released by death, while Arthur is carried to Avalon by the ladies of the lake (including, in some myths, Guinevere herself). Blodeuwedd takes the form of an owl, the grandmother of winter, which links her with the old goddess who predominates at the next change point on the wheel.

Place on the wheel

Alban Elued is Gaelic for 'light on the water' and refers to the sun moving away over the water to shine on the Isles of the Blest, leaving the world with encroaching darkness.

Ancient tales tell of the death of the old hunter god at the hands of his successor or by offering himself to the huntsmen in the form of a magnificent stag. The early hunter gods were often portrayed with antlers, for example the Celtic and Gallic Cernunnos.

If you follow the other myth, the slain corn god is now in the underworld, the womb of the mother, awaiting rebirth.

While the goddess of the slain grain god mourns for her love she must prepare for the harvest over which she presides. But she is tired herself and getting heavier with the light child.

The dark twin finally challenges and kills the light brother who returns to the earth or the womb, as the two legends merge again.

The gathering of the second or green harvest of fruit, nuts and vegetables takes place at this time; also the final grain harvest, the storing of resources for the winter and barter for goods not available or scarce. The forerunner of the modern harvest festival, these feasts of abundance and the offering of the finest of the harvest to the deities were considered part of the bargain between humans and deities.

Marking the festival in the modern world

❋ Make a list of what needs to be done urgently, a second list of less pressing but necessary tasks and a final list of those matters that are best left, some of which may be things you did not want to do anyway. Throw away the third list and draw up a realistic timescale for the completion of the other tasks.

❋ Contact an old friend or a family member with whom you have lost touch. Also decide if there is anyone with whom you would like to reduce or cease communication who is undermining your confidence or making you feel unnecessarily guilty.

❋ Give up a bad habit or work to overcome a fear or phobia that is holding you back from doing things.

❋ Buy or make seasonal fruit jam and hold an old-fashioned tea or coffee party to bring different generations together.

❋ Visit a seasonal farmers' market or art and craft fair and maybe take along something you have created to sell.

❋ Have a sale on eBay, go to a local car boot sale or set up a garage sale to offload items you do not want to dust or store through the winter (a pre-winter clear-out).

❋ Hold an auction of hoarded personal treasures and send the money to a charity that relieves famine.

❋ Stand by the sea or flowing water at sunset and cast pebbles or shells into the dying light on the water to cast off all regrets, resentments, sorrows, failures and unfinished business from the previous months that you do not wish to carry forward into the winter. Look for something on the shore or riverbank to take home as a token of the gifts you carry forward with you from the previous months.

❋ Take a bowl containing equal numbers of nuts or berries and seeds and work outdoors. Name a success or achievement from the previous months that has materialised by the autumn equinox and eat a nut or berry; then name a failure or loss and cast a seed into the ground. Continue until you have eaten and shed the same number and can think of no more; bury the rest beneath a fruit or nut-bearing tree.

✤ Sweep up autumn leaves into a pile; jump up and down in it as you did when a child, expressing joy at the promise of the coming days, naming opportunities and all you can and will achieve in winter. Finally, scatter the leaves and let the good and the bad, the gains and the losses be carried equally on the wind.

✤ Prepare a feast of fruit and vegetables, of bread, cider and barley wine or fruit cup and warming soups and hold an equinox party. Make offerings to the land of barley wine, ale or mead and bread by scattering a little on the ground. Pass round a communal cup to everyone present or fill everyone's glasses and ask them to drink and make a blessing on the occasion or on people and places where there is hunger or poverty.

✤ Contact anyone from whom you are estranged, sending autumn flowers or a plant you have nurtured or a small basket of produce as a peace offering. If your reconciliatory gestures are rejected, at least you can move forward, knowing you have tried. Alternatively, help an organisation concerned with peace.

✤ Climb to the top of a hill at sunset on equinox night and, as the ancients did, say goodbye to the animals who will soon be hibernating and to any birds who are or will be migrating, and wish them well.

Samhain, the beginning of the Celtic winter and the Celtic New Year (31 October–2 November)

Focus of the period: Remembering the family ancestors; for looking both backwards to the past and into the future; for protection, psychic and physical; for overcoming fears, especially of ageing and mortality; for retired people and those in their 70s and 80s; for marking the natural transition between one stage of life and the next; for laying old ghosts, psychological as well as psychic

Key words: Letting go of the need for total control, mortality and immortality

Emphasis of the festival: Honouring and learning from the past, nature spirits, fey energies

Energies of the season: Waning, the temporary rule of chaos over order

Symbols: Apples, pumpkins, nuts and autumn leaves, mingled with evergreens as a promise that life continues, salt, scary masks, fantastic costumes and lanterns, statues of fairies and magical animals like unicorns

Tree: Silver fir

Incenses, flower and herbs: Cypress, dittany, ferns, garlic, nutmeg, pine, sage, thyme; large white flowers, rose petals and rose fragrances, spices

Candle colour: Orange, purple

Crystals: Dark amethyst, jet, lapis lazuli, obsidian (apache tear), smoky quartz, sodalite

Festival foods: Roast beef, salted fish and pickles, pumpkin pie and soup, baked and toffee apples with spices, baked potatoes, spiced or mulled wine, candies and sweets of all kinds in dishes. Cook and eat the favourite foods of relatives who have died or use old family recipes

Angel: Cassiel, archangel of compassion and silence. He is pictured as bearded, riding a dragon and wearing dark robes, with indigo flames sparking from his halo. He rules over good luck and games of chance, so competitive games and divination are popular at this time

God and goddess: The crone or grandmother goddess, for example the Scottish and Irish goddess Caillieach who rules the winter months. She cares for the animals that live on open moorlands during the winter and older people who may feel the cold but do not have enough money for adequate heating. The god energy is divided between the slain grain lord in the underworld awaiting rebirth and the trickster twin Goronwy. Goronwy takes advantage of the goddess's absence from the world when she visits the underworld to share the sorrows of death with her man, to ascend the throne, misrule and cause chaos through the world

The place on the wheel

Samhain means summer's end, the time when the herds were brought down from the hills and family members returned to the homestead for the winter. It was believed the ancestors would likewise return and be welcomed at the family hearth.

The animals were either slaughtered or cleansed ritually by the Halloween fires and then kept in barns. Being the Celtic New Year and the time when the Goddess leaves her creation for three days (all the time that is allowed to her), this is when the otherworld releases fairies and mischievous spirits not just the benign family ancestors.

The Christianised Halloween is called All Hallows Eve. This and the following two days, All Saints and All Souls days (1 and 2 November), are, especially in lands where Catholicism is strong, occasions when the family dead are remembered and honoured. For example, in France families dress in their finest clothes and visit cemeteries where graves are adorned with displays of flowers and photographs. It was once believed the dead returned to the Isle of Mont St Michel in Brittany on 1 November as what is now the church on top of the mount and the golden statue of Michael was once considered an entrance to the Celtic otherworld guarded by the wise druidesses who made their home on the island for hundreds of years.

It is this reverence for the ancestors that neopagans emphasise on Halloween and the days after, though some still have a fun spooky party for children and friends. So too do many neopagans practise divination on Halloween night to discover the opportunities for the year ahead at a time when past, present and future are so close.

Marking the festival in the modern world

* In traditional style, hollow out a pumpkin and place a lighted candle inside. Set the pumpkin in a window facing the road for the three days until dusk on 2 November. This will protect you from all harm but will welcome home the family ancestors. The light will connect you emotionally with living relatives who are far away.

* It was believed that if you listened to the wind at a crossroads on Halloween just before midnight you would hear all you needed to know for the year ahead. Spend time outdoors on Halloween Eve, listening to the wind in the trees, the sound of the sea, water running over stones or birdsong. You may hear words in the leaves or wind or in your mind that explain matters that have been troubling you.

* Alternatively, stay indoors and make eight holes (instead of a face) in the sides of a second hollowed-out pumpkin. Each window represents one of the eight festivals. Place a lighted candle inside. Peer through each hole to see into other dimensions and receive wisdom about each of the six-week periods in turn, beginning with Halloween. Revolve the pumpkin anticlockwise to look into each. Stare hard into each window, blink and an image will flash before you to reveal an opportunity or unexpected assistance or strengths for the approximate six-week period ahead. Begin with the six weeks after Halloween.

* If you are seeking love, eat salted herring before bed and it is said you will dream of your true love bringing you a drink of water in your dream.

* Alternatively, play the traditional druid apple-bobbing game of picking an apple by its stalk with your teeth from a bucket of water. Take the apple home and at midnight eat the apple while brushing your hair and looking into a mirror by candlelight. It is said that the image of your true love will appear in the glass at the first stroke of midnight.

* If you are playing apple bobbing with others, the first to pick an apple will be the first married.

* You can, of course, use your favourite form of divination, such as Tarot cards or runes, to ask questions about the 12 months ahead. Do this at 10 pm or just before midnight as these are the most potent times.

❈ Find out about a family ancestor with whom you feel a strong connection. During the week before Halloween, try to visit the place where the person lived, to connect with your historical roots. Alternatively, go to an industrial or local history museum where you can see the kind of implements and tools your chosen ancestor would have used and the clothes and shoes they would have worn. Either in the place they came from or once lived, or in the museum, sit quietly and picture your ancestor in your mind. Focus especially on an image of their feet and shoes, and say softly or think,

May I walk in your shoes for a while?

Stand up and begin to walk slowly, imagining your ancestor walking beside you until gradually your footsteps and feet merge. You may experience flashes of scenes from their life that you never knew about before and you may share their emotions. Finally, you will feel the connection fading and your footsteps separating. Say,

Go in peace and with thanks and blessings.

❈ If you have not already started to do so, resolve to research your family tree in the days after Halloween or find a family member who would enjoy doing so. Then, by next Halloween, you will have a much fuller picture of your roots.

❈ On Halloween Eve or on one of the two evenings afterwards, cook favourite family recipes passed down through the generations, get out old photographs and tell family stories and legends. If you are alone, recall these stories or record some of them for the future, maybe even as the basis for a short story or novel. The recipes and customs could be written down as a cookery book.

❈ At a quiet time on the evening of 1 November, place a protective clove of garlic on a west-facing window and light an orange candle, saying,

May only goodness and love enter here.

Hold a favourite possession of a beloved deceased relative and speak words of love. Then ask the relative to give you a sign that they are with you. The candle may flicker or you may feel their presence or a soft touch on your shoulder or hair. Your relative will not frighten you by appearing unless this is what you want but you may hear soft words in your mind. After a few moments the connection will fade. Blow out the candle and say,

Go in peace and blessings and with my love.

You may dream of the person during the night or hear their favourite music or smell their favourite flowers somewhere unexpectedly the following day.

✤ Gaze into a fire or candle flame and sprinkle sandalwood, cedar and juniper berries on to the flame or flames. Images of past worlds and maybe past lives will emerge spontaneously in the embers or flame or in your mind. These fragrances are believed to have been used to bring visions of the past from the Archangel Azrael.

✤ On 2 November, if you do not have one already, set up a small table covered by a white cloth where you can keep mementoes of loved ones who have passed on. For example, you could display a piece of jewellery or watch belonging to the loved one and pictures of your family ancestors. Keep fresh fragrant flowers there and on a special family anniversary, at Halloween or, if you wish, once a week on a Friday or Saturday light a white candle, send your deceased relatives blessings, perhaps read aloud their favourite poem or prayer or play their favourite music and ask for their blessings on your life and family. The Ancient Egyptians had altars where they left offerings for the Ka or soul of their deceased relatives and sent blessings that the ancestor's name might live on.

Alban Arthuran, Yule or midwinter solstice (20–22 December)

Focus of the festival: The rebirth of light and hope; for domestic happiness and security, family togetherness, anything to do with the home and property and for financial security; for long-term money ventures; for patience and accepting what cannot be changed; for very old people; for carers of the elderly, sick or vulnerable; for welcoming home travellers and the return of people you miss from the past; for restoring enthusiasm and health in those worn down by illness or lack of hope

Key words: Hope, security and stability

Emphasis of the festival: Rekindling extinguished flames, light in the darkness

Energies of the season: Turning point as the energies begin to rise again from the lowest point

Symbols: Evergreen boughs, especially pine or fir; small logs of wood, especially oak, pine and ash; holly and ivy sprigs; gold coins and jewellery; red, green, white and gold candles; silver, red, green and gold ribbons and baubles; tiny wrapped presents to be opened on the solstice or a pre-Christmas celebration

Tree: Holly

Incenses, flowers and herbs: Bay, cedar, feverfew, frankincense and myrrh mixed, holly, juniper, pine, rosemary, sage and all spices, poinsettias, scarlet and white flowers

Candle colours: White, scarlet, gold, green, purple

Crystals: Amazonite, garnet, malachite, opal aura, snowflake obsidian, snow quartz

Festival foods: Roast pork (more recently turkey), thick meat and vegetables stews, mulled wine, cakes with marzipan and icing, rich fruit cake and puddings to represent the fruits, grains and riches of the Earth Mother (traditionally with silver and gold charms or coins hidden within), mince pies (in Christian tradition to represent the crib of Jesus), marzipan, a sweet rice and cinnamon pudding mix for the nature spirits (in Scandinavian countries), dates, small oranges, figs

Angel: Gabriel, archangel of the moon, who took the news to Mary that she would have a son, Jesus. Picture him in silver or clothed in the blue of the night sky with a mantle of stars and a crescent moon for his halo, holding a golden horn and a white lily or, alternatively, a lantern in his right hand and a mirror made of jasper in his left

God and goddess: The three sisters of Fate, known in different traditions as the Matrones in Ancient Rome, the Norns in Scandinavia or the midwives who deliver the new sun king. In some legends the Celtic maiden goddess or Saint Brighid acts as midwife. The infant sun king or light twin and his mother, the Virgin Mary of Christianity, or the Ancient Egyptian Isis who gave birth to her son Horus in a cave in secrecy on the midwinter solstice

The place on the wheel

Alban Arthuran is Gaelic for 'the light of Arthur' and refers to the rebirth of Arthur as the divine child called the Mabon in Celtic spirituality. The festival celebrates the restoration of the power of the sun and the almost imperceptible return of the light and with it hope of lighter and longer days and even spring.

The sun god is reborn after the fear that the world will be overwhelmed by darkness on the shortest day of the year.

As the dark twin knows his power is on the wane, he watches jealously the attention being paid to his newborn brother.

At this time, in hunting and agricultural societies, there was a natural fear about food supplies not lasting the rest of the winter, especially if the weather ahead was hard.

At the midwinter solstice and during the later 12 days of Christmas, people held feasts of the finest of the food as a magical gesture to attract abundance. In the Norse tradition, this feast was shared with the deities and ancestors. People from time immemorial hung lights from evergreen branches to encourage the trees and vegetation to sprout greenery again and to give power to the sun.

In passage graves throughout the world, such as at Newgrange in Ireland, people waited in darkness for the first shaft of light on the solstice morning to illuminate the inner shrine. Their lanterns were then relit from a single flint.

Marking the festival in the modern world

* On the shortest day, as the day fades, either alone or with a group of friends or family, light from a small central gold candle, a circle of white candles. Light one from the other and say,

    > I/we will walk into the darkness in total trust, knowing that the light will return.

    Blow out the candles one by one round the circle in reverse order of lighting until only the central candle is alight. Wait in the growing darkness, trusting that all will be well and not worrying about the future. I once did this in the old stone circle at Avebury in Wiltshire with other druids. The only sound was the sheep and the only light a small flickering one in the centre of the shadowy stones. One of the three druidesses acting as the midwives asked,

    > Who will walk into the darkness with me? Who will take my hand?

    When you are ready, relight each candle, one from the other, beginning from the central gold one, naming for each candle relit what you seek as enlightenment, and the light you will offer the world in return.

* Alternatively, light a dark-coloured candle on the solstice eve or the night of the solstice day to represent the past that is gone or matters that now must be accepted. From it, light a white or gold candle for the future and then extinguish the dark candle. Let the white or gold candle burn, allowing the cosmos to send what you most need.

* Make or buy small dried herb sachets or bath products for friends and family as a gift in the build-up to Christmas, just to say 'I appreciate you'.

* Leave the Christmas shopping and, on the day of the solstice, go out into the countryside or local urban woodland and, if allowed, gather evergreen boughs with friends and family. Alternatively, find or buy sprigs of holly, ivy and mistletoe to represent the potential of new life. Make this also the evening you put up and decorate your solstice or Christmas tree, rather than doing it weeks beforehand, and mark the tree decorating and lighting as a special occasion. Choose a tree with roots that you can plant outdoors after Christmas. I have several of our family Christmas memory trees in the garden that I adorn with outdoor fairy lights.

* As you decorate the house, sing your favourite Christmas carols from childhood and some of the old songs with pagan overtones, such as 'The Holly and the Ivy', 'The Cherry Tree Carol' and 'Green Grow the Rushes'. Some of the modern commercialised recorded Christmas music has little to do with the old festival but is often

taught, even in schools, instead of more popular folk heritage songs that span different religions and cultures. Learn and sing songs from other winter festivals of light such as the Hindu Divali.

* As darkness falls on the day of the solstice, create a small fire outdoors or in a tiny metal pot and burn sprigs of yew, oak and holly. Alternatively, indoors, light a big white candle embedded in soil from Mother Earth and burn pine needles and rosemary. As you toss on each fragrant handful of sprigs or pinches of herbs, name someone who cannot be with you and those causes dear to your heart that will benefit from the renewed power of the sun.

* On solstice night also fill a metal bowl with cold water and either alone or with friends or family, in the age-old tradition, take it in turns to drip wax from the Christmas candles on to the surface of the water. Use candles that are the same colour all the way through, and hold one in each hand. Either ask specific questions or allow the images that appear to suggest opportunities in the weeks ahead. You will see a moving image as the molten wax falls on the surface of the water and a second more permanent image as the wax sets. The first will indicate an area of life or situation that will bear fruit over the coming days and weeks; the second will show ways in which you can maximise the energies of the ascending light of the season. Wash out the bowl between readings if you want to ask more questions.

* If you are seeking love, on solstice or Christmas Eve walk upstairs backwards while eating a piece of Christmas cake and place the crumbs beneath your pillow. You will dream of your true love or a secret admirer.

* French villagers, especially in Provence, once created their own *santons*, tiny nativity figures made from clay and often including village characters and local tradespeople. Take time with children or friends and family to fashion from self-hardening clay your own *santons* to paint and display. Include family members, pets and local characters. The scene can be adapted to illustrate the rebirth of the sun king or goddess myths. Set the *santons* around your tree or in a cave made from rocks and crystals.

9 The Pagan Workplace

The workplace can be more difficult to make and keep harmonious than the home, largely because we do not choose our colleagues. While good friendships and romances may spring up quite naturally at work, there may be people we would not wish to see out of office hours and one or two who seem deliberately to make the working day as hard as possible for us and others. We still have to co-exist and co-operate with these people during what may be a large part of our week, however, and so it is necessary to minimise the effect of any negative behaviour or unnecessary intrusion into our personal workspace and time, however well meant this may be. Often the most irritating interruptions are benignly intended, but if you work in a highly competitive environment and if you are naturally gentle and helpful, you can become exhausted or frequently upset by unfair criticism, gossip and pressure to fulfil unrealistic targets.

Applying neopagan principles in the workplace

Some workplaces are naturally supportive of the neopagan viewpoint of co-operation, integrity and valuing every person no matter how complex and time consuming or how little they can do for us in return. However, you may find it hard to maintain ethics and tolerance in larger impersonal organisations or multi-nationals with limited interest in local variations, which encourage conformity to some corporate ideal that seems to take little account of the people involved. Even if you work in the caring professions, concern and time for the needs of vulnerable individuals may be constrained by financial targets, under-resourcing of co-workers and equipment and top-heavy administration.

It may be that some day you will be able to work for or by yourself or with a partner, applying the standards you value and perhaps, if you wish, developing creative, therapeutic or spiritual gifts as a full-time occupation. With the opportunities offered by the internet, many people now run businesses from home that have worldwide connections, and it is immensely satisfying and in the tradition of early people to keep yourself and a family with what you produce, whether it be websites, film scripts, fine crafts, paintings or organic fruit and vegetables. However, as I have discovered, self-employment and working from the living-room table can bring different pressures, such as a less-than-structured day that can spill over into evenings and weekends and constant telephone, personal and mail intrusion.

Even if you do work in a large company, you can improve the energies in your own space and the positive effects will spread to improve the general atmosphere and certainly bring a more favourable response towards you and your work.

Neopaganism and business

Many neopagans are successful in business precisely because they are people-centred, are on the whole honest and try to see the best and the potential in every situation. They are also more likely to trust their intuition about opportunities and people, and to realise that what you put into your job in terms of time and effort brings personal satisfaction even if others seem to do very little and get away with it. Whether you are a therapist, or would like to open a New-Age store, write self-help books, run classes, make or sell herb and flower beauty products or healing remedies or run a wholefood restaurant or catering company, you will have daily pleasure in producing what you love.

Many neopagans do succeed in business, and if this is your dream I would recommend you make a start, even if only in a small way. Spend a few months working in a New-Age store before opening your own or, if you would like to run a home-based therapy or life-coaching business or to practise clairvoyance or mediumship, rent a room in a therapy centre or successful New-Age store while you are building up a client base. You can then gradually increase your hours through word of mouth, the best form of advertising. Book a table at any alternative health or psychic fair within reasonable travelling distance of your home and, even if at first you just break even, you can take along a pile of business cards, printed very cheaply, to distribute among already interested people. Take every chance to do lectures, for free if necessary in return for advertising and perhaps a table to sell your goods and services. Offer your products to local stores, take them along to any fairs or exhibitions, not just New-Age ones, and start your own mailing list.

The internet is the gateway to the wider public, so persuade a technologically minded teenager or employ a good web designer whose work you know or who is recommended, to advertise your events, services and goods (whether physical items or online courses or readings).

There is a misconception that if you follow pagan principles you should not charge for your expertise or ask a realistic price for what you sell, and that poverty equals spiritual worth. In fact, the more successful you are, the more you can help deserving people for nothing or cheaply. You also need to charge an economically viable rate for your time, services and expertise if you are to be taken seriously and thrive in an increasingly overcrowded market.

Finally, remember alternative-based businesses are businesses like any others and those few who wait for inspiration or for the cosmos to provide will not succeed – and in not succeeding, will miss the chance to do good as well as to earn a living.

The aura of the workplace

Your workplace will have an overall energy field or aura just like an individual human aura that has built up over years. If there is a lot of electrical or technological equipment, then the workplace aura will be highly charged and volatile, even before you add the personalities of the workers and the joys and sorrows of their lives in and out of work that make up their individual energy fields.

Highly charged does not necessarily equal efficient and even in a place where there are daily deadlines, a calm, relaxed and friendly atmosphere makes focus and accuracy easier than if everyone is constantly screaming, rushing round with one ear clamped to a mobile phone and worrying about the task after next before the current one has been completed.

In a recent UK survey of more than 1000 office workers carried out by Office Angels, 26 per cent wanted the re-introduction of a tea, coffee, sandwiches and cakes lady instead of machines or having to go out for snacks, 39 per cent wanted the revival of the full-hour lunch break and 33 per cent asked for an annual work outing. Half did not want to eat lunch at their desks while a third disliked open-plan offices. All these are indications of the need for workplaces to become more friendly and homely but also to allow for privacy and space.

Improving the energies of your workplace

As in the home, informal Feng Shui in the workplace has become very popular. A number of the most widely adopted principles are identical to those embedded in Westernised folk custom as sound principles by which people have traditionally organised their lives.

* ✤ If you have sympathetic employers or managers, campaign for frequently refurbished work and rest areas in lively but relaxing colours with comfortable furnishings, softer lighting instead of fluorescent overhead lights, greenery in workspaces and perfumed soap in wash rooms. Ask for toasters, refrigerators, good-quality coffee and juices, and basic foods, such as fruit, for workers to prepare nutritious, energy-giving snacks. In workplaces where people feel at home, there is a definite increase in productivity and less absenteeism and temper flare-ups.

- ✤ If you have a very metallic, high-tech Air-orientated office (see page 211), try to soften the atmosphere with gentle earth colours (yellow and brown) and where possible thick, comfortable fabrics or even a cushion or two.

- ✤ Regular de-cluttering and spring cleaning your workspace not only helps the energies flow, but is a psychological boost to efficiency and, on a practical level, saves you time as you don't have to sort through e-mails and piles of papers for vital information. If you have messy colleagues, you should not act as their parent, but if you keep your personal area and any essential communal places tidy, you may influence them to be more organised in time.

- ✤ Put aside a time each week for archiving or removing old e-mails and responding to any that you have been avoiding.

- ✤ Plants in your office will absorb harsh electrical impulses from computers, phones and so on and if positioned on the window ledge will stop pylon or phone-mast pollution entering the room. Remember to care for them and to rotate them to rest, particularly hard-working ones. Workplace energy fields generally respond better to greenery and growing pot plants than cut flowers.

- ✤ Do not have sharp or spiky plants like cacti near your phone or computer, or a paper shredder or cutter near them or the main door as in both Feng Shui and Westernised energy balancing these are considered bad for harmonious relations. Watch and you will notice that many people do seem to get irritable around cacti or when shredding paper.

- ✤ Keep clocks in good working order and accurate, especially after a change to summer or winter times. Keep their faces dust free and polished.

- ✤ Gentle sounds encourage the flow of the life force, and a small wind chime or bells as part of a mobile over your workspace will encourage good fortune energies, opportunities and possible promotion or advancement.

- ✤ Use background fragrances, such as lavender and rose to encourage gentle words and empathy between people, orange to promote a sense of well-being and lemon bergamot for overcoming lethargy.

- ✤ Have a computer screensaver of your children, grandchildren, partner or pet looking happy or a beautiful place you have visited or are aiming to travel to one day, to give you extra positive vibes.

❋ If you work in a restrictive environment or regularly stay in impersonal hotels on business trips, try to imprint something of your own personality on the space. Use as a focus a small personal item you have had for years that makes you happy, a small framed photograph or two and a few favourite crystals. Try to pick up some brightly coloured flowers or a pot plant on the way from the station or airport. You can leave the plant for the next guest or the person who cleans your room.

Overcoming bad energies in the workplace

Sometimes buildings, especially in cities, near docks or on industrial estates may be built on land with soured energies, whether caused by unhappy events on the land in the past or earth energies that have become blocked because of a main road, phone mast or major industrial development in the area. Converted prisons, factories or hospitals, especially mental hospitals, carry a lot of accumulated sadness, particularly if conditions were bad within them during their former use.

If you notice a lot of workplace absence or feel frequently unwell or exhausted yourself at work, amethyst crystals (especially small geodes) and green plants are the best remedies. Place them on window ledges, wash the amethysts weekly, leaving them to dry naturally, and make sure the plants are well watered. Even if used only in your own area, amethysts and green plants can be more effective than you might imagine in lifting the general energies.

People in the workplace

❋ Be active in planning regular works' barbecues and family events so that you get to know your colleagues and their families out of work. In this way you will be more supportive of one another in times of family crisis and also tend to have more family support for your workplace. Regular teen days when older children come to work for the day and help out are another way of bringing work and home closer.

- If you are an employer or manager in a smaller workplace make sure you share breaks with your workers where possible, bring cakes on birthdays and take your turn in making coffee and fetching the sandwiches.

- The simplest but most effective way of improving a workplace atmosphere is to smile when you greet people and to offer praise and positivity, as this is self-fulfilling and soon spreads.

- Personal contact is not always possible in a larger workplace. If you find that you tend to communicate with colleagues in the same office by phone or e-mail, try whenever possible, to walk across the room or even down a floor to talk to them. Talking face to face often solves problems in a fraction of the time and avoids possible misunderstandings.

- Think about the message you are giving to a client or colleague if you interrupt a conversation with them to answer your phone or check an e-mail.

- Believe in yourself, your products and your value, and take each situation as it comes and each person as you find them. Do not be over modest and undersell your abilities as that is undervaluing the client who has trust in you and believes that you are the best person to help them.

Crystals in the workplace

- A clear crystal sphere or a glass paperweight near a telephone or on top of a computer, is considered fortunate in both Eastern and Westernised energy balancing. The perfect spherical shape and the sparkling crystal bring in advantageous business calls and e-mails and when it catches the sunlight the quartz radiates fresh energies and clears stagnant ones. It will also prevent negative energies filtering into your aura. Wash the sphere or paperweight regularly and leave it to dry naturally.

- Green and black malachite crystals will guard you from the more adverse effects of modern equipment. Have one at each of the four corners of your computer or any other technical machine you regularly use.

- Use pastel crystals such as amethyst, rose quartz and blue lace agate to improve the energies in an Air-orientated office.

- Kunzite or sugilite, both recently discovered stones, should be kept in any vehicle you use in connection with work to keep you safe while commuting and to prevent road rage.

- If you work for yourself and have a shop or store room for items that will be sent out to customers, you can guide business to your company premises by hiding a pointed clear quartz crystal on either side of the door or gate. Position these so that they point inwards slightly and then use more pairs at regular intervals, always hidden and pointing inwards, to mark an invisible pathway of energy to guide people into and round your premises (even if they are actually ordering online). I have used this method successfully, hiding two pointed crystals, pointing inwards, in the two front corners of a shop window.

- In a shop, use more hidden crystals to direct the feet and eye gaze of your customers. Think about the way customers walk around the shop, stopping finally at the till to pay. Experiment with positioning crystals on either side of the invisible path, pointing towards any special displays where you would like customers to pause.

- You could put pictures of inward-pointing crystals as decorations on catalogue or web pages for the same effect.

- If you use a computer in your business, direct one crystal point diagonally towards your computer on the left as you face it and one pointing diagonally outwards on the right-hand side of the computer, again at the front, to encourage internet business.

- Keep a sparkling yellow citrine, called the merchant's stone, in a till or cash box and if you have a new business, display the first money you are given for a sale in a glass frame on the wall.

Workplace protection

The psychic shield technique is ancient. On his travels through the Near East, the Ancient Greek general Alexander the Great discovered a valley filled with huge diamonds that were guarded by poisonous serpents. Alexander ordered his soldiers to polish their shields so that they became like mirrors. As the soldiers advanced, the serpents saw their own reflections, became confused and stung one another to death, leaving the way clear for Alexander to take the treasure.

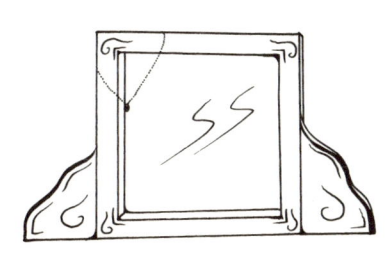

Use this same technique to create a protective shield around yourself in the workplace.

- ✤ If you are suffering spite or gossip, any shiny object on your desk between you and the approaching perpetrator is effective as a shield. Try the mirror of an open make-up compact, a small ornamental or swivel mirror or a stainless steel desk tidy. Alternatively, set a spare pair of spectacles, facing outwards on your desk or hang a long, unfastened necklace of clear glass or crystal beads behind you as a single strand from a high window catch or from a hook on the wall. This will reflect back any negativity moving towards you, especially when light catches the beads.

- ✤ As the person who is unfriendly, bitchy, bullying or super critical approaches, imagine the light from the reflective surface becoming incredibly bright and forming a shield in front of you, so that any negative words bounce back. Sit and smile calmly at the person as they speak to you, and they may move back involuntarily as the reflected force of their own tirade or sarcasm hits them. If you still feel intimidated, as they leave, pick up your chosen reflective surface and hold it towards their retreating figure, saying out loud or in your head if you can be overheard, 'You can have that back.' When possible, splash water on your chosen reflective surface.

- ✤ Alternatively, raise the hand you write with slightly so the palm is vertical and facing the person who is causing you problems, and push the air back towards them. This is one of the oldest protective gestures known to humankind, and pushes the negativity back to the sender. You are not cursing them, just sending back the negativity that rightly belongs to them.

- ✤ Use the same hand gesture towards the screen of your computer if you have received an unpleasant memo or e-mail.

- ✤ When you need to enter the lair of the office dragon or an autocratic executive, wear a silver- or gold-coloured pendant, necklace, bracelet or earrings, a shiny buckle or spectacles on a metal chain round your neck or carry a folder with a metallic cover or edges. Silver, copper and gold are very protective metals.

* If you feel angry or feel undervalued, compose an e-mail to the perpetrator saying exactly why you feel bad. Do not worry how petty it seems or how many grievances you list, but do not add any adverse comments, just state what you feel. Then read it through, delete it and wait. Sending the negativity back in your mind may, under the threefold law, cause a change of heart or even a climbdown by the perpetrator as you have sent back the energies. As a result you will feel better and even if you still have to deal with the matter, you will have had time to calm down and the other person may realise that they overreacted. I wish I had learned this years ago.

* In a noisy or stressful environment try occasionally to build in some peace, however brief, before you get a headache or lose your cool. Build in a quiet break somewhere green, maybe in a local city square away from the office at lunchtime. Invent, if necessary, a solitary routine task where you fetch files from the basement, check a book reference rather than going online or deliver something by hand. If all attempts to escape fail, go to the cloakroom and splash ice cold water on the centre of your hairline, your brow centre, your throat and wrist points to send an infusion of energy through your chakra energy system.

Crystalline protection

Ideally, you should have some clear quartz crystals and some darker stones in your workspace. If you cannot display your crystals because of the nature of your work, keep a single gently protective crystal such as an amethyst or smoky quartz in your left pocket or on your left side and a more active one, such as sparkling citrine on the right. This should balance the energies.

Light-reflecting crystals

* Choose clear crystal quartz, a sunny sparkling citrine and warm glowing orange carnelian or amber, all symbols of courage and confidence (the latter is even said to contain the souls of many tigers). Keep these in a dish in your workspace so you can run your fingers through them in order to keep your defences and self-confidence charged.

* Obtain two or three small clear quartz crystals with a point at one end that you can set along the three outer sides of your workstation. You can then turn the points outwards when trouble or intrusion appears on the horizon.

- ❀ Keep the points of the crystals facing inwards the rest of the time to transmit positive energies towards you during the day.

- ❀ If possible, position your crystals to allow natural sunlight, or in winter artificial light, to flow through them and make them sparkle.

- ❀ Hold your clear crystal sphere between your hands to fill you with confidence and optimism if you are expecting a difficult phone call or face-to-face meeting. Picture the crystalline sphere enclosing you during the conversation.

- ❀ Wash your protective crystals regularly under running water, especially after a hostile assault, and allow them to dry naturally.

Darker crystals

- ❀ Keep some darker semi-transparent stones within your work area to filter out depressing comments or discouraging remarks that can sap energy and enthusiasm. I call these my misery stones and they absorb unhelpful responses that come by phone or e-mail as well as teenage angst or whining cats passing through my workspace. Especially effective are amethyst, grey or brown smoky quartz, golden rutilated quartz with its tightly packed needles of light, rainbow or gleaming black obsidian or its softer sister semi-transparent Apache tear.

- ❀ These darker stones should be rounded and can be kept permanently on display in a dish or in a protective semicircle in your workspace to absorb noise, pollution, stagnant energies, highly contagious inertia and the vibes of those who constantly complain.

- ❀ Wash these stones regularly and bury them in the soil of a plant pot for 24 hours over the weekend or on your day off if they have had to absorb a lot of doom and gloom.

- ❀ If there is a lot of hostility or gossip or you have a bullying boss, use darker smoky quartz points or obsidian arrows (narrow arrow-shaped pieces of black obsidian, traditionally used in sevens, and sacred to the Ancient Egyptian lion-headed fire goddess, Sekhmet).

- ❀ As with the clear points, arrange the dark points in a semicircle, outwards to repel harm, inwards to enclose you in a low profile when you want to be left alone to work.

The Westernised elements and the workplace

Whether you work from home or go into a specific workplace, the same rules of elemental harmony apply as to the home. By harmonising your workspace you can maximise your opportunities and minimise any stress or negative effects from those you work with or who visit the workplace, or phone or e-mail you.

The psychotherapist Carl Gustav Jung, who was fascinated by the elements and the spiritual world, gave the elements a modern psychological spin. He hypothesised that everyone had a predominant elemental trait, a secondary one, a third shadow element that we find difficult and identify as a fault in those we dislike and a fourth element that is generally undeveloped. Earth is, in his theory, the sensations mode, Air thinking (logic), Fire intuition and Water feeling (emotions).

As you read the list of positive and negative qualities and elemental excesses in the lists below, you may identify your employer, partner, colleague, new recruit or yourself as possessing the characteristics of a particular element.

Your predominant element will act as an anchor and energise you if you keep your special elemental symbols (whether as crystals or a fragrance) in your workspace at all times. You can connect with them when you feel drained or anxious to restore your self-esteem and inner harmony. The element that you display the most will represent the way you show yourself to the world and interact with other people especially at work.

The lesser subsidiary element, your alter ego, signifies strengths that complement your main good qualities. Build up this element in lesser amounts in your workspace if you are being taken for granted or feel that you are stifled by your present role.

The other element to consider strongly is the one whose faults and excesses annoy you most in others. There may be a particular person at work who infuriates you. Add just very small quantities of this opposing element to your workspace and gradually you may become more tolerant of the person you dislike and maybe understand yourself (and your hidden nature) better. You and your enemy may even become friends as you discover what a lot you have in common.

The element that is fairly absent could offer you unexpected strengths to develop your working life in new ways and master those skills you have dismissed as not for you or beyond your capabilities. Again, introduce these only little by little and new doors of opportunity will open as you become skilled in different areas.

Finally, consider whether there are any particular work situations that trigger off your own or the elemental excesses of others. Perhaps a monthly visit from Head Office makes everyone excessively Fire-biased and irritable or bombastic so that the company does not show itself at its best. In this case, for example, you could try introducing some extra Water symbols the day before and the day of the visit to help the situation flow more easily. This may even help the more difficult personalities to act in harmony and thus effectively.

The lists below are similar to those in Chapter 3 (see pages 74–81) where the four elements are used for spiritually cleansing the home. Here, however, the elemental qualities are applied to the workplace. Thus, the character of each element is the qualities the element-biased person will display at work and a list of particularly suitable occupations for each element is also given. This may explain why you have always felt drawn to a particular career and perhaps could work towards it.

Earth

Character: The facilitator, protector, nurturer

Key words: I make welcome, I offer security

Activities to encourage Earth qualities in a team: Working on a practical project such as preparing for visitors; walking or trekking involving practical challenges

Workplaces and careers: Daycare centre workers, caring for older people and the disabled, caring for your own family full or part time, animal welfare and veterinarians, animal trainers and communicators, crafts persons, sculptors and potters, wood carving, carpenters and furniture makers, midwives, bankers, accountants, tax inspectors, house sales agents, government officials, land and property surveyors and developers, house renovators, painters and decorators, factory workers, funeral directors, family-run businesses, forestry and environmental workers, farmers, the food industry, bakers, gardening, mining and minerals

Colours: Green or golden brown

Crystals: Most agates, especially moss and tree agate, amazonite, aventurine, emerald, fossils, jet, malachite, petrified or fossilised wood, rose quartz, rutilated quartz, smoky quartz, red and golden tiger's eye, all stones with holes in the centre

Fragrances: Cypress, fern, geranium, heather, hibiscus, honeysuckle, magnolia, patchouli, sagebrush, sweetgrass, vervain, vetivert

Materials and substances to increase Earth: Dishes of salt, pots of herbs or dishes of dried herbs, flowers, miniature trees, ceramics and clay ornaments and vases, coloured and natural sand and ornamental gravel, pot pourri, crystals and gems, stones, bowls of fruit and nuts, anything made of wood, fabrics, cushions, mosaics, paper, account files and books of all kinds, animal symbols and images, forest or animal call music, anything green or brown

Excess Earth is manifest as: Inertia, sluggishness, constant tiredness, meanness with money from a usually generous person, obsession with details, inability to grasp the wider picture, unwillingness to consider alternative approaches, secrecy, obsessive tidiness, excessive home-making or nest-building at work, pessimism, territorial tendencies (own special chair or coffee mug)

Counteract excess Earth with: Air

Lack of Earth: See Excess Air (page 212)

Related sense: Touch

Positive qualities of Earth people: Patience, stability, generosity, reliability, endurance, perseverance, respect for others and traditions, protectiveness, acceptance of others as they are without needing to change them, common sense, groundedness, tolerance, caretaker of the environment

Use Earth to bring into the workplace: Protection, security and stability, a steady infusion of money and customers, success with official and legal matters, a happy workplace, contented fellow workers, love of traditional work practices and crafts, respect for older workers, hospitality, inter-generational harmony, a welcome for new workers

Air

Character: Thinker, planner, evaluator

Key words: I calculate, investigate and communicate

Activities to encourage Air qualities in a team: Visualisation, music, mantras

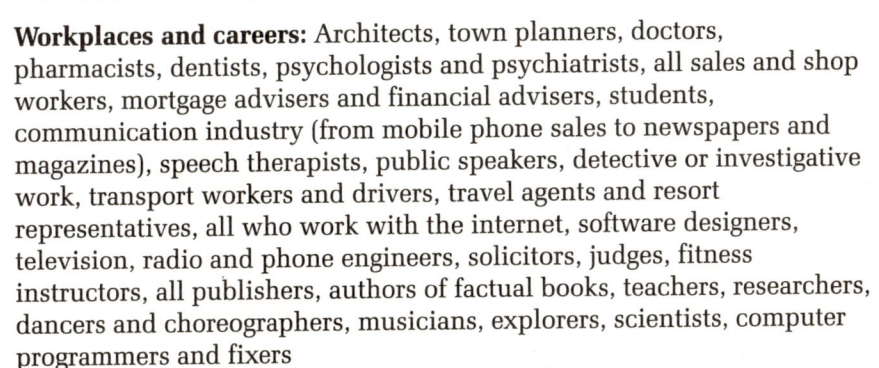

Workplaces and careers: Architects, town planners, doctors, pharmacists, dentists, psychologists and psychiatrists, all sales and shop workers, mortgage advisers and financial advisers, students, communication industry (from mobile phone sales to newspapers and magazines), speech therapists, public speakers, detective or investigative work, transport workers and drivers, travel agents and resort representatives, all who work with the internet, software designers, television, radio and phone engineers, solicitors, judges, fitness instructors, all publishers, authors of factual books, teachers, researchers, dancers and choreographers, musicians, explorers, scientists, computer programmers and fixers

Colours: Yellow or grey, also purple

Crystals: Amethyst, angelite, blue lace agate, citrine, diamond, danburite, Herkimer diamond, lapis lazuli, sapphire, sodalite, sugilite, turquoise

Fragrances: Acacia, almond, anise, benzoin, bergamot, fennel, lavender, lemongrass, lemon verbena, lily of the valley, peppermint, sage, sandalwood

Materials and substances to increase Air: Feathers, feathery grasses, stainless steel and chrome, paper clips, scissors and knives, electric fans, pencils and pens, pins, helium balloons, all technological equipment including computers and phones, tools or instruments, ceiling mobiles, seeds, wind chimes, bells, keys, fragrant flowers and fragrance sprays, musical instruments, open windows, bird call, classical or dance music, fairy, bird and butterfly statues, symbols and images

Excess Air is manifest as: Being super-critical, sarcastic or witty at the expense of others, rushed or inaccurate work, incoherence, unwillingness to explain thinking or ideas, crankiness, gossiping, being liberal with the truth, poor timekeeping, losing data or forgetting appointments, changing the focus without reason, inability to finish a task or give realistic deadlines, impatience with details and boring tasks

Counteract excess Air with: Earth

Lack of Air: See Excess Earth (page 211)

Related sense: Smell, sound (hearing)

Positive qualities of Air people: Communication skills, persuasiveness, joy, focus, intelligence, fair-mindedness, logic, independence, clarity, good memory, mental dexterity, optimism, teaching abilities, musical gifts, concentration, commercial and technological acumen, versatility, healing abilities through orthodox medicine or from higher sources

Use Air to bring into the workplace: Skill in passing tests and examinations, learning new skills, meeting deadlines, successful travel, changes and improvements in career (especially self-employment), obtaining justice, just rewards for efforts made, advantageous career relocation, money-spinning ventures, curiosity, better health and healing, new beginnings, following opportunities and meeting new helpful people, anything to do with science, technology or the media

Fire

Character: The creator, action man or woman, the crusader

Key words: I inspire, I carry through and I get results

Activities to encourage Fire qualities in a team: Adventure days, barbecues and orienteering challenges

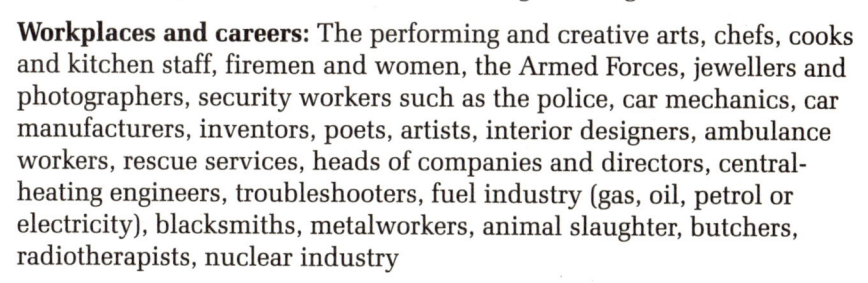

Workplaces and careers: The performing and creative arts, chefs, cooks and kitchen staff, firemen and women, the Armed Forces, jewellers and photographers, security workers such as the police, car mechanics, car manufacturers, inventors, poets, artists, interior designers, ambulance workers, rescue services, heads of companies and directors, central-heating engineers, troubleshooters, fuel industry (gas, oil, petrol or electricity), blacksmiths, metalworkers, animal slaughter, butchers, radiotherapists, nuclear industry

Colours: Red, orange or gold

Crystals: Amber, blood agate, boji stones, carnelian, desert rose, fire agate, garnet, heliotrope, hematite, iron pyrites, jasper, lava, obsidian, ruby, topaz

Fragrances: Allspice, angelica, basil, bay, carnation, cedarwood, chamomile, cinnamon, cloves, copal, Dragon's Blood, frankincense, juniper, lime, marigold, nutmeg, orange, rosemary, tangerine

Materials and substances to increase Fire: Candles and tea lights, lights of all kinds (especially fibre optic and lava lamps), sun catchers (sparkling or clear crystals on strings or chains hung at windows to catch the light), crystal spheres (especially clear quartz that reflect rainbows), mirrors (sometimes regarded as Water), essential oils and oil burners, natural sunshine, rainbows, oranges and all orange fruit, sunflowers and all golden or orange flowers, radiators, stoves and furnaces, dragon images and statues (especially gold ones), mobiles and images of dragonflies, natural sunshine, music from hot lands, gold jewellery, anything that is gold, orange or red in colour or made of gold

Excess Fire is manifest as: Irritability and impatience, temper tantrums, being autocratic or dictatorial, forcing an unrealistic pace of work for self and others, sudden loss of interest in a project without good reason, inability to switch off from a subject or from work, becoming increasingly accident prone, empire building, carelessness with property, unnecessary risk taking, inappropriate sexual remarks or jokes, inflaming dormant office passion

Counteract excess Fire with: Water

Lack of Fire: See Excess Water (page 215)

Related sense: Vision and survival instincts

Positive qualities of Fire people: Courage, inspiration, idealism and altruism, loyalty in adversity or a major crisis, striving for perfection, defence of the weak, creativity, leadership, potency, fertility in all aspects of life, generosity, breadth of vision, generation of enthusiasm in others, transformation of raw idea or product into a marketable creation, ability to see possibilities in even an unpromising situation or project

Use Fire to bring into the workplace: The fulfilment of ambitions, dynamic leadership, all creative and artistic ventures, ethical and spiritual principles, success in sports and competitive games, fame, wealth and unexpected good fortune, courage, pleasure in achievements (of self, others and the company), the removal of what is no longer needed, protection against vicious attack or threats

Water

Character: The peacemaker, counsellor and creator of beauty and harmony

Key words: I bring people together and can flow with the situation and adapt to the needs of the moment

Activities to encourage Water qualities in a team: Meditation, sharing experiences and feelings, role playing

Workplaces and careers: Social services, the export trade, alternative medicine and therapy, nurses and therapists, mental health workers, psychotherapists, play therapists, beauty and fashion consultants, florists, water industry, hydroelectric power, fishermen and sailors, counsellors, writers of fiction and children's books, customer service advisers, clairvoyants and mediums, the hotel and hospitality trade (also Earth), production or sale of alcohol, laundry workers, cleaners, refuse disposal workers, plumbers, swimming pool workers (instructors or maintenance or other staff), glass makers and glaziers, ministers of religion

Colours: Blue and silver

Crystals: Aquamarine, calcite, coral, fluorite, jade, kunzite, milky quartz, moonstone, opal, pearl, selenite, tourmaline

Fragrances: Apple blossom, apricot, coconut, eucalyptus, feverfew, heather, hyacinth, jasmine, lemon, lemon balm, lilac, lily, myrrh, orchid, passionflower, peach, strawberry, sweet pea, thyme, valerian, vanilla, violet

Substances and materials to increase Water: Milk, water, tea, coffee, juice; sea shells; water features; vases; nets or webs of any kind; fish in tanks (in Feng Shui eight goldfish for prosperity and good luck and one black one to absorb negativity); mermaid, sea creature and dolphin images and statues; flower and tree essences; glass or crystal bowls filled with water; sea, river or dolphin music; silk scarves; transparent drapes; glass; mirrors; silver bells on cords; Tibetan singing bowls; silver or copper jewellery or anything made of silver or copper

Excess Water is manifest as: Becoming over-emotional about a professional matter, being manipulative, playing favourites, inappropriate role-taking at work (for example, helpless little girl, big sister or father knows best), attention-seeking, constant need for reassurance or praise, excessive socialising during working hours, instigating rivalries, jealousy, over-sensitivity to constructive advice, inability to be objective about people or situations, over-identification with the boss or the workplace

Counteract excess Water with: Fire

Lack of Water: See Excess Fire (page 213)

Related sense: Intuition, taste

Positive qualities of Water people: Love of beauty, compassion, empathy, harmony, love, forgiveness, unconscious wisdom, imagination, lover of nature, willingness to negotiate and compromise, peace-making skills, ability to work with others, gentle good humour, uncanny power to anticipate the needs of a situation and thoughts of other people

Use Water to bring into the workplace: Trust, friendship, loyalty and commitment to the workplace and co-workers, the mending of quarrels and slowness to take offence, adaptability to changing circumstances, versatility, fun and spontaneity, gentle good humour and ability not to take self too seriously, respecting everyone's opinion and feelings, spiritual values, healing differences and old rivalries

Making elemental modifications

An elemental imbalance at work may affect everyone but will be most noticeable in individuals who normally display that element prominently in their character. The excess may also become obvious during a meeting or in remarks made and behaviour observed during a break when everyone comes together.

The excess may have been triggered by an event such as a wave of redundancies, a lost order for the company or new people joining an established team. Elemental imbalances tend to spread like wildfire but are easily remedied.

The excess of an element may make the atmosphere of the workplace strained and may result over time in an unusually high number of stress-related absences or even resignations. The lists above will help you to identify the element of which there is an excess.

On the other hand, there may be a lack of a particular element, especially if you work alone or for yourself and have to be a self motivator. This can greatly deplete your overall elemental energy.

For example, if your office displays signs of excess Water, you might require additional Fire power if you have to get a project finished urgently. Water will calm down stressed individuals trying to meet deadlines, who are in overload and making mistakes. Likewise, extra Air will bring sudden focus and concentration when creativity is in overdrive and extra Earth ensures somebody is sorting out the practicalities, such as supplies and delivery, without which nothing productive will result in spite of extra efforts by the workforce.

Refer to the lists above to identify the crystals, colours or materials that are suitable for dealing with the elemental imbalance in your workplace. Choose one of the methods below and you will find that, even if you can only change the balance in your own workspace, the effects will be experienced more widely, and often quite rapidly.

- ❋ Crystals, colours and fragrances are the fastest and easiest extra input. Use natural sources such as fragrant flowers in different colours, essential oil fragrances on oil burners or fresh fruit to eat.

- ❋ Keep a set of one or two of each of the elemental crystals in a drawer or locker to put on your desktop or workspace as required.

- ❋ Soak an elemental crystal in water for a few hours and use the crystal-infused water in juice, tea or coffee. Keep a small bottle of an appropriate water to drink or splash on pulse points. Old mineral water bottles are ideal for this purpose.

✤ Herbal teas, for example, chamomile for Fire, are a natural source of instant elemental energy.

✤ Keep a collection of small coloured ribbons or coloured wools so you can knot a single strand around your chair or workbench or in a driving cab to give you a gradual infusion of elemental strength. Alternatively, make watchbands from appropriate colours.

✤ If you know what kind of a day lies ahead, dress in particular elemental colours or wear the appropriate metal to keep you harmonious and focused.

✤ Breathing in the colour of fresh flowers or crystals is highly restorative and can be practised unobtrusively in a busy office. As you breathe in slowly and regularly, picture the flower colour entering your body on the in-breath and filling it with coloured light. On the out-breath, visualise dark- or misty-coloured energies flowing out. Continue until you feel filled with light.

10 A Pagan Treasury of Wisdom and Healing

The pagan way can bring all manner of good things into our lives. This chapter looks at how a closer relationship with nature can bring tranquillity into a hectic modern lifestyle and how wisdom can be passed to us through clouds and water. If there are areas of our life that need healing, such as low self-esteem, exhaustion, cravings or even medical problems, this chapter offers pagan solutions that concentrate on restoring balance through ancient rituals and the use of natural resources.

The power of nature

There are many ways we can bring a more natural focus to our lives, for example by exploring the countryside or city wildlife areas at weekends rather than spending time and money on activities organised by other people. The patience involved in sitting for what seems like hours in a red-squirrel or deer hide or waiting for a badger or hedgehog to potter round our garden at night, is rewarded when we see the creature moving close yet within its independent universe. On a visit to a wolf sanctuary, I once had the experience of a female wolf licking my hand. The conservator said she may have remembered me from earlier encounters but, whether or not that was true, I felt immensely privileged to be so close to an animal that was still essentially wild, yet by choice momentarily interacted with me.

The greatest skill we can teach ourselves and our families is to be still and quiet, to watch and listen and not feel the need to fill every available second with chatter, movement or stimulation. As an ex-teacher and a mother I am convinced that many of the modern problems that children experience, such as Attention Deficit Hyperactivity Disorder, are at least partly caused by the continual background of noise they live with. These intrusions include televisions in every room that are never turned off, games consoles with simulated gun fire and screams, supermarket tannoy music and announcements, and the constant reminder on some trains by a tinny automated voice of the station you have just passed, the one you have not reached and that there is still not a buffet car on the train. There are even junior treadmills and exercise machines, which take children into a noisy indoor gym atmosphere rather than outdoors into nature where the emphasis is on exploration and play with nature's own toys: sticks, stones, water and shells.

Listening to the voices of nature

Unless you were training to become a diviner, priest or priestess and so worked with more complex forms of prophecy, ordinary people in earlier times gained insights from the voices and images of nature. They listened to the voices in the wind, watched the pictures in the clouds or patterns made on the surface of water. Whether you live in town or country, you can still use these ways today to get in touch with your own inner knowledge and hidden wisdom and to guide you to the right course with no formal divinatory tools or training. Children and family members can join in identifying pictures in water or clouds and sometimes this can be a good way of talking round family problems and coming up with original solutions in a non-confrontational way.

People from the beginning of time have looked up at the clouds and the sky for messages and signs of favour from the deities. Rainbows, wind and storms are still used as omens and guides to wise action among indigenous people like the Maori of New Zealand and those in parts of sub-Saharan Africa whose culture and customs date back thousands of years.

Messages in the clouds

When looking for pictures in the clouds, your best options are the high, thin, wispy cirrhus clouds that can appear in fabulous colours when the sun is low on the horizon or the lower, cotton-wool, fluffy, fair-weather cumulus clouds seen against a blue sky. Many other cloud conditions, some of which may only last a relatively short time, also naturally form pictures.

Before you begin asking questions and seeing how the cloud images answer them, spend time cloud-watching in different locations and at different times. Scan fast-moving clouds over a plain before a storm or on a windy day; watch clouds heavy with snow, sudden small black clouds in an otherwise blue sky and white or grey clouds in the night sky. Try cloud-watching from the window of a plane, especially on a relatively clear day when shadows are cast on the land or sea by the clouds and plane. Look down through the different levels at the shapes formed by natural land formations of forests, fields and lakes. Indeed you do not have to ask questions, but can just enjoy identifying cloud images with friends or family on a picnic.

A single cloud may create an image, or two or more clouds may seem closely connected as a single idea. For example, you may see a cat chasing a bird who is constantly hopping or flying just out of the pouncing cat's claws as one cloud pursues the other across the sky.

For each image or idea, extract as much information as possible. For example, if you see a cloud dragon, ask yourself: Is it fire-breathing and fierce or guarding treasure? Is it a young dragon, newly emerged from its egg? Does the dragon represent in your life, a relative, a partner, an employer, a difficult child, or you? What message does the dragon have for you? Of course, if the clouds are moving fast, all this may be quite instantaneous, but that will prevent your logical mind from intruding.

Messages on the water

In almost every culture, water is the oldest and also one of the most popular sources of nature's clairvoyant or psychic visions. Throughout the ages, women have seen psychic images in water as they washed clothes in pools or rivers. According to St Augustine, who lived around 500 CE, in Germany ordinary women frequently studied the whirls and swirls of fast-flowing rivers, especially the Rhine, to gain wisdom from the water spirits. Needless to say, the saint did not approve.

Industrial rivers and canals flowing between warehouses and new office and apartment blocks are just as good as still lakes in deep countryside for seeing images in water. In a town you will benefit from all kinds of lights and shadows flickering and glinting on the surface, including street lights along the embankment and the reflection of lighted windows.

Traditionally, before water divination or scrying (seeing pictures in reflective surfaces), a coin or small gold or silver earring is dropped in the water in honour of the essences or spirits of the waters.

A slight breeze in soft light, morning or evening, are the best conditions for gazing into any water. You will find that the images are very fleeting and subtle. Keep looking on the surface and ask the water to tell you what you need to know. The light and shadows on the surface of the water will be transformed into a series of images in your mind and, with practice, in the water. Most importantly, you will receive impressions and feelings in your mind. Practise water scrying in your daily life, using some of the methods suggested below.

- As you sit in a bath of warm water, illuminated by candles, relaxing at the end of the day, move the bath foam around with your fingers to make shapes, patterns and pictures.

- Half fill a washing-up bowl or clear cooking dish with cold water and squirt a trail of washing-up liquid on to the surface of the water, allowing it to form swirling images.

- Go to a swimming pool in the early morning or evening when it is quiet and use the pool lights or natural sunlight filtering through windows to make images. As you swim you can break up the water patterns and allow new ones to form. This is a good way of seeing how changes might be possible and feeling them as you constantly move through the changing images.

- Outdoors, stir a pool with a branch of a water tree, such as willow, rowan or alder, and focus on the area in the centre of the ripples.

- A fountain will also cast pictures, especially if you watch the kind that looks like a giant, constantly forming, bubble and the sun is shining on it. Fountains that change colour at night are also excellent for scrying.

- Try the ancient three-stones method that was popular in Ancient Greece. Throw three stones fast, one after the other, into the same spot in still water. (The original format advocated a square, a triangular and a round stone, but I think that three round stones, all the same size, are best.) As the ripples form, a scene will emerge on the surface of the water and then fade as the ripples fade. Keep throwing in threes until you have your answers. Stony beaches by small lakes are ideal for this method or you could take a bag of pebbles with you if the shore is sandy or grassy. Get friends and family to keep throwing and calling out ideas about a current question or family issue. This is a brilliant way of brainstorming.

In any water scrying, you may get impressions of what you sense you saw, but may be unaware of actually seeing an image. This is because your inner psychic or clairvoyant eye is transmitting information too fast for your conscious mind to process the imagery in situ. In time, the images will remain longer on the surface and your processing abilities will become more accustomed to dealing with psychic material within the water.

The healing path

I believe many modern ills, such as food disorders, alcohol abuse, overuse of prescription as well as illegal drugs and compulsive disorders, are increased and sometimes even caused by the frantic commercial world that we live in today.

When one part of our life is out of balance, we may reach for a quick fix, whether it be cigarettes, a food binge or a few glasses of wine to relax us after work. The problem is that the quick fixes do work in the short-term and so tend to be the first port of call in times of stress or overload. Munching your way through a packet of chocolate biscuits while fuming over the selfishness of others, blunts the anger for a time as you swallow the resentful words rather than say them. However, the negative effects of the quick fix actually tip the balance even further as you soon feel bloated, headachy and weak willed, and are still left with the negative and usually justifiable feelings that caused the binge in the first place.

One media food guru says that you are what you eat and so, by implication, if you eat the wrong things, such as that packet of chocolate biscuits, then you are a pretty useless human being. In contrast, the neopagan belief is that you should love and respect your body and yourself *as you are*, for the body is the home of your spiritual self. Compare this with the current media emphasis on the body beautiful as the route to happiness and being a better person in the eyes of the world. The magazines and television programmes devoted to this concept create an over-valuation of the external rather than the inner person.

Of course, I am not advocating overeating or any other quick fix. Food imbalance is one of the major problems in the modern world with large parts of the world's population starving and elsewhere record levels of obesity, health-related problems even among young children, and food-related psychological disorders among children, especially girls, as young as seven or eight.

As parents or anyone connected with children, and indeed in our own lives, it is important to emphasise the value of the child or adult as they are now and as they look now. When a person stops making food or any other oral satisfaction the centre of their universe and focuses on what really would make them happy or less frustrated, cravings diminish and weight drops naturally to the balanced optimum weight for that person.

Except for overindulged pets, you rarely see overweight animals or birds – and they don't count calories.

A ritual for boosting self-esteem

The first step towards regaining balance in your life is to boost self-esteem. I use this simple routine myself and use it with others to help build up the self-liking that is at the centre of personal balance.

Even truly beautiful slim people can have low self-esteem, often because someone they love or loved told them they were fat or ugly. This causes imbalance that can lead to excess dieting or over-exercising – and still the critical person is not satisfied. Of course, it is all about power and control by the critical person but it is all too easy to see in the mirror what the other person tells us we are.

- When you get up and before you go to bed, stand in front of a mirror. Either position the mirror so that you are framed in natural light or, if this is not possible, light a candle and position it so that it shines in the mirror.

- Look at yourself in the mirror, smile and say,

> *Mirror, mirror on the wall,*
> *I demand respect from all.*
> *I am worthy of admiration;*
> *I am worthy of consideration.*
> *I love myself as I am and for who I am.*
> *I am a beautiful human being*
> *And so I claim the right to my place in the sun.*

Blow out the candle if you are using one.

- Whenever anyone, no matter how loved, tries to diminish or unbalance you, imagine yourself framed with light and repeat in your mind,

    I am a beautiful human being and I claim my place in the sun.

- It may be that in time you move away from the critical person quite naturally, but that will be easier if you believe in your own value.

- You may like to hold a sparkling yellow citrine in your hand as you speak into the mirror and then carry it with you as a reminder that you are worthy of consideration whenever you feel under threat.

The Three Treasures

In Oriental tradition, there are three essential forces or energies that work together to sustain human life. These are called the Three Treasures (San Bao) of Shen, Jing and Qi. They are interdependent and need to be balanced in order for life to be lived at peak capacity.

When Jing is at a sufficiently high level, it is said Qi will be at optimum capacity and when the Qi is strong, Shen will flourish. Conversely if Jing is depleted, Qi will be weak, then Shen will be weak.

Shen is sometimes referred to as spirit and is closely connected with the condition of the mind and heart. If a body is lacking in Shen, the person's hair, skin and eyes are usually dull and lacking in lustre, and the person feels exhausted and at the mercy of fate.

In an adult, dwelling on misfortunes rather than trying to fix them or let them go can sometimes contribute to a stress-related illness or make the original misfortunes worse. Long-term negative emotions as well as repressed emotional states can deplete natural vitality and may be manifest either as restlessness and insomnia or more usually as compulsive and obsessive behaviour. This can lead to drinking or smoking too much or binge eating and yo-yo dieting in the hope of gaining control over weight and, so it is thought, of life. Consequently, the maintenance of a healthy Shen is vital to well-being, to successful and effortless weight balance and to reduce other orally-related cravings.

Jing is the fundamental substance, which in the Oriental tradition is said to form and maintain life. Jing can be viewed as the material basis of Shen and provides the strength of one's constitution. There are two forms of Jing, the Jing of reproduction, growth and development and the Jing of nutrition, which is derived from foods as well as water.

Signs of a malfunctioning Jing include, it is believed, a general lack of energy, poor memory, back and joint aches and tension, a weak back, fear or nervousness, ringing in the ears, night sweats and for women PMS and troubles with menstruation and menopause. The lack can lead to mood-swing eating and comfort eating as well as apparently motiveless over-indulgence in other ways.

Qi or **Chi** is a vital form of energy, which manifests itself in many different forms according to its place of distribution and function in the body. There are many forms of Qi. The Chinese symbolise Qi through an image of vapour rising from steaming rice. Qi is thought to be the basis of all the body's functions: breathing, speaking, moving, eating, drinking and thinking.

Produced from the food we eat and the air we breathe, Qi circulates throughout the body, replenishing it with vital energy. When the body's balance is disrupted, the Qi becomes disturbed by emotional aggravation and symptoms of dysfunction and leads to a sense of things not being right or being out of balance. This can make it hard to follow a healthy eating pattern and can lead to feeling exhausted and dispirited and seeking a sugar or fat lift to restore vitality temporarily.

Both Confucianism and Taoism, traditional systems of Chinese belief, stress that we should nourish Qi by being even-tempered, generous to the self and others, not overworking, not arguing or worrying excessively and by healthy eating and digestion and breathing pure air.

Some Chinese doctors say that modern life is a prime cause of diminishing Shen, Jing and Qi and that whole generations are growing up in conditions inimical to a sense of well-being and balance.

Using the Three Treasures to restore balance in your life

If you are feeling out of sorts, restless, anxious, over-stressed or exhausted or are struggling with bad habits or obsessions of any kind, you may need to restore the free flow of your Three Treasures. It may be that you have been overworking, worrying, bingeing, crash dieting, relying on fast foods, coffee, alcohol or cigarettes to keep up your energy levels or even over-exercising and pushing yourself too hard. You may be experiencing constant food cravings or terror at the thought of eating anything at all. If any of these describe your present state, stop before indulging or depriving yourself and try the following visualisation exercise to restore balance to your life.

Afterwards you will be in a better position to decide what you really need in order to deal with your feelings, overcome the obsession or make the craving go away – and maybe it is some approval. If you are not getting it, you can decide whether you need to move on in your life from the person or situation making you feel bad about yourself or if you can give yourself the love and esteem you deserve.

At first it may take up to 15 minutes to work through the visualisation but, in time, you will be able to move faster through the steps, taking just two or three minutes if necessary when you are in a hurry. You may need to do the exercise many times.

- ❦ Find a quiet place where the air is relatively pure, preferably out of doors but certainly away from air-conditioning that can transmit many impurities and even illnesses if it is not well maintained.

- ❦ Choose a view of nature – a lake, a hill or even a painting or computer screensaver – and sit where it fills your whole view.

- ❦ Slowly drink some green or herbal tea without milk or sugar. If you are working outdoors, take it in a flask. Peppermint is a specially cleansing flavour. Tea ceremonies in the Orient provide a sacred space and stillness and the slow action of sipping tea while meditating restores natural rhythms to the whole system as well as aiding natural digestive processes. If you hate tea use a diluted juice or spring water.

✤ When the cup is empty, close your eyes and picture the Three Treasures before you, as three huge bowls made of gold set on different levels, resting on ascending steps of shining green jade, the crystal of calm, healing and immortality.

✤ If you wish, at home you can use actual small jade crystal or glass bowls as a focus, the Jing bowl filled with dried green herbs, the Shen with fragrant oils or dried rose petals and the Qi with pure water with a single flower floating on it. If you are using actual bowls, create three different levels for the bowls.

✤ Imagine or place the Jing bowl on the lowest level and concentrate on green light emanating from plants within it, being transformed into ruby red liquid which flows upwards like a fountain into the Qi bowl. Feel a gentle, pulsating warmth making your heart beat regularly and your pulse even and calm but strong. You will start to feel the tensions and cravings decreasing.

✤ See the red liquid flowing into the Qi bowl and becoming clearer until it rises as steaming white water. Imagine your worries, self-dislike or unfulfilled need for approval (all the things that make you overeat, deprive yourself or push yourself too hard) as dark mist leaving your mouth.

✤ Breathe in gently the white and clear vapour of the hot Qi spring through your nose.

✤ Breathe easily as you watch the Qi bowl and let the gentle vapours clear any inner hunger or any suppressed anger that makes you bite into food, drown your sorrows or choke your lungs with smoke rather than speak out.

✤ Let the steam rise as a waterspout into the Shen bowl which is filled with golden light and watch as it flows back into the Jing bowl making the plants a rich pulsating green. Imagine the gold expanding as sunbeams and flowing into you, filling your whole body with energy, self-love and confidence.

✤ Repeat this visualised cycle until you feel calm but energised and your exhaled breath is quite clear and free of tension and tinged with gold. Say,

I value myself as I am and I can be what I want to be.

- ❋ If you are hungry, eat some pre-prepared small fruits, chopped raw vegetables, nuts, seeds and raisins.

- ❋ If you are in the open air, walk to the place you were viewing while you were drinking your tea or go out into the fresh air breathing regularly. Walk or run until you are tired.

- ❋ When you return, sleep until you wake naturally, which may be a few minutes or hours later. See the golden bowls in your mind's eye as you drift away into the golden cloud.

- ❋ If you are at work or when you cannot rest, press your hands over your eyes for a minute or two, relax and imagine the beautiful place. Then splash your hands and face with cold water.

- ❋ In time you will be able to imagine the bowls and the process anywhere, even in the office, using your beautiful screensaver to stimulate your imagination.

The power of stones

The druids and the Vikings believed in the power of stones and this ancient ritual can be used to remove pain, fear, resentment, guilt, illness or bad habits from your life. Traditionally, bones were used in the same way and were buried as a sign of burying a quarrel. You can either follow the steps below or carry the process out in your mind.

- ❋ Either find a perfectly round black stone or picture one in your mind and imagine it representing pain or fear or whatever it is you want to get rid of.

- ❋ As you hold or picture it, imagine the stone getting heavier as it is filled with your pain, fear or anger. You may physically feel the stone getting heavier and your negative feelings or pain slowly ebbing away.

- ❋ When the stone feels too heavy to hold or you sense it is full, cast it into water or bury it in earth where nothing grows.

- ❋ If you are picturing the stone in your mind, throw it high into the air where it is transformed into a shimmering sunbeam. Alternatively you can imagine the stone getting smaller and smaller and either dissolving or crumbling into earth.

The power of water

Water can be empowered for many purposes using our own energy system and the power of thought. The following technique, which is still practised in modern healing, comes from a much earlier time when people believed that it was possible, by calling on various deities and using water from a sacred source, to bring healing and fertility by drinking empowered water.

In more modern times we know that we can draw through our own energy systems the necessary strength to overcome a craving, to help our immune system or innate natural pain-blocking mechanisms to kick in, to relieve panic or anxiety or to fill ourselves with power and energy for a particular purpose.

- All you need is a glass (if possible, not plastic) of water, either mineral or from a running tap.
- Hold the glass of water between your hands to connect the water to your own inner energy system through your palm energy centres. These are linked to the heart energy centre that, in turn, draws strength from nature and from the earth and cosmos.
- If you can be outdoors, the visualisation is even more powerful but you can do this in the office, in the home or even while sitting on a crowded plane if you start to panic.
- As you hold the water, say either aloud or in your mind what it is you most need, for example,

    I am of worth and do not need to eat this junk to prove it.

    Or

    My headache is lifting and I am full of energy.

    In a pub you might say,

    I do not need excess alcohol to make me feel happy.

    Or before you light up a cigarette,

    I can easily fix the situation and do not need this cigarette to calm my nerves.

- Keep your hands in position cupped round the glass for about two minutes, picturing light entering the glass from all round as the water become infused with the purpose. If you can be in sunlight or natural light, so much the better.

- ❦ Slowly sip the water. Speak or think as if the desired result has been achieved. You will slowly feel yourself filled with the desired power and it may be that you no longer need the junk food or cigarette, that the panic or pain is lifting or that you can speak calmly and firmly to someone who is trying to bully you rather than over-reacting or saying nothing and absorbing the unfairness.
- ❦ If you suddenly need to carry out this ritual, you can use a plastic bottle of purchased mineral water. Alternatively, carry a bottle of mineral water with you, so that you are always prepared.

The power of crystals

Crystals are a concentrated form of healing power from the earth. They amplify the innate healing abilities we all possess, whether we are healing ourselves or someone we love. Though crystals do seem to have beneficial physical as well as emotional and spiritual effects, there are none of the dangers of taking pills or surgical intervention as the healing takes place on some intangible level.

The crystalline healing energy is experienced as warmth, as what has been described as liquid light flowing through the whole body, not only the part being healed. A similar sensation, as well as tingling, may be experienced while holding crystals for healing, as your own energy system makes a connection with that of the crystal.

Some people like to add a third power into the equation, in the form of an angelic or higher healing guide. Indeed, when using a crystal for healing, you may feel that you are being gently guided as to the best place to hold and the best way to move the crystal.

What crystals cannot do

I do not claim to be a medical doctor and would urge anyone who becomes ill or has a sick family member to seek medical care. We should not ignore conventional medical care for urgent or acute conditions or chronic conditions that need expert monitoring, nor should anyone claim that with crystals they can cure cancer or halt or reverse a degenerative condition.

Crystal healing may, however, reduce pain and improve life quality even in difficult cases and can sometimes seem to make people more responsive to conventional medical or surgical treatment. For headaches or stomach ache, crystals can be faster acting and more effective than medication – and with fewer side effects. You may find if you use crystals that your health does seem to improve, because of the, as yet, hardly understood connection between mind, body and spirit. Try crystal healing for a condition where the treatment seems slow to take effect or you are waiting for a consultation, and you may be pleasantly surprised.

Healing with crystals

Start by choosing an appropriate crystal from pages 232–237. You will notice that some crystals are effective for a number of problems. You might like to buy some that you use often or favourites of each colour and keep them in a drawstring bag for healing work. If you are uncertain of the nature of the illness or the obvious crystal does not feel right, pick one from the selection in your bag without looking to allow your unconscious mind to indicate what other crystal energies would be helpful to balance your system.

Once you have chosen your crystal, you can then carry it with you, sleep with it under your pillow or hold it against a point of pain, either gently warmed in your hands or dipped in cooling water as most appropriate. The steps below can be used for healing yourself or another person.

As with many innate spiritual gifts, the key to healing with crystals is to relax and allow the crystal to find its own movements and pathways.

- When healing, experiment to determine the hand in which the chosen crystal feels most natural. This may vary according to the nature of the problem. Trust yourself.

- Hold the crystal a short distance (2.5 cm/1 in) away from the body as you work.

- Pass the crystal over the body, letting the crystal guide your hand and not the other way round.

- The key to movement is anticlockwise to remove pain, tension and unhappiness and clockwise to add light, warmth, energy and hope. This holds true whether the problems is physical, emotional, spiritual or, as most often, a mixture of all three.

- Sometimes you may instinctively want to hold the crystal over a seemingly unrelated part of the body from that suggested by the described or perceived symptoms. You may be surprised to find your migraine is rooted in your stomach, but the result will prove your instinctive movement right. Listen to the crystal and it will take your hand to the source of the trouble.

- You may want to move the crystal constantly or feel it suddenly pull down over a particular spot. This may be because the crystal has detected a knot of trapped energy. Unblock this with the crystal as you would a physical tangle of thread.

✤ Your crystal may also pause over a place on the body and you will feel in your fingers as if it has momentarily run out of energy. This indicates a lifeless area where the energy has drained away or maybe not reached because of an energy knot that is nearby. Infuse lifeless areas with energy with smooth clockwise circular movements until you can feel the energy buzzing harmoniously again.

✤ Afterwards, wash the crystal under running water and leave it to dry naturally.

✤ The power of water can be combined with that of crystals by using crystal waters. Soak a well-washed crystal in a small jug of water from dusk until dawn, or when you get up, if you want to remove chronic pain, illness or worry, or from when you wake to noon to energise or bring optimism. Remove the crystal and filter the water into a small bottle that you can carry with you to drink. The water can also be poured into a bath to aid an ache or pain.

Crystals for particular problems

Abuse of any kind: Chrysocolla, desert rose, jade, orange calcite, rose quartz

Addictions (smoking, overeating, alcohol, etc): Amethyst, angelite/celestite, carnelian (for all food-related disorders), golden tiger's eye, kunzite (good for women), laboradite, rhodochrosite (good for over-reliance on prescription drugs and food-related disorders), ruby in zoisite, unakite

Ageing: Emerald (especially for women), fossilised or petrified wood, iron pyrites, lepidolite (especially for problems with degeneration of memory and functioning), pearl, rutilated quartz (good for older men), sodalite

Anaemia, blood disorders: Heliotrope, haematite, orange jasper, red agate, red jasper

Anger, irritability: Amazonite, amethyst, orange aragonite, ruby, sodalite

Anxiety, panic attacks, phobias: Amethyst, angelite/celestite, aquamarine (for fear of boat travel), aventurine, desert rose (good for claustrophobia and agoraphobia attacks), garnet, kunzite (good for women), kyanite, opal aura, rose quartz, sodalite (fear of flying), sunstone

Appetite, loss of: Amber, apatite, carnelian

Arteries: Blue lace agate, crazy lace agate, picture jasper, tourminalated quartz, tree agate

Arthritis, rheumatism, bone and joint pains: Carnelian (especially for men), coral (good for women), garnet, green calcite, green fluorite, jade (especially for hips), orange jasper, red jasper, turquoise, any crystals with holes

Asthma: Olivine/peridot, pietersite, rhodochrosite, sodalite, tektite

Autism, Asperger's syndrome: Aqua or cobalt aura, lapis lazuli, tourminalated quartz

Baby and childhood illness: Blue chalcedony, blue opals, green opals, jade, mangano or pink calcite, mother of pearl (soothes a baby or child when the mother is not present), pink chalcedony, pink opals, any crystals with holes

Back, spine: Amazonite, citrine, blue howlite, jet, petrified or fossilised wood, white howlite, yellow calcite

Balance, inner ear, also unsteadiness walking: Coral, jade, onyx, turquoise

Bedwetting: Citrine, any fluorite, jade

Bites and stings: Bowenite or new jade, brecciated jasper, jet, leopardskin jasper, olivine/peridot, onyx, snakeskin agate

Bladder: Aquamarine, aventurine (good for genitourinary problems), jade, mookaite, rainbow quartz

Blood pressure: Blue lace agate (counteracts high), carnelian (low), charoite (high), haematite (high), pietersite (high or low), sodalite (high)

Blood sugar disorders: Amethyst, bowenite or new jade, chrysocolla, jade, mookaite, sodalite

Bones, including dislocation: Apatite, coral, fossilised or petrified wood and all fossils, green calcite, snow or milky quartz, white howlite, any crystals with holes

Bowel disorders and constipation: Amber, banded agate, dalmatian jasper (especially good for irritable bowel syndrome), rainbow quartz

Brain: Amazonite, aqua aura, Herkimer diamond (slows brain waves to slower, deeper patterns and so avoids burnout physically or emotionally), lapis lazuli, opal aura, rutilated quartz, turquoise

Breasts: Amazonite, mangano or pink calcite, milky quartz, olivine/peridot, rainbow moonstone, white chalcedony

Bronchitis and respiratory complaints, lungs: Aquamarine, emerald, green jasper, jade, lapis lazuli, pietersite, yellow aragonite

Bruises: Amethyst, rose quartz, smoky quartz, sodalite

Burns scalds: Jade, red agate, rose quartz, sodalite

Cell, tissue and bone marrow: Amber, boji stone, coral, iron pyrites, kyanite, moss agate (wear next to skin), rutilated quartz, snowflake obsidian, sugilite, white sapphire

Childbirth and post natal: Blue opals, fossils, green opals, heliotrope, jet, kunzite (helps post-natal depression), mangano calcite (helps mother to bond with babies and for post-natal depression), pink chalcedony (good for first-time mothers, those who have had surgical intervention and post-natal problems), pink opals

Circulation: Carnelian, garnet, ruby, snowflake obsidian, yellow aragonite

Colds and coughs: Aquamarine, green jasper, moss agate, orbicular or ocean jasper, turquoise, yellow aragonite

Colon: Banded agate, jet, red agate, rose quartz, yellow calcite, yellow jasper

Cramps: Turquoise, any crystals with holes

Cuts, wounds: Haematite, heliotrope, mookaite, rhodonite

Degenerative conditions: Lepidolite, sugilite, titanium aura

Depression: Apache tear, citrine, clear quartz crystal, jet, ox or red tiger's eye, rainbow quartz, smoky quartz, sunstone (especially in the winter)

Detoxifying of system: Aqua aura, bowenite or new jade, cobalt aura, green fluorite, heliotrope, rhodochrosite (especially good for purifying blood and liver)

Ear infections and earache: Amber, lapis lazuli, onyx, purple fluorite, turquoise

Exhaustion, lack of energy: Bowenite or new jade, carnelian, citrine, clear quartz crystal, golden tiger's eye, ox or red tiger's eye, rainbow quartz, red agate, red and orange jasper, ruby, smoky quartz, sunstone

Eyesight, eye infections and night vision: Amethyst, blue sapphire, cat's eye, chrysoberyl, emerald, golden tiger's eye, laboradite, lapis lazuli, ox or red tiger's eye, pietersite

Feet, legs: Jet, any of the sandy yellow or brown patterned jaspers

Fertility problems or to restore cycles of ovulation after artificial contraception: Amber, coral, moonstone, orange and red jasper, rhodochrosite (good for IVF and artificial insemination), rose quartz, any crystal eggs

Fevers: Blue lace agate, blue sapphire, chrysocolla, clear fluorite, pietersite, snow or milky quartz

Fluid retention, bloating: Blue calcite, blue chalcedony, green calcite, moonstone, selenite

Gallstones and gall bladder problems: Amethyst, blue chalcedony, citrine, garnet, golden tiger's eye, olivine/peridot, orange calcite

Glands, swollen and glandular disorders: Blue lace agate, emerald, lapis lazuli, moonstone, selenite, sodalite, sugilite (balances and improves functioning of the all important pineal, pituitary and adrenal glands)

Hair: Bowenite or new jade, rose quartz

Hay fever and plant allergies: Blue chalcedony, moss agate, prehnite

Heart: Aventurine, bowenite or new jade, emerald, red jasper, sodalite

Hernia: Mookaite

Hormones: Bowenite or new jade, chrysocolla, moonstone, opals, pearl, pietersite (especially growth hormones), selenite

Indigestion and stomach acidity: Amber, amethyst, angelite/celestite, any chrysoprase, ruby in zoisite, yellow jasper

Inflammation anywhere in the body: Blue chalcedony, clear fluorite, lapis lazuli, ruby in zoisite

Influenza: Aqua aura, garnet (helps to build up resistance and speeds recovery), green garnet, green jasper, moss agate, obsidian, snowflake obsidian

Insomnia and nightmares: Amethyst, charoite (good for sleepwalking and sleep disturbances), moonstone, rose quartz, smoky quartz

Intestinal and abdominal problems, also internal parasites: Angelite/celestite, banded agate

Kidneys: Aquamarine, blue calcite, carnelian, green calcite, green fluorite, heliotrope (good for kidney stones), jade, moonstone, smoky quartz (good for kidney stones), yellow calcite

Lactation, nursing mothers: Blue chalcedony, blue howlite (good for mothers of twins, triplets or premature infant), clear fluorite (good after Caesareans), milky or snow quartz, pink chalcedony, white chalcedony

Liver: Amethyst, banded agate, citrine, golden tiger's eye, heliotrope, malachite, olivine/peridot, orange calcite, yellow calcite, yellow jasper

Menstrual difficulties: Chrysocolla, coral, heliotrope, laboradite (especially excessive), moonstone (irregular or scant), opal, ox or red tiger's eye, pearl, rainbow quartz, red and orange jasper, selenite

Metabolism: Citrine, clear quartz crystal, opal aura, rainbow quartz, unakite

Migraines and headaches: Amethyst, charoite, lapis lazuli, malachite, moonstone (especially when hormonal or stress related), rose quartz, sodalite, titanium aura, turquoise

Muscle weakness: Haematite, lemon chrysoprase, serpentine

Nausea: Citrine, desert rose, lemon chrysoprase (good for morning sickness in pregnancy as well), sodalite

Neck: Amazonite, blue howlite

Nervous system: Amazonite, lapis lazuli, leopardskin jasper, opal aura, orange aragonite

Ovaries, womb: Moonstone, opal aura, orange or brown aragonite

Pain, chronic: Boji stone, chrysocolla, haematite, lapis lazuli, rainbow obsidian

Pancreas and spleen: Banded agate, citrine, emerald, green fluorite, smoky quartz, yellow calcite

PMS and menopausal disorders: Chrysocolla, emerald, green fluorite, heliotrope, kunzite, moonstone, red and orange jasper, rose quartz, selenite, all crystal eggs

Pregnancy: Angelite/celestite, blue opals, green opals, jade, kunzite, moonstone, opal aura, pink chalcedony, pink opals, rose quartz, selenite, white chalcedony

Prolonged medical, chemical or surgical treatment: Aqua aura, banded agate, malachite, rainbow moonstone (good for women after operations), titanium aura

Prostate: Aventurine, brown aragonite, desert rose, orange and yellow aragonite

Psychosomatic conditions: Kunzite, ox or red tiger's eye, sugilite

Pulse and heartbeat, irregularities: Aventurine, banded agate, ruby in zoisite

Recovery after illness, trauma, accident or surgery: Amber, carnelian, any chrysoprase, ox or red tiger's eye, red agate, red and orange jasper, ruby

Scars and birthmarks: Green fluorite, rhodonite, rose quartz, tourminalated quartz, white howlite

Sexual dysfunction in men, male genital disorders: Carnelian, orange aragonite, ox or red tiger's eye, ruby

Sinus: Clear and purple fluorite, sodalite, tourminalated quartz

Skin inflammation, eczema or rashes and allergies: Blue lace agate, bowenite or new jade, coral, desert rose, emerald, lapis lazuli, leopardskin jasper, moss agate, red agate, snakeskin agate, titanium aura

Speech problems: Angelite/celestite, blue lace agate, blue sapphire, blue topaz

Stomach, including upsets: Chrysoberyl (good for diarrhoea), chrysoprase (lemon is good for diarrhoea, green for stomach ulcers), desert rose, golden tiger's eye, golden topaz, orange aragonite, any crystals with holes

Stress: Amethyst, angelite/celestite, blue lace agate, jade, kyanite, laboradite, purple fluorite, rose quartz

Swellings and growths: Aqua, cobalt or titanium aura, jet, olivine/peridot, sugilite

Teeth and gums: Apatite, aquamarine, blue howlite, malachite, white howlite

Throats sore and tonsillitis: Amber, blue howlite (good for recurring infections), blue lace agate, green fluorite, purple fluorite, turquoise

Thyroid: Amazonite, chrysocolla, emerald

Travel sickness: Amethyst, aquamarine, desert rose, gold topaz, jade

Ulcers: Green fluorite, rhodonite, tourminalated quartz

Veins: Blue or crazy lace agate, tree agate

Viruses and infections: Garnet (especially in autumn and winter), green calcite, iron pyrites, leopardskin jasper, opal aura, orange and yellow aragonite (good against super bugs resistant to antibiotics), purple fluorite, ruby in zoisite, any stones with holes

Warts and skin or hair parasites: Desert rose, leopardskin jasper, turitella agate

Weight loss, to achieve: Kunzite, lemon chrysoprase, moonstone especially blue, sugilite, topaz

Whole mind and body health and healing/immune system: Aqua aura, clear quartz crystal, green jasper (helps body to absorb vitamins and minerals), Herkimer diamond, jade, laboradite, rainbow moonstone, rainbow obsidian, rhodonite (good for immune system problems), tektite (for autoimmune system)

The Pagan Path

Living by the cycles of nature is remarkably easy and takes no major life changes, just following what feels instinctively right and authentic to you. It is about listening to your body, your mind and your spirit – voices that can get drowned out by the noise and bombardment of often conflicting information and promises of instant popularity and success if you buy the right brands or sign up to the right network.

You may decide to go along to a neopagan gathering at a seasonal change point or find out more about one of the more nature-based forms of spirituality. However, the purpose of this book has been to introduce some of the best of the old ideas that can be incorporated into the busy world of today that has its benefits as well as its drawbacks. Paganism, like every other form of spirituality, has to evolve and to opt in rather than opt out of the modern world in which most of us must live.

This has been an appropriate book for me to write at this point in my life. At nearly 60, with grown-up children, only now have I realised that I can travel anywhere with just my computer and hand luggage, and that a lot of the items of material security I thought essential for happiness are merely trappings. As I clear the junk of 30 years in a house I must soon leave, I realise the only lasting and necessary treasures are my children and my happy memories, and how truly lucky I am to have those.

I finally watched my now floorless caravan, the setting for so many happy days with the children and a writing sanctuary away from my DIY-mad neighbours, being towed away to the caravan park in the sky. As the wild geese from the local bird park practise their flight before migration, as I have seen them do so many times, I know that autumn in my life as well as the season is rapidly approaching. I have to gather in what is of worth and accept that some things did not work out and that becoming 60 is not as frightening or old as I thought it would be. I am a Travelodge druidess through and through, a crushed-velvet witch (as one welly-booted pagan described me) and so, for me, neopaganism will always be mixed with home comforts.

But true paganism is what you feel in your heart, what you say and how you make every day count. Whether you celebrate the passing seasons in a neon-lit discotheque or on a wild hillside, whether you dance or walk more sedately or uncertainly through the year and your life, you leave your sacred footprints for future generations.

Cassandra

Useful Contacts

This is a representative sample of organisations that offer a starting point for more information on and contacts for neopagan forms of spirituality described in this book.

Druidry

The Order of Bards, Ovates and Druids
Based in the UK but with international connections; a huge amount of information on nature spirituality, training courses and meetings and useful links
www.druidry.org

Manannan mac Lir Grove of The Order of Bards, Ovates, and Druids
Based in the San Francisco Bay area of Northern California; good for general information and contacts
www.druidry-sf.org

Druid Groups: Oceania
An excellent starting point for details of Druidry in Australia
http://druidnetwork.org/directory/groupsoceania.html

Goddess spirituality

Fellowship of Isis
Worldwide organisation imparting knowledge about goddess spirituality, with training courses, literature and information
www.fellowshipofisis.com

Heathenism

American Vinland Association
Heathen association offering helpful links, events and information on all matters heathen
http://freyasfolk.org

Anglo Saxon Heathenism
Good historically based site on Anglo Saxon Heathenism and the runes
www.englishheathenism.homestead.com

Wodens Harrow
An excellent source of art, literature, myths and useful information about the ancient Norse world and its religions
http://home.earthlink.net/~Wodensharrow/

Neopagan contacts

Pagan Awareness Network, Australia
Provides useful information and contacts for individuals and groups within the pagan community
www.paganawareness.net.au

Pagan Federation International, USA
Connections in the USA and with other pagans worldwide
www.us.paganfederation.org

The Pagan Federation, UK
UK and international information and contacts for pagan individuals and groups; a good starting point
www.paganfed.org

RowanCraft
For healing, shamanic and magical workshops and hand-crafted bespoke products under the gentle guidance of Jane Rowan and Robin Oak
www.rowancraft.co.uk

Spirituality

Spheres magazine
A very useful journal for the southern hemisphere and beyond on all matters spiritual, with useful contacts and details of events
www.spiritguide.com.au

Wicca and witchcraft

Children of Artemis
An excellent source of information and a meeting base for Wicca and witchcraft in the UK and beyond
www.witchcraft.org

Covenant of the Goddess
Old of the oldest and best US-based Wiccan organisations, with excellent international resources and links
www.cog.org

The Spirit Guide to Spellcraft
Useful and excellent journal for the southern hemisphere and beyond, with information, contacts and details of events
www.spellcraft.com.au

The White Goddess
Community of Wiccans, witches and pagans; online forums for exchange of information and resources
www.witchweb.org.uk

The Witches' Voice
US-based international site with just about everything including political commentary, resources and knowledge
www.witchvox.com

History of witchcraft

The Museum of Witchcraft in Boscastle, Cornwall, UK
Reopened after bad floods in the town; an excellent website with online artefacts and descriptions of the old ways
www.museumofwitchcraft.com

The Museum de la Sorcellerie
Located in the Central Loire Valley of France; website has English language information
www.musee-sorcellerie.fr

Salem Witch Museum
The website also offers information about local events related to witchcraft
www.salemwitchmuseum.com

Cassandra Eason can be contacted via her website, which contains a great deal of information about magic and nature spirituality as well as details of courses
www.cassandraeason.co.uk

Further Reading

Neopaganism

Aswynn, Freya, *Northern Mysteries and Magick*, Llewellyn, 1998

Briggs, Robin, *Witches and Neighbours: The Social and Cultural Context of European Witchcraft*, Blackwell, 2002

Blain, Jenny, *Nine Worlds of Seid-Magic: Ecstasy and Neo-shamanism in North European Paganism*, Routledge, 2001

Cowan, James, *Aboriginal Dreaming, An Introduction to the Wisdom and Thought of the Aboriginal Traditions of Australia*, HarperCollins, 2002

Crowley, Vivianne, *Wicca: The Old Religion in the New Age*, Robert Hale, 1998

Eason, Cassandra, *The Modern-Day Druidess*, Piatkus Books, 2004

Eason, Cassandra, *Complete Book of Natural Magick*, Quantum, 2005

Fries, Jan, *Helrunar*, Mandrake Press, 2002 (about the Norse tradition)

Gardner, Gerald B, *Witchcraft Today*, Citadel, 2004

Harvey, Ralph, *The Last Bastion: The Suppression and Re-emergence of Witchcraft, the Old Religion*, Zambezi Publishing, 2004

Hutton, Ronald, *The Pagan Religions of the Ancient British Isles: Their Nature and Legacy*, Blackwell New editions, 1993

Jacq, Christian, *Magic and Mystery in Ancient Egypt*, Editions du Rocher, Monaco, 1983, Translation, Souvenir Press, 1998

Malidama, Patrice, *Of Water and the Spirit: Ritual, Magic and Initiation in the Life of an African Shaman*, Penguin Arkana, 1994

Matthews, John, *The Druid Source Book*, Blandford, 1997

Murray, Margaret Alice, *The Witch-Cult in Western Europe: A Study in Anthropology*, (1921), R A Kessinger Publications, 2003

Nichols, Ross, *The Book of Druidry*, HarperCollins, 1992

Paxson, Diana L, *Essential Asatru: Walking the Path of Norse Paganism*, Citadel, Kensington, 2007

Pennick, Nigel, *Secrets of East Anglian Magic*, Robert Hale, 1995

Rabinovitch, Shelley, *An Ye Harm None: Magical Morality and Modern Ethics*, Citadel, 2005

Starhawk, *The Spiral Dance: A Rebirth of the Ancient Religion of the Great Goddess*, Harper, San Francisco, 1999

Thorsson, Edred, *Northern Magic: Rune Mysteries and Shamanism*, Llewellyn, 1992

Amulets and charms

Ball, Pamela, *Spells, Charms, Talismans and Amulets*, Castle, 2002

Budge, E A Wallis, *Amulets and Superstitions*, Dover Publications, 1978

Kunz, George Frederick, *The Magic of Jewels and Charms*, Dover Publications, 2003

Lippman, Deborah & Colin, Paul, *How to Make Amulets, Charms and Talismans*, Citadel Press, 1994

Angels

Davidson, Gustav, *A Dictionary of Angels*, Simon and Schuster, 1994

Eason, Cassandra, *Touched by Angels*, Quantum/Foulsham, 2006

Newcomb, Jacky, *An Angel Treasury*, Element/Thorsons, 2004

Parisen, Maria, *Angels and Mortals: Their Co-creative Power*, Quest Books, 1994

Candles, herbs, oils, incenses and magical foods

Cunningham, Scott, *Encyclopedia of Magical Herbs*, Llewellyn Publications, 1997

Cunningham, Scott, *The Complete Book of Incense, Oils and Brews*, Llewellyn Publications, 2004

Eason, Cassandra, *Candle Power*, Blandford (Octopus Books), 1999, Sterling US, 2000

Eason, Cassandra, *Smudging and Incense-Burning*, Quantum/Foulsham, 2001

Eason, Cassandra, *Fragrant Magic*, Quantum/Foulsham, 2004

Flandrin, Jean-Louis; Montanari, Massimo, *Food: A Culinary History*, Columbia University, 1999

Gamache, Henri, *The Master Book of Candle Burning, How to Burn Candles for Every Purpose*, Original Publications, 1998

Higley, Connie & Alan; Leatham, Pat, *Aromatherapy A–Z*, Hay House, 2002

Kinkele, Thomas, *Incense and Incense Rituals: Healing Ceremonies for Spaces of Subtle Energy*, Lotus Books, 2004

Larkin, Chris, *The Book of Candlemaking: Creating Scent, Beauty and Light*, 1998, Sterling

Reppert, Bertha, *Herbs for Weddings and Other Celebrations: A Treasury of Recipes, Gifts and Decorations*, Storey Communications, 1993

Vickery, Roy, *A Dictionary of Plant-Lore*, Oxford University Press, 1995

Celtic and ancient spirituality

Carmichael, Alexander, *The Carmina Gadelica: Hymns and Incantations*, Lindisfarne Press, 1994

Frazer, Sir James, *The Golden Bough*, Penguin, 1996

MacLeod, Fiona, *By Sundown Shores – Studies in Spiritual History*, George Loring Press, 1902

Matthews, Caitlin, *Celtic Devotional*, Godsfield Press, 2003

Ross, Anne, *Pagan Celtic Britain*, Routledge and Kegan Paul, 1967

Chakras, colours and auras

Davies, Brenda, *The Seven Healing Chakras Workbook*, Ulysses Press, 2000

Eason, Cassandra, *Chakra Power for Healing and Harmony*, Quantum/Foulsham, 2001

Karagulla, Shafica; van Gelder Kunz, Dora, *The Chakras and the Human Energy Fields*, Theosophical University Press, 1994

Klotsche, Charles, *Color Medicine: The Secrets of Color/Vibrational Healing*, 1993, Light Technology Publications

Sun, Howard & Dorothy, *Colour Your Life*, Piatkus, 1999

Crystals

Cunningham, Scott, *Encyclopedia of Crystal, Gem and Metal Magic*, Llewellyn, 1991

Eason, Cassandra, *The Illustrated Directory of Healing Crystals*, Collins and Brown, 2004

Gienger, Michael; Astrid, Mick, *Crystal Power, Crystal Healing: The Complete Handbook*, Cassell Illustrated, 1998

Dream meanings and symbols

Browne, Sylvia; Harrison, Lindsay, *Sylvia Browne's Book of Dreams*, E P Dutton, 2002

Buchanan-Brown, John, *et al*, *The Penguin Dictionary of Symbols*, Penguin Books, 2004

Cooper, J C, *An Illustrated Encyclopaedia of Traditional Symbols*, Thames and Hudson, 1979

Eason, Cassandra, *Cassandra Eason's Modern Book of Dream Interpretation*, Quantum/Foulsham, 2005

Jung, Carl Gustav, *Man and his Symbols*, Laurel Press, 1997

Tresidder, Jack (ed), *The Complete Dictionary of Symbols in Myth, Art and Literature*, Duncan Baird Publishers, 2004

Elements

Hobson, Wendy, *Simply Feng Shui*, 1999, Quantum/Foulsham

Lipp, Deborah, *The Way of Four: Create Elemental Balance in your Life*, Llewellyn, 2004

McArthur, Margie, *Wisdom of the Elements, the Sacred Wheel of Earth, Air, Fire and Water*, Crossing Press, 1998

Parsons, Sandra, *Seeking Spirit, A Quest through Druidry and the Four Elements*, Capall Bann, 2000

Rupp, Rebecca, *Four Elements: Water, Air, Fire, Earth*, Profile Books, 2005

Twicken, David, *Four Pillars and Oriental Medicine: Celestial Stems, Terrestrial Branches and Five Elements for Health*, Writers Club Press, 2000

God and goddess traditions

Budapest, Zsuzsanna, *The Holy Book of Women's Mysteries*, Wingbow, 1997

Farrar, Janet & Stewart, *The Witches' Goddess*, Phoenix Publishing Inc, 1987

Forrest, M Isadora, *Isis Magic: Cultivating a Relationship with the Goddess of 10,000 Names*, Llewellyn 2001

Graves, Robert, *The White Goddess*, Faber and Faber, 1988

Jackson, Nigel, *Masks of Misrule, the Horned God and his Cult in Europe*, Capall Bann Publishing, 1998

Richardson, Alan, *Earth God Rising: The Return of the Male Mysteries*, Llewellyn, 1991

Starhawk, *Circle Round: Raising Children in Goddess Traditions*, Bantam (US), 2000

Trobe, Kala, *Invoke the Goddess: Visualizations of Hindu, Greek and Egyptian Deities*, Llewellyn, 2000

Healing

Angelo, Jack, *Your Healing Power: A Step-by-step Guide to Channelling your Healing Energies*, Piatkus, 1998

Dobbs, Horace, *Dolphin Healing*, Piatkus, 2000

Kavasch, E Barrie; Baar, Karen, *American Indian Healing Arts*, Thorsons/Bantam US, 1999

Simpson, Liz, *The Healing Energies of Earth*, Gaia Books, 2005

Meditation and personal empowerment

Eason, Cassandra, *Cassandra Eason's Complete Book of Spells*, Quantum/Foulsham, 2004

Eason, Cassandra, *Pendulum Dowsing*, Piatkus Books, 2004, as *The Art of the Pendulum*, Red Wheel/Weiser, 2005

Eason, Cassandra, *Becoming Clairvoyant: Develop Your Psychic Abilities to See into the Future*, Piatkus, 2007

Farrell, Nick, *Magical Pathworking, Techniques of Active Imagination*, Llewellyn, 2003

Lonegren, Sig, *Spiritual Dowsing*, Gothic Images, 1986

Weiss, Brian L, *Meditation: Achieving Inner Peace and Tranquility in Your Life*, New York: Hay House, 2002

Moon, sun and stars

Cashford, Jules, *The Moon: Myth and Image*, Cassell Illustrated, 2003

Guiley, Rosemary Ellen, *Moonscapes: A Celebration of Lunar Astronomy, Magic, Legend and Lore*, Cynthia Parzych Publishing Inc, 1991

Guttman, Ariel; Johnson, Kenneth, *Mythic Astrology: Internalizing the Planetary Powers*, Llewellyn, 1995

Lieber, Arnold L, *How the Moon Affects You*, Hastings House, 1996

McCrickard, Janet, *Eclipse of the Sun: Investigation into Sun and Moon Myths*, Gothic Image Publications, 1990

Paungger, Johanna; Poppe, Thomas, *Moon Time: The Art of Harmony with Nature and Lunar Cycles*, Rider, 2004

Townley, John, *Dynamic Astrology: Using Planetary Cycles to Make Personal and Career Choices*, Inner Traditions, Vermont, 1997

Nature spirits and sacred places

Campanelli, Dan & Pauline, *Circles, Groves and Sanctuaries: Sacred Spaces of Today's Pagans*, Llewellyn, 1993

Carmichael, David L, *et al*, *Sacred Sites, Sacred Places*, Routledge, 1997

Devereux, Paul, *The Sacred Place: The Ancient Origin of Holy and Mystical Sites*, Cassell Illustrated, 2000

Eason, Cassandra, *A Complete Guide to Faeries and Magical Beings*, Piatkus, 2002, Red Wheel/Weiser 2003

Froud, Brian, *Good Faeries, Bad Faeries*, Simon and Schuster, 1998

Hawkins, Jaq D, *Spirits of the Water*, Capall Bann, 2000

Palmer, Jessica Dawn, *Animal Wisdom*, Element, 2001

Romani, Rosa, *et al*, *Green Spirituality*, Green Magic, 2004

Rites of passage

Neasham, Mary, *Handfasting: A Practical Guide*, Green Magic, 2003

Speyer, Josefine; the National Death Centre; Wienrich, Stephanie, *The Natural Death Handbook*, Rider and Co, 2003

Starhawk; Nightmare, M Macha, *Pagan Book of the Living and Dying: Practical Prayers, Rituals, Blessings and Mediations on Passing Over*, Harper, San Francisco, 1997

Wind, Linda Heron, *New Moon Rising: Reclaiming the Sacred Rites of Menstruation*, Windrush Press, 1996

Seasons, days and times

Crowley, Vivianne, *Celtic Wisdom: Seasonal Festivals and Rituals*, Sterling, 1998

Duggan, Ellen, *7 Days of Magic: Spells, Charms and Correspondences for the Bewitching Week*, Llewellyn, 2004

Ellwood, Taylor, *Space/Time Magick*, Immanion Press, 2005

Hutton, Ronald, *Stations of the Sun: A History of the Ritual Year in Britain*, Oxford Paperbacks, 2004

Luenn, Nancy, *Celebrations of Light: A Year of Holidays Around the World*, Simon and Schuster Inc, 1998

Nichols, Mike, *The Witches' Sabbats*, Acorn Guild Press, 2005

Old Moore's Almanack, Foulsham, annually

Pennick, Nigel, *The Pagan Book of Days: A Guide to the Festivals, Traditions and Sacred Days of the Year*, Destiny Books, 2001

Singer, Marian, *Dancing the Fire: The Ins and Outs of Neopagan Festivals and Gatherings*, Citadel, 2005

Space clearing and psychic protection

Eason, Cassandra, *Psychic Protection Lifts the Spirit*, Quantum/Foulsham, 2001

Harbour, Dorothy, *Energy Vampires: A Practical Guide for Psychic Self-Protection*, Inner Traditions Bear and Company, 2003

Kingston, Karen, *Clear your Clutter with Feng Shui*, Piatkus, 2000

Matthews, Caitlin, *The Psychic Protection Handbook*, Piatkus, 2005

Mickaharic, Draja, *Spiritual Cleansing, a Handbook of Psychic Protection*, Red Wheel/Weiser, 2003

Workplace spirituality

Canfield, Jack, *Chicken Soup for the Soul at Work*, Vermillion, 1999

Eason, Cassandra, *Alchemy at Work*, Ten Speed/Crossing Press, 2004

Pierce, Gregory F A, *Spirituality @ Work*, 10 ways to balance your life on the job, Loyola University Press, 2001

Index

Page numbers in **bold** indicate major references; those in *italics* refer to lists of contacts and further reading

abundance 40, 160–161
adoption ceremonies 139–140
aetts 100–104
air element
  cleansing a home 71
  purifying a home 75–78
  in the workplace 211–212
Alban Arthuran 194–197
Alban Eiler 167–170
Alban Elued 185–188
Alban Heruin 174–177
amulets and charms *246*
ancestors **179–181**, 192–193
  see also family archives
angels *246*
animals and birds 24, 32
auras *247*
  workplace 201
autumn equinox 185–188

babies
  Baby-naming ceremony 136–139
baptisms 28–29, 135–136
blessings 133–136
balance, restoring
  Using the Three Treasures 226–228
Bean-Tighe 55
bedtime 90, **99–100**
Beltane 171–173
bereavement ritual 152–153
birds 24, 32
  as souls of the dead 149
birthdays 44, 133
blessings
  baby 133–136
  house 81–83
  mealtime 50–51
brownies 57
burials 148–153
business *see* self-employment; workplace

candles 74, *246–247*
celebrations *see* rites of passage; seasons; wheel of the year

Celts *247*
  baby blessings 134–136
  lunar calendar 121–125
ceremonies *see* rites of passage; rituals
chakras *247*
children 34
  mealtimes 51
  and moon cycles 109–110
  and noise of modern life 219
  see also babies; family life
chime hours 101
choices 26
christenings *see* babies
Christmas 163, **195–197**
cleansing 68–73
cloud messages 220–221
clutter clearing 62–65
Coligny calendar 121–122
colleagues 203–204, 209–210
colours *247*
condiments **46–48**, *246–247*
consumer society 34
cosmic
  energies 22, 25
  exchange principle 29
crescent moon 111–112
crone 190
crystals *247*
  healing 230–237
  meanings of 43
  power of 230
  protective 207–208
  workplace 204–205, 207–208

dark of the moon 116
darkness, embracing 34, 88
dawn 27, 90, **92–94**
daytime
  aetts 100–104
  see also Sun, The
death 29, **148–153**
deities, pagan 14–17
destiny 26
difference, importance of 30
Dísir 54–55
divorce 154
  Breaking the cord 155–156
  Ritual to end a marriage or committed relationship 156–157

253

Index

domovoy 58
dreams *248*
Druids 11, *241*
Duendes 55
dusk 90, **96–98**

Earth Day 25
earth element
  cleansing a home 70
  purifying a home 79
  in the workplace 210–211
Easter 168–170
elements 62, *248*
  cleansing a home 69–73
  purifying a home 74–81
  and the workplace 209–217
endings, rites of 154–157
energies
  cosmic 22, 25
  cumulative 25
  in the home 61–62
  lunar 110
  personal 11
  plant 36
  positive and negative 25
  seasonal 11
  solar 89
  workplace 201–203
equality of people 23
essential oils *246–247*
  meanings of 42, 80–81
  sprays 80–81

fairies 64
family archives 64–65, 147
  see also ancestors
family life 35, 39, 41
  changes in 37
  disagreements 42
  mealtimes 44–45, 50–51
  welcoming new members 139–142
  see also hearth; rites of passage
Far East, guardians 52–53
Fate, sisters of 195
Feng Shui 62, 201
fertility 106–107, 114
festivals *see* seasons; wheel of the year
fire element
  cleansing a home 72
  purifying a home 74
  in the workplace 213–214
flowers, meanings of 42

food *246–247*
  customs 44–45
  disorders 223
  mealtimes 44–45, 50–51
  properties of 45–49
  shopping for 33
fragrances *see* essential oils; flowers; incense
full moon **112–115**, 119, **120, 126**
funerals **148–153**, 180
future, influencing 26

gnomes 57–58
gods and goddesses 14–15, 163, *241, 248–249*
guardians (household) 52–59
  Calling on the protection of your household guardians after dark 55–56

Halloween 190–193
handfastings 28–29, **143–147**
harm none 24
harvest *see* Alban Elued; Lughnassadh
healing *249*
  crystals 230–237
  moon water **114–115**, 116
  path 223
hearth, The **37–39**, 52, 54
  Creating a magical hearth 40–41
  Creating a special place 42–43
heathenism *241*
herbs **46–48**, *246–247*
Hestia 38
homes 37
  blessing 81–83
  clutter clearing 62–65
  energy fields 61–62
  household guardians 52–59
  purifying 74–81
  spiritually cleansing 68–73
  spring cleaning 62, **65–68**
  see also family life; hearth
hot cross buns 44–45
house elves 56–58
  Living with and attracting house elves 58–59
house wights 53–54
hunter god 186

imagination 87–88
Imbolc 164–166

incense **75–77**, *246–247*
interconnectedness of life 22, 26–27

Jing 225
Jung, Carl Gustav 32, 209
Jupiter 14

Lammas 182–184
leisure time 9, **35**
  time out of time 34, **85–88**
life
  cycle of 22, 26–27
  rites of passage 28–29
  sacredness of 23–24
lifestyle, spiritual 12–13
light
  artificial 33, 85
  and dark 163
Llew 182, **185–186**
Lughnassadh 181, **182–184**
lunar
  calendars 121–125
  energies 110
lunchtime 90, **95–96**

marriage 28–29, 133, **143–147**
May Day 162, **171–173**
mealtimes 44–45
  A mealtime blessing 50–51
meditation *249*
menstruation 106–107
midday 102
midnight 90, **99–100**, 103–104
midsummer solstice 174–177
midwinter solstice 194–197
money, attracting 41
Moon, The *249–250*
  energies 107–108
  and fertility 106–107, 114
  harmony with 28, 33, **105–107**, 109–110
  phases of 110–120
  and plants 107
  void of course 120
  water **114–115**, 116
moral dilemmas 19–21
Mother Earth 10
mothers 55

Native North Americans 12, 106, 139
  lunar calendar 121–125
natural rhythms 85–88

nature *250*
  connecting with 35, 36
  listening to 220
  messages in 220–222
  power of 219
  and spirituality 31
negativity 25
  washing away 67–68
neopaganism 9, **10–11**, *242, 245–246*
  and business 200–201
new moon 118
New Year 39, 65–66, **189–197**
night *see* aetts; solar periods
noon 90, **95–96**

Orlog 26

paganism
  21st-century 7–8, 9, 11–13
  and daily life 32–36
  deities 14–17
  general principles 21–31
  history of 10
  and perfection 15–16
  see also neopaganism
past influences 26
people   *see* children; colleagues; family life; relationships
plants
  energies 36
  and the moon 107–108
polishing, magical 67
polytheistic religions 10
positive vibes 25
power
  animals 24
  of crystals 230
  of nature 219
  of stones 228
  of water 229–230
protection, psychic *251*
  at work 205–208

Quaker blessings 134
Qi 225–226

relationships, ending 154–157
rites of passage 28–29, **133–157**, *250*
rituals 11
  seasonal 26–27, 36, **159–163**, 180

salt 79

255

Index

Samhain 189–193
scrying 221–222
seasonal
　energies 11, 163
　rituals 26–27, 159–163, 180
seasons *250–251*
　celebrating 26–27, 36, 162–163, 180
　wheel of the year **159–162**, 179
self-employment 199, **200–201**
self-esteem 224
shamanism 12
Shen 225
shield, psychic 205–207
Shinto 53
silence 87
smudge 75–76, 78
solar energies 89
solar periods 90–100
souls of the dead 149
spirituality *242*
　creating your own 30
　focus 16–17
　and lifestyle 12
　and location 31
　male and female 15
spiritually cleansing 68–73
spring 164–166
　cleaning 62, 65–68
　equinox 167–170
stars *249*
Stonehenge 27
stones, power of 228
summer solstice 27, **174–177**
Sun, The 88, *249–250*
　daily cycle 27, 33–34, 86
　energies 89
　solar periods 90–100
symbols *248*
synchronicity 32

technology, impact of 9, 35
Three Treasures 224–228
threefold law 25
time 27
taking time out of time 34, **85–88**
totem animals 24

undorne 102

vacuuming, psychic 67
vegetarianism 23–24
Vikings 180

waking up 90, **92–94**
waning moon 28, 109, 110,
washing negativity away 67–68
water
　messages on 221–222
　power of 229–230
water element
　cleansing a home 73
　purifying a home 80–81
　in the workplace 214–216
waxing moon 109, 110, **111–112**
weather, enjoying 34, 87
weddings 28–29, 133, **143–147**
wheel of the year 159–162, 179
Wicca 11, 12, 15, *242–243*
　funerals 180
Wiccan Rede 24
wildlife 24, 32
witchcraft *see* Wicca
workplace *251*
　aura 201
　colleagues 203–204, 209–210
　crystals in 204–205, 207–208
　elements 209–217
　environment 201–203
　and neopagan principles 199–201
　protection 205–208

Yule 194–197

zodiac signs 127–132